MO
DOE
MAKE A DIFFERENCE?

Wayne G. Johnson

University Press of America,® Inc.
Lanham · Boulder · New York · Toronto · Oxford

Copyright © 2005 by
University Press of America,® Inc.
4501 Forbes Boulevard
Suite 200
Lanham, Maryland 20706
UPA Acquisitions Department (301) 459-3366

PO Box 317
Oxford
OX2 9RU, UK

All rights reserved
Printed in the United States of America
British Library Cataloging in Publication Information Available

Library of Congress Control Number: 2004114177
ISBN 0-7618-3081-2 (clothbound : alk. ppr.)
ISBN 0-7618-3082-0 (paperback : alk. ppr.)

∞™ The paper used in this publication meets the minimum
requirements of American National Standard for Information
Sciences—Permanence of Paper for Printed Library Materials,
ANSI Z39.48—1984

To my parents, Gust J. and Ruth H. Johnson,
who gave me life and grounded me in basic trust;

to Dr. Ronald V. Wells
who mentored me during a life transition;

and to Jeanne
who brought fulfilling dimensions to my life.

CONTENTS

Preface	vii
1. A Theory About Moral Theories	1
2. The Point of Morality	17
3. Moral Theories and Worldviews Hebrew Prophets, Pre-Socratic Greeks, Protagoras, Epicurus, Plato, Aristotle, Augustine, Aquinas, Hobbes, Hume, Kant, J. S. Mill, Marx, Nietzsche, Sartre, A. J. Ayer	29
4. Religion-Based Morality: An Overview	91
5. How "God" Makes a Difference	105
6. Self, Others, and Rights	125
7. The Challenge of Ethical Relativism	145
8. Why Be Moral?	161
9. Evolution and Ethics	181
10. Issues in Religion-Based Morality	199
End Notes	213
Bibliography	223
Biographical Sketch	231
Index	233

PREFACE

The intersection of religious and philosophical thought has long been an object of my academic as well as my personal interests. This intersection becomes highlighted when the question of the nature of morality arises. In what has been termed a "culture war," there are strident voices raised in a variety of religious camps today. Philosophy, perhaps, fares no better. In his influential *After Virtue*, Alasdair MacIntyre suggested that there is a "slightly shrill tone" in much philosophical debate about morality. He also noted that the roots of this tone lie in the premises with which a philosopher begins. Various positions have their own logical structure, given the premises from which they proceed, MacIntyre observes, but there appears to be no way to make a rational evaluation of the premises themselves. This book is an attempt to enter into the conversation by arguing that the basic premises to be identified are ontological in nature and lie at the roots of various worldviews. Hence, the title of this work: *Morality: Does "God" Make a Difference?* The term "God" is put between quotation marks to indicate a broad concept—God, Allah, Yahweh, Law of Karma, Brahman. As I shall note, when the concept of God is fleshed out in various specific ways the moral content related to that concept can vary a good deal.

In my answer to the question posed in the title, I shall agree with many religious as well as non-religious thinkers in maintaining that belief in God *does* make a difference. The question that remains is whether or not the difference that belief in God makes is constructive, for many agnostics and atheists assert that religious morality is fundamentally flawed. This book neither defends nor attacks religion-based morality. I will not assert that one must be religious in order to be moral, and I leave the existence of God as an open question. What I do seek is an *explanation* of just *why* belief in God shapes a moral perspective—for good or ill. Beyond explanation, I will *claim* that theism provides a basis for a kind of morality that cannot be rationally defended on non-religious grounds. That claim, however, does not imply that theistic morality is necessarily superior to a non-religious one.

Chapter One sets forth my Broad Theory about moral theories and explores the various phenomena that my Broad Theory seeks to explain. Chapter Two examines the *point* of morality, noting that moral patterns are expressed in every civilization or culture in some way. But just why is that the case? Why do moral systems develop at all? I will conclude, following William James, that moral reflection is an attempt to find a way to *appropriately* arbitrate between the competing wants, needs and desires (WNDs) of sentient creatures. The challenging moral issues, then, develop when both resources and human sympathies are limited.

In seeking to appropriately arbitrate between competing wants, needs, and desires, two related issues must be considered. The first relates to one's own manifold WNDs. Which deserve to be honored and which rejected? This is the question of what constitutes a truly fulfilling human existence. All classical moral systems, religious or non-religious, address this question. They assume not only that it is entirely rational to pursue fulfillment, but also that the moral pathway is an essential part of the quest for fulfillment. The second issue is the question of whether or not individuals, while seeking their own fulfillment, have any obligation to help others find *their* fulfillment. This is basically the question of moral obligation.

Chapter Three provides a brief summary of the ethical views of influential philosophers. I demonstrate how answers to both of the above questions are shaped by the religious or non-religious beliefs held by that thinker. Chapter Four describes in some detail the nature of religion-based morality in its variety of forms. In Chapter Five, after reviewing the various views concerning the nature of human fulfillment, I describe how belief or non-belief in

God shapes such views. The question of moral obligations toward others is explored in Chapter Six, with analyses that illustrate how belief or non-belief in God shapes answers to that question.

Chapter Seven reviews the issue of ethical relativism and the relationship of ethical relativism to the basic theory I seek to develop. It involves a number of formally structured arguments that may be a challenge to those with little background in logic. This chapter can be skipped without losing the major thrust of my theory and argument. Chapter Eight explores the question "Why Be Moral?" In that chapter I examine psychological egoism and challenge a position called "the moral point of view." Chapter nine considers whether or not evolutionary theory can provide something like moral insight. Finally, Chapter Ten explores a variety of criticisms leveled at religion-based morality as well as the advantages these moralities may provide. Having borrowed from William James in my opening chapter, I borrow again from him in the closing one. And, in the spirit of William James, I invite you, the reader, to consider my arguments and then reflect on the two basic issues in morality: 1) What type of fulfillment do you seek? And 2) What is the nature of your obligations toward others?

CHAPTER ONE

A THEORY ABOUT MORAL THEORIES

Though in theory we might think that a people could construct a wholly autonomous value system independent of any metaphysical referent, an ethics without ontology, we do not in fact seem to have found such a people.

Clifford Geertz[1]

There does seem to be some connection between anthropology and ethics, that is, between what it is believed that man is and what it is believed that he ought to do.

W. D. Hudson[2]

Why do people act the way they do? This question may well have been raised by reflective human beings since the dawn of our species. For possible answers to that question I have been drawn not so much to sociology and psychology—though these fields help shed light on that issue—but to philosophical and religious traditions that seek not to explain *why* we do what we do but to advise us about what we *ought* to do. The field of ethics or moral philosophy has been central in this attempt to advise. This work will not presume to provide the reader with advice about proper morality. For those who seek such advice, the store of books available is bountiful if not always compelling. I will, instead, seek to analyze the nature of moral advice offered by various thinkers and to show why such advice has varied so remarkably from thinker to thinker and from time to time.

Throughout history, advice about the proper moral pathway has been offered by deeply religious persons as well as by those who reject religion. This history of morality prompts the central question of this work: Does a religious worldview support a view of morality which cannot be rationally grounded in a non-religious worldview? In short, does the idea of God make a difference?

Since the role of worldviews is central to the analysis and argument that is to follow, some clarification of their nature and function should be offered. To hold a worldview is to possess a web or system of beliefs that constitutes one's understanding of the nature of the universe and of human life. Traditional religions represent such worldviews, as do various non-religious systems of thought. Typical contemporary worldviews would include beliefs established through science. And yet a worldview is more than a mental picture of the empirical universe; it also encompasses what William James called "overbeliefs"—those about the ultimate nature of reality and about what is meaningful or valuable. For James the empiricist, these matters are overbeliefs since they are neither justified nor entailed by empirical evidence. Nevertheless, James claimed, all of us necessarily hold a variety of such overbeliefs that, true or false, function as basic guidelines for our goals and actions.

Central to the nature of such overbeliefs, and consequently central to the nature of worldviews, is the question of whether or not anything exists above, beyond or prior to the physical universe. Hence, a basic issue in the construction of a worldview is whether or not something like God exists or whether only the physical universe exists. In the history of philosophy, this constitutes a fundamental ontological issue regarding the nature of being.

Our Western cultural traditions provide us mainly with a choice between two worldviews—theism (or some modified form of such) or naturalism. Both are theories in the sense that they are conceptual constructs designed to explain aspects of our experience just as scientific theories attempt to explain natural phenomena. Thus, theism and naturalism may be thought of as conceptual maps that serve as explanatory systems—as basic beliefs used to explain and interpret our world of experience, to ascertain what is valuable, and to guide our actions.

The most common forms of theism in our culture are expressed in three related religions—Judaism, Christianity and Islam. If you fall roughly into this camp, you believe that God (Yahweh, Allah) is the ultimate ground of all existence. God is eternal, non-material, beyond space and time, and all-powerful. This God brought the universe into being out of nothing, *ex nihilo*, and sustains the universe and all its inhabitants. Furthermore, according to this worldview, the history of the universe and of humanity moves toward some ultimate and glorious culmination under the guidance of the Divine power. Because we are created by this God and are called into relationship with our Creator, our lives are meaningful and significant. Obedience to the Divine will, which is usually understood by way of some form of revelation, promises to lead us to the highest form of human fulfillment. The journey through this world may be troubled and dark at times, but the promise of fulfillment and various gifts of grace keep us from despair during our earthly journey

The worldview just described is, of course, traditional theistic religion. For several decades, we have witnessed a curious shift in beliefs as various individuals claim to be "spiritual" but not "religious." Since the entire scene of this spirituality in our society is so amorphous and vague, I have elected not to venture into that particular arena. Instead, I shall use traditional religious positions for reference purposes and illustrations. While these positions may or may not be accurate worldviews, at least we have a fairly clear idea of their meaning and structure.

Naturalism is the major alternative to theism as a worldview in our culture. An increasingly live option for persons in our culture, naturalism is the theory that only nature exists; that is, only the universe and the physical realities contained therein. There is no God or similar reality, and nothing beyond, prior to, within, or under nature. To put the matter in a slightly different way, naturalism is usually an expression of ontological materialism, a philosophical theory that asserts that matter, or matter/energy, is the fundamental, uncreated and eternal reality and the basis for all existing entities. This should properly be seen as a philosophical theory rather than a scientific theory since the claim runs beyond what scientific method can, in principle, pursue. Most modern forms of naturalism hold that nature is made up of forces and particles that can be studied by physics and that bring forth living creatures through the process of evolution. Since these particles and forces are uncreated, basic and eternal, evolution within a naturalistic worldview is usually seen as a random process with no particular aim and certainly no divine guiding hand in control. Nature does what it does according to the causal structures described by natural laws that explain the workings of natural processes.

Naturalism, then, implies that our human life is the product of a causal universe ordered by natural laws and acting through a random evolutionary process. Human beings are wholly physical entities with no separate reality such as mind or soul that lives within or parallel to the physical body. Consciousness and its various activities, such as thinking, feeling, remembering, choosing, reading, are phenomena generated by the physical brain. We do not *have* bodies, we *are* bodies. When the body dies and the life processes cease, our consciousness shuts down and our bodies return to a more basic form of matter. There is no personal life possible beyond the death of the body. The meaning or point of our lives, if there is one, is to be found within this physical universe during the limited years of our existence.

With this brief explanation of worldviews in place, we now return to the central question of this book: Can a theistic worldview support a view of morality that cannot be rationally justified on the basis of naturalism? Does "God" make a difference? Many voices of the past would answer that with a resounding "yes," and these voices would include not only religious thinkers, but also atheists and agnostics. Influential theologians in the Christian tradition have long argued that human reason on its own can neither grasp moral truth nor provide the motivation needed for the moral pathway. Philosophically inclined theologians, as saints Augustine and Aquinas, always appealed to revealed truth in the form of scripture to anchor their final vision of morality. Luther and Calvin, the major Protestant reformers, were convinced that human beings, distorted by original sin and the Fall, were turned in upon themselves and blind to moral truth. Without grace enabling faith, persons could neither see the good nor find the motivation to do the good.

On some issues, the inner logic of a religious position is quite clear. If, for instance, Joe believes that God teaches the faithful through the Church; and if Joe knows that the Church teaches that a fertilized ovum is a human person endowed at the time of conception with an eternal soul; and if Joe knows the Church teaches the taking of an innocent life is morally wrong, then he would certainly believe that an abortion is morally wrong. This logic is clear within the circle of the basic faith judgments in Joe's tradition.

On the other hand, many non-theistic philosophers have argued that belief in God *does* makes a difference, but any morality based on religion fails both rationally and morally. Plato, for example, held that the gods presented in Greek mythology were basically corrupt and should not serve as role models for the young. In his philosophy, however, Plato employed a view of God that supported his own moral theory. Aristotle, on the other hand, constructed an ethical theory that is still influential but had nothing of significance to say about the role that the gods might play. And Epicurus, while he thought that gods might exist, held that they are irrelevant to our moral quest and that we should, as mere mortal creatures, pursue pleasure for the self.

Other thinkers have leveled harsh judgments against morality that is rooted in the religious traditions. While proclaiming that "God is dead," Nietzsche also dismissed Christian morality as a form of slave morality adopted by the weak and cowardly. Other more contemporary philosophers share, in part, Nietzsche's view. Richard Taylor, in his *Ethics, Faith, and Reason*, "repudiates the debilitating egalitarianism of modern ethics" (and its religious roots) "in favor of the ideals of the ancient pagan moralists."[3] The late John Mackie, in his *Ethics: Inventing Right and Wrong*, takes a more moderate position. He held that, if true, the theistic position could make a "significant difference to moral philosophy." But he argues that the theistic position has little by way of cogent argument to support it and that it remains largely incoherent. Hence, human beings must invent morality.[4]

By way of clarification, I will *not* claim that belief in God is necessary for living a morally decent life. Little empirical evidence would support such a claim.[5] Nor will this work attempt to defend or defeat religious worldviews and the moral systems linked to them. No moral advice will be given. What I seek to develop is a theory that acknowledges and clarifies the differences between religious and naturalistic moral theories and also explains *why* these differences occur. Instead of critiquing standard moral theories or developing and defending one in particular, I seek to construct a general theory *about* such moral theories.

While no detailed analysis of the nature and role of theories will be developed here, some basic characteristics will be noted. To begin, a common distinction between "fact" and "theory" will be helpful. This distinction is reflected in our everyday use of language, for while it seems appropriate to speak of a theory as being either true *or* false, it would be odd to speak of a false fact. Of course one's belief that some X is a fact may be a false belief; but the claim that X is a fact implies the claim that X is true. The major distinction can be expressed as follows: A statement of fact is a statement about something directly presented to our sensory experience or about a logical relationship. Thus, it is a fact that the page you are reading has black print on white paper. And it is a fact that two plus two equals four. On the other hand, a theory is not a statement about what is directly presented to us, but is, rather, a construct designed primarily to *explain* certain facts. We do not experience theories directly by way of our sensory experience; we use theories to help us explain such experiences. While it is a *fact* that a ball drops to the ground when released from my hand, Newton's *theory* of gravity explains *why* the ball falls to the ground.

The main function of any theory is that of explaining certain phenomena, events or states of affairs. When a coroner, for instance, seeks to ascertain the cause of someone's death, he or she develops a theory, based on the facts of the case, that explains the cause of death. Newton's theory (or law) of universal gravitation explains a variety of phenomena such as why a rock will return to the earth even when hurled upward into the air, and why an apple falls down instead of up when it breaks from the stem. When a physician prescribes a treatment, she is acting on a theory related to the factual observations obtained by the physical examination of her patient. It is clear, then, that theories are not to be taken lightly. To say of some theory that it is "only a theory" is to fail to see that most human actions are predicated on some theory that a particular person holds. We live by our theories—and sometimes die because of them.

If the function of any theory is to explain certain phenomena, then it is successful to the degree that it explains phenomena relevant to that theory. Rather than developing an analysis of just how theories do explain, or what constitutes an explanation of some fact by way of a theory (How does Newton's theory of gravitation "explain" why an apple falls to earth?), I will trust the reader's own understanding of this matter.

If my theory about ethical theories is to be successful, it must explain a variety of phenomena related to morality. The most significant phenomena to be explained include the following: 1) Fact: Human beings and human cultures tend to develop systems of morality or codes of ethics. What is there about the human situation that leads to such systems or codes? 2) Fact: Thoughtful human beings have generated a wide variety of views about the nature of morality. How can so much variety be explained? 3) Fact: It seems to be difficult if not impossible for all thoughtful people to come to agreement about moral principles and rules. What accounts for this difficulty? 4) Fact: Religion-based moral systems often have a substantially different view of morality than do non-religious systems. What accounts for these differences?

At this point, I present what I shall call my "Broad Theory" formulated to explain the various facts listed above. Following the formulation of that broad theory, I will state four basic claims linked to it. No defense of the theory or the basic claims will be made in this chapter, but the remainder of this work will serve as such a defense.

Broad Theory: *Normative ethical systems are best understood as attempts to seek out and justify ways of living a fulfilled human life in terms of the kind of fulfillment one believes to be possible given one's beliefs about human nature and the ultimate nature of all things. Furthermore, any normative ethical system must also indicate just how one's own quest for fulfillment is related to the experiences of other people and sentient beings, given, again, one's view of human nature and the ultimate nature of all things.* In short, I claim that any normative ethical system must suggest a pathway to human fulfillment and must also indicate just how one's *own* fulfillment is related to other beings who also seek their fulfillment.

Two clarifications are in order. By a normative ethical system I refer to one that sets forth and defends certain moral norms as the correct ones to be adopted. Such systems differ from a *descriptive* approach to ethics that would *describe* moral views held by people but would not attempt to support a specific set of principles. An anthropologist may, for example, describe the moral views held by certain groups of people, but would not, as anthropologist, propose that some such moral views are to be adopted and others rejected. By beliefs about the "ultimate nature of all things," I have in mind certain metaphysical beliefs or ontological commitments, such as materialism, naturalism, or a kind of transcendentalism or theism—that is, some type of worldview.

Four basic claims are linked to this Broad Theory:

1) The principle aim of any rationally justifiable moral theory is to identify paths of action that will result in a fulfilling existence for anyone walking that pathway. "Fulfilling," here, remains vague intentionally. The same point could be made by substituting "flourishing" for "fulfilling." I have deliberately avoided the term "happiness" as the most basic aim of a rational person, even though a number of important philosophers have used that term. While happiness is a significant dimension of human experience, it is too superficial or insubstantial to qualify

universally as the most fulfilling of life's quest.[6] One implication follows from this first claim. If the principle aim of a moral theory is to *identify a pathway that leads to fulfillment*, then that moral theory would also claim that straying from the moral pathway would in some way hinder or undercut the fulfillment of the one who so strays. In short, every moral theory includes some theory of sanctions such that failure to live morally leads inescapably to lack of fulfillment. Sanctions, of course, can take many forms. In traditional Western theism, moral failure can be sanctioned by either temporary or eternal punishment. In Far Eastern thought, the sanctions are applied through the working out the Law of Karma and various levels of reincarnation. For Epicurus, the sanction would be that of failing to experience the life of pleasure; while for Aristotle, ethical failure would entail the failure to be a truly excellent man. Or perhaps moral failure leads to a sense of personal disgust with one's own life—"Am I really that kind of person?" Any attempt to remove sanctions from a moral theory would, it appears, strip it of its human seriousness. Without sanctions of some kind, moral requirements might be interesting but trivial.

2) Normative ethical theories differ largely because differing metaphysical beliefs or worldviews held by the theorist since these commitments determine, in part, not only beliefs about what *kind* of fulfillment is possible, given the nature of things, but also beliefs about how proper moral principles are related to that fulfillment.

3) Normative moral theories differ also in part because of various views regarding the question of how other human beings (or other sentient creatures), in their quest for fulfillment, are related to one's own quest. Some persons (or creatures) count for us because their fulfillment is intimately related to our own. Others do not count in the same way.

4) The substance of a morality rooted in theistic religious traditions cannot be successfully defended on non-theistic or naturalistic foundations. Since many theists as well as atheists assent to this claim, it implies neither an endorsement nor a rejection of a religion-based morality.

I need, now, to guard against one possible misinterpretation. My theory is not to be construed as a defense of certain positions declared in the current culture war. Nor is it to be understood as a claim that moral degradation must inevitably follow from the demise of religious belief. Any such implication or claim would run far beyond the *descriptive* intent of my theory. I have my own convictions and commitments; but I give no advice and make no judgments in this work. Consequently, the adequacy of a morality rooted in a theistic worldview or one rooted in a naturalistic worldview will remain an open question.[7]

Since my theory attempts to explain a variety of facts about morality and historical ethical theories, two important distinctions often made in moral philosophy will be clarified. If the Broad Theory is to be successful, it must be able to explain not only the facts cited on page seven, but also the bases for the two distinctions now explored. First, the distinction between teleological and deontological moral theories will be made. This will be followed by developing the distinction between morality as "discovered" and morality as "invented."

A teleological (Greek *telos*, for "aim" or "goal") view of morality holds that the moral goodness of an act depends on certain non-moral value (pleasure, peace, happiness) resulting from the act. For instance, utilitarianism maintains that an action may be certified as morally good if it produces a greater quantity of general happiness than unhappiness. From this perspective, you may be morally obligated to lie to an angry man waving a gun who has just asked you where your son could be found. In contrast, a typical deontological (from Greek *deon*, for "duty" or "obligation") view of morality would hold that the moral quality of an act does not depend its results, but on some intrinsic value of the act itself. A deontological position may hold, for instance, that there is something morally wrong about telling a lie even if it would produce more general happiness than truth-telling. Lying about your son's whereabouts to the angry man waving a gun would be morally wrong from this perspective. The moral philosophy of Immanuel Kant reflects such a deontological perspective. Most formulations of the "divine command" view in religious ethics would also reflect a deontological position in that this theory holds that an act X is morally right only insofar as God commands X, and an act Y is morally evil only insofar as God declares Y to be evil. An act is to be evaluated, not on the basis of its results, but on the basis of a Divine Command. X is right only because God declares that X right.

Another significant distinction in moral philosophies can be made between those who hold that moral structures can be *discovered* in the very nature of things, and those who argue that moral structures or rules are human *inventions* designed to serve some human purpose. It is, of course, logically possible for one to actually *invent* ethical directives while believing that one has *discovered* them. Is the claim of knowing some divinely revealed moral truth, for instance, an invention of some kind or is it an actual discovery? The answer to such a question may necessarily be cast in terms of a certain faith judgment.

How, then, can morality be understood as an aspect of the very structure of reality, of the very nature of things? The most familiar view is presented in a variety of religious systems. Theists generally hold that the God who brought the world into being has also set forth a set of objective moral structures to be followed by morally responsible created creatures. The Ten Commandments, for instance, are believed by some theists to be revealed by God to Moses and represent an objectively true moral pathway that applies to all human beings. With these commandments comes the promise that those who obey will find themselves blessed in a variety of ways. On the other hand, Far Eastern religions, as Hinduism, Jainism and Buddhism, hold that certain basic moral realities are part of the very nature of being and are expressed through the Law of Karma. Good deeds result in some form of reward for the faithful and evil deeds bring about some form of punishment, according to Karmic Law. But such Biblical laws or Laws of Karma are not seen by believers as inventions of human beings; these laws are, instead, part of the very structure of reality to be discovered, accepted and obeyed.

Others have argued that morality is not to be discovered in some revealed divine law or Karma, but through a rational analysis of human nature. If, for instance, human beings have an *essential* nature and if fulfillment or happiness is best achieved only through expressing that essential nature, then moral philosophy must consist in describing that essential human nature and showing how that nature can best be expressed or developed. Thus Aristotle, for instance, held that human beings are essentially rational animals and their happiness, the appropriate end for which they act, comes through the exercise of this rationality. Epicurus reflected a similar pattern of analysis in his egoistic hedonism whereby he claimed that right actions are those which maximize pleasure over pain for the one who so acts. This claim, too, was grounded in a belief about the essential nature of human beings. People, he taught, are strictly mortal creatures with no meaningful existence beyond death and who appropriately and rationally seek to avoid pain and to experience pleasure during their limited years of existence.

The Buddha, or the "Enlightened One," arrived at his "Noble Truths" through an analysis of our essential human condition. "To live is to suffer" was the first of his four noble truths. The remaining Noble Truths identified the cause of suffering and the remedy for it. The remedy, the "noble eight-fold path," involved a number of moral instructions. The point, here, is that neither Aristotle nor Epicurus nor the Buddha believed that they were inventing rules to help human beings through life. Instead, they believed they had discovered and described the essential nature of human beings. Furthermore, the point of the advice given by each was that of maximizing personal fulfillment for those who followed this advice. To be sure, their views of the nature of such fulfillment were strikingly different. Aristotle's ideal man (and only a male can be such an ideal for Aristotle) in his quest for happiness has little resemblance to that of the Buddha's.

Another highly influential expression of the claim that morality is discovered, not invented, came from Immanuel Kant, the highly influential eighteenth century German philosopher, in his analysis of human reason. He shared with Aristotle and many others the assumption that our essential human nature is linked to the capacity to reason. In brief, Kant argued that reason was "given" to human beings so that they could be creatures with moral responsibility and a destiny. He believed that the features of a truly objective morality could be clarified by examining just how human beings do, in fact, think about matters moral. The conclusion of his argument led to his claim that a "categorical imperative" exists as the basic moral principle: "Act only on that maxim that you can, at the same time, will to be a universal law." Kant's subtle theory will be more fully developed in Chapter Three. In this context, his view is presented as another example of the claim that morality is an objective aspect of the nature of things and that the central truth of this morality can be discovered and clarified.

On the other hand, a significant number of philosophers have defended the view that moral codes and moral theories are *invented*. Their claim is that morality is not some objective aspect of the way the world is constructed or the way in which human reason necessarily works. Rather, they believe that morality is a purely human invention designed to help people cope with the world as they experience it. Protagoras may have been one of the earliest supporters of this position. He is famously noted for his claim that "Man is the measure of all things, of things that are, that they are, and of the things that are not, that they are not." In ethics, this claim led him to a form of ethical relativism in that he claimed there was no uniform moral law to be discovered that rightly pertains to human beings everywhere. Instead, each society or culture develops its own moral patterns and laws. He also asserted that there is no rational way to discern which of the varying rules and laws are right and which are wrong since no criteria exists, in principle, independent of particular cultures or societies. His advice, as a conservative, was to generally honor the patterns of one's own society since such rules are probably as good as any others. His analysis, critiqued by Plato, set the stage for arguments about ethical relativism all the way into the twenty-first century.

A more recent view of morality as "invented" was expressed by the French existentialist, Jean Paul Sartre. Having rejected both the existence of God and the view that there is some type of essential human nature to be expressed in life, Sartre concluded that there can be no objective way of validating moral choices. Yet life presses us into situations where we must make such choices. But in making these, he argued, we are "condemned to be free." We must choose, but we have no way of rationally or objectively justifying or defending the morality of an action. According to Sartre, then, our own moral decisions derive entirely from our own subjectivity which eliminates the possibility of any claim that we have somehow attained an *objective* moral truth.

The so-called emotive or "boo-hurrah" theory of ethics, intensely debated in the mid-twentieth century, gave the entire argument about moral principles a radical reconstruction. Traditional moral philosophy generally considered moral judgments such as, "killing innocent persons is wrong," to be either true or false. Hence, the task of the moral philosopher was that of showing how such judgments can be construed as true or false. The surprising claim of the emotivist view was that moral judgments are neither true nor false since they are merely *expressions* of emotions, not factual judgments of some kind. To assert that "killing is wrong," for instance, is the equivalent of uttering "Boo to killing." Such "boo" utterances *express* emotions, but such expressions are neither true nor false. If someone utters "Boo to that team," it would not make sense to reply, "That's false" or "That's true." Though one might respond, "I feel differently about the team." This position will be developed more fully in chapter three. At this point, I list the emotive theory among those that deny moral truths can discovered in the nature of things since there are no such entities to be found. This would appear to leave the emotivist in the camp of those who hold that moral claims are invented since there are none to be discovered. But what is invented, then, are not moral claims that can be true or false, but merely expressions that reflect our disapproval (boo) or approval (hurrah) of certain actions or states of affairs.

The emotive theory of ethics could suggest another theory that would explain how human beings invented ethics. Let us call it the "projection theory of ethics." Such a theory would grant that moral judgments are accompanied by certain emotional states.

A THEORY ABOUT MORAL THEORIES

Thus, the judgment "That was an immoral deed" would be accompanied by a feeling of disapproval which could be expressed as "Phooey on that deed." Or, "That was a good deed" would be accompanied by a feeling of approval expressed as "Hurrah for that deed." But given that we experience these feelings of approval or disapproval, we then come to invent ways to explain them or, more significantly, we invent ways of justifying the *feelings* we do have. (Most therapists would grant that human beings have a great propensity for fabricating explanations that appear to justify their feelings or actions.) And what could more adequately justify our feelings of approval or disapproval than the theory that such feelings are reflections of a basic moral order that exists in the universe?

Certain parallel cultural patterns and the myths that sustain them reflect this kind of inventive rationalization. In traditional Hinduism, the feeling of superiority that the higher caste person has over the lower caste person--as well as the actions which flow from such caste structure--is neatly justified by the theory of the Law of Karma. "I am properly in this position of higher caste and you in the lower precisely because of the difference in the Karma which resulted, necessarily, from our deeds in our previous incarnation." Or, in the Biblical tradition, the first command given by God to the first man and woman could be seen as the attempt of the ancient Hebrews to give divine sanction to those activities they found to be central to their life experience. "Be fruitful and multiply, and fill the earth and subdue it; and have dominion over the fish of the sea and over the birds of the air and over every living thing that moves upon the earth" (Genesis 1:28). Hence, the fruitfulness and dominion they *experienced* as factual become justified and explained as actions endorsed by God. This theory of ethics may then help explain how the very idea of moral rules came into being: Since I enjoy being treated in just and loving ways, justice and love must be fundamental principles built into the very nature of existence; therefore, God commands love and justice. And since I abhor theft and adultery, such actions must run counter to the fundamental nature of life and the commands of God.

Two observations about this "projection theory" need to be made. First, even if this theory is correct—and I have no idea just how one might verify such a theory—this would still not falsify any moral theory that developed. A basic logical principle holds that the origins of an idea in no way falsify (or justify) the idea itself. The genetic fallacy identifies just such a faulty inference. Thus, a moral theory could well be correct even if it grew from the dynamics just described. Sigmund Freud recognized this principle when he granted that even if he could show that religious belief was grounded in fear and the need for a father figure, this would not, in itself, falsify religious beliefs that developed as a response to such needs. When Freud claimed that religion was an "illusion" he meant that religion results from wish-fulfillment, not that religious beliefs are false. He did, of course, argue that religion should be considered false on other grounds.

My second observation about this "projection theory" of ethics would be to grant that such a theory would be completely compatible with the major arguments put forward in this book. What I aim to show is that there are certain logical relationships between a moral system and the broader explanatory worldview in which this moral system is rooted. The logical connection could run in either direction. Given certain *beliefs* about the nature of things--a worldview--then some moral patterns appear to follow and would thus produce certain *feelings* about deeds deemed to be morally good or bad. Conversely, given certain *feelings* of compassion, sympathy, or anger, for example, we then *invent* beliefs about the nature of things—worldviews—that would justify the feelings we experience.

While I have described the distinction between deontological and teleological theories of ethics in this chapter, I have not committed myself to either theory. And while I have suggested a number of ways in which morality can be discovered or invented, I have not committee myself to the truth of any such view of the origins of morality. As my argument moves forward, I must necessarily make some theoretical commitments of my own.

CHAPTER TWO

THE POINT OF MORALITY

... *the concepts of moral and ethical arise because of conflicts of interest, and ... moral systems have been designed to assist group members and explicitly not to assist the members of competing groups.*

R. D. Alexander[1]

Is it not significant that those who advocate self-sacrifice usually present it as a path to self-realization? 'He who loseth his life shall find it.' ... If a man used moral language to commend not doing whatever would give rise to the flourishing of man as what he took man to be, then we should consider him irrational.

W. D. Hudson[2]

Ordinary language involves a variety of terms, such as "good," "bad," "right," "wrong," " ought," and "obligated" that usually reflect moral judgments of various kinds. We are aware not only of these judgments, but also of various laws, principles and rules presumably employed in making them. Furthermore, we are familiar with the apparent authority these rules have in directing deliberate human actions as well as the many disagreements among people about them. As we live out our lives, most of us operate with some semblance of a moral system that largely reflects the patterns of those who nurtured us and helped shape our beliefs. We tend, intuitively, to trust these beliefs and call on them whenever we seriously engage in decisions about matters moral. Generally, we try to avoid being moral failures by our own standards, even by employing transparent rationalizations such as, "Everybody is doing it."

The theory outlined in the previous chapter was formulated in order to explain certain phenomena related to the moral judgments that people make. One basic phenomenon is that human societies appear, universally, to create moral systems and codes. What is there about our human situation that prompts us to develop such systems? Just what is the point of morality for human beings? What function does it have? These questions can be answered by constructing a series of scenarios, originally suggested by William James, that will help illuminate the point of morality by showing how experience forces human beings to make moral judgments.[3]

The first scenario presents a universe completely devoid of sentient creatures—creatures or beings that have wants, needs, desires, pleasures, pains, or interests of some kind. Hereafter, I shall refer to these "wants, needs, desires, etc." as WNDs. Such WNDs would include not only physical or bodily WNDs but also the entire potential range of human experience—emotional, psychological, aesthetic, intellectual, social, spiritual, mystical, and creative. Though this first scenario presents a universe devoid of human beings, animals, angels, and gods or *a* God, there could be a sun, stars, land, sea, clouds, and all related celestial and terrestrial phenomena. Even plants could be part of this universe if we agree that plants are not sentient beings.

Several observations could be made about this non-sentient universe. In the first place, it would clearly not contain any civil or statutory laws since such laws depend on a human or human-like agency to construct them. In the second place, this universe would be one devoid of *value*. In the absence of creatures that want or need or desire or appreciate or value, there would be no object needed, desired, appreciated or valued. In order for something to *have* value, it must *be* valued. In this universe, a rock might be broken or a tree shattered by a stroke of lightening, but these events would neither increase nor decrease value— assuming, again, that trees are non-sentient. An object could have *potential* value in the sense that it could potentially become the object of some sentient creature's valuing if such a sentient creature came into existence. Finally, this proposed universe would also appear to be devoid of morality or of moral issues.

Even if some *Karma* or moral law of cause and effect, as in Hinduism, existed in this universe, such *Karma* would have no application since no actions that had moral significance could take place.

A second scenario would be constructed by adding to that originally non-sentient universe one (but only one) sentient being that has WNDs. In this scenario, it is also assumed that no future potential sentient creatures would come into existence and that no gods or God exists. The addition of that one sentient being would bring other dimensions to the scene. There would now be a universe with *value* since any object or state of affairs wanted, desired, or enjoyed by that creature would have positive value just because that creature valued it. What that single being experienced as good *would* be a good. "Good" is used here in its non-moral sense, as we speak of a "good" cake or a "good" automobile. What that being experienced as bad (non-moral "bad") would be bad. If the being added to the universe were godlike, value would also be added if the god valued that universe or preferred certain states of affairs in that universe to other possible states of affairs.

Certainly this new universe would not yet include civil law since no authoritative civil body existed to legislate such laws. It would also be a universe without moral dimensions. The choices made by this one being could increase or decrease the amount of value experienced by *that* being, but the choices would have no moral implications. In that one-sentient-being universe there would be no meaningful role for moral laws or moral decisions. And this would be the case even if that one sentient being possessed those characteristics which are generally assumed to be necessary for moral capacities, such as freedom of action and the ability to understand the nature of moral obligation. In the absence of other human beings or other sentient creatures, and if no future human beings or sentient creatures were to ever exist, a lone human being in that universe would have no moral obligations. Furthermore, that lone human being would appear to have no moral obligation to herself. Her choices could produce increasing or decreasing satisfaction for her, but such choices would have no moral significance. Even that creature's suicide would seem to have no *moral* implications. We are still assuming that no divine Mind or Reality exists in this second scenario and that no future sentient beings will some day exist.

For the third scenario, one more sentient creature is added to the universe, but there still does not exist a god-like being or the potential for future sentient beings aside from the two introduced. There is, now, increased value in that universe since there are *two* creatures that can value objects or states of affairs. Also, this universe would have the potential of morally significant actions. If these two creatures never interacted in any way, this universe would still be devoid of moral significance. Creature A could presumably pursue its own goals without any concern for or impact on creature B's goals and vice versa. No moral situations would appear, no moral decisions would be made. If, however, A's quest for its own good did interact or intersect with B's quest for its good, then a new dimension has clearly appeared. Given such an interaction, a happy unity could exist if the WNDs of A were completely supportive and compatible with the WNDs of B—say, for instance, a truly perfect marriage in a truly perfect world. All the WNDs of both A and B could be honored and no moral choices need to be made. But if a clash of WNDs occurred with the interaction of A and B—if A desires to eat B and B desires not to be eaten by A—then the scene is radically altered. At that juncture, some desires must be sacrificed if other desires are to be affirmed. In order for some good as a fulfilled desire to come into being, another good must be set aside; hence, we have a value conflict between sentient beings pursuing their WNDs. However, this setting may not yet have *moral* implications. Would a moral dimension exist if creature A were a human being and creature B a rabbit? Or what if creature A were a lion and creature B a human being?

Most readers will probably agree that a morally significant situation would exist in this third scenario if the two creatures were basically human in their make-up—that is, if both of them had the capacities and experiences which made it possible for them to think and act in moral terms and if some type of moral structures or laws existed. Here, we leave open the question of what capacities and experiences are required for such thinking and acting. Though no god-like being has been introduced into this universe, we also leave open the question of just what kind of moral laws or structures could exist in this third universe. If the interests of the two human-like beings are in competition, a cluster of questions arises that tests our moral intuitions: How would such a clash of interests be arbitrated in that setting? Would a *moral* arbitration be possible? If A felt threatened by or experienced a deep distaste for B, would it be *immoral* for A to take B's life? If so, why so? Or would it be immoral for B to enslave A if B found that to be both advantageous and possible? Again, if so, why so?

This brings us to the final scenario which shall be called "Our Moral Setting." This scenario is our present universe that is currently teeming with sentient creatures including some six billion human beings and possibly gods or a God. Occasionally, the WNDs of the sentient beings that exist in Our Moral Setting interact in positive and cooperative ways; at other times there are dramatic and bloody clashes of interest, as the struggles between certain species and the history of human warfare both bear witness. It is this final scenario that establishes the issues to be faced by any moral philosopher or system of ethics. Given Our Moral Setting, it is clear that not all the WNDs of all beings can be honored; indeed, some must be denied so that others can be affirmed. But how are these clashes of interest to be arbitrated? To reflect on morality is to come to terms with just such issues. In the end, the task of moral reflection is that of puzzling out how to *appropriately* arbitrate the many conflicts among the multitude of WNDs of various sentient beings existing in the world.

Given the scenarios we have examined, it seems intuitively clear that not all decisions or choices would fall into the category of *moral* judgments. Whether I eat an apple or a pear would not appear to constitute a moral choice since it does not involve the WNDs of other sentient creatures. On the other hand, if I decide to eat well while fully aware that another human being with whom I could share such food is malnourished or starving, then it would appear that a moral situation is involved since there would be conflicting WNDs. In pursuing my desire to eat well, I am also frustrating the desires of those in need of food.

If my interpretation of the scenarios described above is cogent, then any action that has moral significance will have at least six characteristics. 1) Such an action involves the WNDs of human beings and perhaps other sentient beings from animals to God or gods. 2) Such an action must in some way involve at least two sentient creatures with WNDs. A totally isolated creature cannot perform an action with moral significance. 3) Such an action requires a setting where there is a *conflict* between two (or more) sentient beings. Actions in an *ideal* world with no such conflicts would not have moral significance. An ideal world would, presumably, be one where the WNDs of various sentient creatures do not come into conflict and there are sufficient resources to meet all of the existing WNDs. In that world, no WNDs would need to be sacrificed. Even in the Garden of Eden myth, there were no moral issues until the expressed WNDs of Yahweh came into conflict with the WNDs of Eve, Adam and the serpent. Paradise was broken by conflicting WNDs. 4) Such an action must be performed by a being with the capacity for making moral judgments. Such a being would be *aware* of the WNDs of other beings that are in conflict with its own (it recognizes a moral issue). This being must consciously raise the issue of the proper prioritizing of the conflicting WNDs (it is aware of possible moral rules or principles). And this being must be aware of the consequences of its actions regarding its own WNDs and those of competing creatures. Without such awareness, no actions would have moral significance, though they could still be "good" or "bad" in a non-moral sense. A lion pursuing a gazelle, we generally assume, is not concerned about any moral issue at stake. Furthermore, *we* would also assume that no moral issue is, in fact, at stake there. Animals are not usually viewed as morally responsible creatures even though we do reward and punish them for their behavior. We may refer to a dog as mean or nasty, but it would seem odd to speak of an "immoral" dog. 5) This being must be able to choose between various options while acting in this sphere of conflicting needs. This does not necessarily imply the need for freedom of the will, since the freedom to do what one wants can be seen as sufficient for moral responsibility. 6) Some type of action-guiding rules or principles or criteria must exist, though these could be either objective or subjective in nature. For instance, the very rational nature of the person may lead him or her to recognize a basic and objective moral principle (Kant). Or, the person may claim that his or her own needs have priority and that such subjectivity is an adequate defense of an action that is purely self-interested or self-referential (egoism). If the individual is not aware of any action-guiding principles, either objective or subjective, that person could not make a morally significant decision.

This analysis of Our Moral Setting and its implications casts a wide net regarding morally significant actions. These actions would run far beyond lying, cheating, killing and adultery. If this analysis holds, then morally significant decisions abound in life. I contend that the following illustrative choices are morally significant, but I am not judging whether a particular solution is immoral or moral. For instance, if I choose to spend my money for costly meals or for elaborate vacations instead of using it to help a child without nourishment or health care, I would be making a morally significant decision since some WNDs are being satisfied while others are being "butchered," to use James' term. Furthermore, I would presumably be willing to defend my choice by appealing to rules, principles or arguments that would justify it. This analysis implies that the vast majority of civil laws and political decisions are morally significant since they almost always involve supporting the WNDs of some while sacrificing those of others. A simple example would be the laws against theft that protect the WNDs of those who own food and frustrate the WNDs of others who could benefit by stealing it. (Was Robin Hood immoral?) The graduated income tax assumes that the wealthier members of society should be taxed so that services beneficial to others, such as free public education or universal health care, can be carried out. Political debate regarding such programs is grounded in a variety of assumed moral principles.

But perhaps the scenarios adapted from James have led us to a mistaken judgment about the nature of moral reality. Conceivably, moral judgments could be unrelated to what we have called the WNDs of sentient creatures. Perhaps moral reality is rooted in some other aspect of the nature of things. For instance, moral reality may be based solely on the commands or laws of a God and have no relationship at all to the WNDs of created sentient beings. What that God commands will be morally right just because that God so commanded. Or perhaps there exists in the natural world certain structures or relationships that not only shape morality but are also independent of the WNDs of sentient beings. Indeed, certain WNDs may be antagonistic to these basic moral structures. Again, perhaps moral reality is grounded in the very nature of human *rationality* rather than in human WNDs, and these rational structures may at times be in opposition to the urgings of desires and wants. My major argument assumes that these alternative approaches to morality are mistaken and that our original interpretation of the moral scene is more compelling.

My basic claim is: "The point of the moral reflection that we *necessarily* pursue is to find *appropriate* ways of arbitrating among the various conflicting WNDs of sentient creatures." Morality and moral reflection, when viewed in this manner, are necessarily part of human experience since we all must devise some method of arbitration that we deem appropriate. The meaning of "appropriate" is, of course, a crucial consideration in any moral theory and must be analyzed in the argument to be developed in this work.

In analyzing the point of morality and moral reflection, I did not attempt a definition of morality. Instead of giving a definition, I consider the *point* or *function* of morality. Two implications of this approach should be noted. First, *any* system of thought which seeks to find appropriate means of arbitrating among conflicting WNDs will be classified as a moral theory. Thus, the egoistic hedonism of Epicurus will be understood to be a moral theory, just as will Kant's formalism. Both Epicurus and Kant developed principles whereby persons could appropriately arbitrate among conflicting WNDs. Clearly, however, Kant's view of "appropriate" varied a good deal from that held by Epicurus.

A second implication of this approach is the rejection of the notion of "*the* moral point of view." This phrase suggests certain necessary conditions involved in holding a moral point of view whereby any theory that lacks those conditions will fail to be a *moral* theory. A developed analysis of this "moral point of view" will be made in Chapter Eight. At this point, I would grant there exists what might be called a "received tradition." Most recent formulations of "*the* moral point of view" reflect such a tradition. But to identify certain aspects of this *received* tradition with *the* moral point of view begs important questions. Some claim for instance, that *the* moral point of view includes the concept of impartiality or of not being egoistic. Such a feature would rule out the hedonistic egoism of Epicurus as a moral point of view. But I suggest that Epicurus' theory should be considered to be *a* moral point of view since his theory was also designed as a means of arbitrating among the conflicting WNDs of sentient creatures in a way *he* deemed appropriate. We may reject his moral theory, but still accept it as *a* moral theory. My theory, then, constitutes a highly inclusive view of just what constitutes a moral theory. Again, a major aim of this work is to explain just why so many varying moral theories exist.

When any moral theory attempts to identify the appropriate way of arbitrating the various conflicting WNDs of sentient creatures, there are two major issues that require analysis. The first issue arises from the possible conflict among one's own WNDs. Which of my varied WNDs should I pursue through my actions? Which objects or states of affairs are the most valuable to me? An individual often discovers that some of her own WNDs come into conflict with certain others; not all of them can be acted upon. One cannot "have one's cake and eat it too." Hence, the individual must decide which of her own WNDs to honor and which to forego. She cannot, for instance, enjoy both the benefits of a married life and the benefits of a single life. She must, therefore, come to some conclusion about which goals and experiences are most desirable for her. If she is choosing *only* from among her own WNDs, and if these choices in no way impinge upon the WNDs of other sentient beings, she would not be making *morally* significant decisions since no conflict between the WNDs of two or more beings is involved. She would, of course, be making decisions about what is valuable for her alone.

In choosing among her WNDs, she will have certain beliefs about what constitutes a truly fulfilling or worthwhile life and, as a rational person, she would choose to pursue just that kind of life. The claim that a rational person would choose to pursue a fulfilling life—as that person understands "fulfillment"—has been made by many significant philosophers including Plato, Aristotle, Thomas Aquinas, Spinoza and J. S. Mill. This claim, however, does not necessarily imply a form of ethical egoism—the theory that a person should always seek her own fulfillment. Nor does it imply a form of psychological egoism—the descriptive theory that people always act to satisfy their own perceived best interests. These two forms of egoism will be considered in Chapter Eight where the question of, "Why be moral?" will be analyzed.

Yet the question of the fulfilling life, which a rational creature would want to pursue, is complex and inescapably linked to certain other questions about the nature of human beings. Six such questions are central: 1) Is there a meaning or a point to the human venture? 2) Are we part of some Divine plan or are we the random products of an impersonal natural process? 3) How do persons best find a sense of significance? We want not only to *be*, but also to be something of significance. 4) Is there meaningful personal experience beyond the death of the body? If death is the end of personal existence, then it would appear that any fulfillment must come during bodily life. 5) Just what kinds of experiences lead to an individual's fulfillment? There are a variety of candidates: pleasure, tranquillity, power, status. 6) Which human beings, or other creatures, contribute to my personal quest for fulfillment and which do not? In this quest, am I linked positively only to those within my clan, family or tribe while other human beings are just "in my way"?

The second issue the moral philosopher must face as she seeks the appropriate way of arbitrating among the competing WNDs is that of her own obligation to others as they seek *their* fulfillment. This differs from question 6) above in that we are now asking whether or not she has some *obligation* to help others in their pursuit of fulfillment as she pursues her own. Question 6) asked not about *obligation* but about how the lives of others contribute to her own fulfillment. This issue of possible obligation to others carries with it the clear ring of moral language. To pursue what one believes to be fulfilling for oneself is to seek the "good life" in the usual non-moral sense of "good." In asking the question of possible obligation toward others, we raise the question of the "good life" in the traditional moral sense of "good."

This second issue is also complex. Do we have this moral responsibility toward *all* sentient creatures such that their quests for fulfillment have some claim upon our own lives? If so, why so? If not, why not? Or do we have moral responsibility only for other *human* beings. And if not for *all* human beings, then which ones? Are there other powers or natural laws or gods or a God such that our WNDs and our quest for fulfillment are related in some meaningful way to the WNDs (commands, laws) of such powers? Do I honor the WNDs of such powers only insofar as they promise to benefit me as well; or must I honor their WNDs even when it involves a genuine cost to my own aspirations, goals, desires and fulfillment?

To sum up, I claim that the point of morality is to find a life pathway which leads to one's own personal fulfillment by pursuing those WNDs that promise to be most fulfilling. But in the quest for my own fulfillment I must also decide just how the WNDs of other sentient creature relate, positively or negatively, to my own. Not all WNDs can be honored—my own or those of others. Some must be rejected if others come to fruition. Thus, the task of moral reflection is to determine the most *appropriate* way to arbitrate between the multitude of competing WNDs. All fully developed moral theories address this task directly or indirectly. Chapter Three will illustrate how this task is worked out in a number classical and contemporary moral theories, while Chapters Five and Six will examine how "God" makes a difference, for good or ill, as this task is pursued.

CHAPTER THREE

MORAL THEORIES AND WORLDVIEWS

"Without religion there can be no real, sincere morality, just as without roots there can be no real flower."
Leo Tolstoy[1]

"We have been so conditioned and enervated by the Beatitudes that we are hardly capable any longer even of understanding... the truth that was so obvious to the pagan moralists: that what is worth having is not the common, but the uncommonly good."
Richard Taylor[2]

In previous chapters, two claims were made about any complete moral theory. First, such a theory must provide an answer to the question of what type of life is most fulfilling for a human being--the question of the fulfilled life. Second, such a theory must show what obligation, if any, a person has to help other persons who also seek a fulfilled life--the question of responsibility. In this chapter, a number of influential moral theories will be reviewed showing how each theory answers these questions from within the context of the philosopher's worldview. This overview is intended to demonstrate that beliefs about the fundamental nature of *reality* (God or not-God) shape the answers to the two questions above. My aim is to be purely descriptive; no attempt will be made to evaluate the views to be presented.

Two major worldviews, theism and naturalism, were described in Chapter One. In the reviews to follow, each philosopher will reflect, sometimes only roughly, one of these. Of course, some worldviews do not fall neatly into either of these two categories. Ancient polytheists, for instance, were neither naturalists nor theists; and while Plato's philosophy was used by later theists to construct systems of religious philosophy and theology, he could not be classified as a traditional theist. While the list could be extended to include the major religious systems of the Far East along with deists and transcendentalists, I narrow the discussion to the two worldviews described largely for the sake of simplicity and illustration. However, views that cannot be neatly classified as naturalistic or theistic could also be shown to exemplify the theory about morality presented in this work.

Ancient Roots:
The Hebrew Prophets and Pre-Socratic Greeks

The cluster of the major prophetic voices in the Hebrew Bible (the Christian "Old Testament") range from the eighth to the fifth century BCE. Moses, seen as the primary recipient of the Law, is usually placed in the thirteenth century BCE. These figures represents what might best be called a divine command theory of ethics. This theory maintains that what God commands is right, and it is right precisely because God commands it. Conversely, an act is morally wrong, if and only if, God prohibits it. These various prophetic voices should not be seen primarily as predictors of the future. Rather, the Hebrew term translated as "prophet" means one who speaks forth God's will to the community. The commands of God put forward were understood neither as the product of rational reflection nor insight into natural moral law. The prophets were not philosophers. Instead, the prophets, functioning as God's mouthpiece, viewed these commands as revealed truth delivered to the believing community. This understanding of morality is still reflected in the conservative traditions of Judaism, Christianity and Islam.

While God's commands clarified the moral pathway, they also contained a promise to those who walked that pathway. The decision to obey or disobey God was a fateful one. "You shall walk in all the way which the Lord your God has commanded you, that you may live, and that it may go well with you, and that you may live long in the land which you shall possess." (Deuteronomy 5:33) The nature of the fulfilled life which results from obedience to God's commands varies within the Biblical traditions and cannot be developed in detail here. Since the Hebrew Bible acknowledges no meaningful existence beyond the death of the body, it idealizes a long life enjoyed with many offspring and much wealth. Disobedience to God's will brings the promise of God's wrath measured out in disease, natural disasters or destruction at the hand of enemies. As the concept of the resurrection of the dead later makes its way into this Biblical tradition, ultimate personal fulfillment was postponed to the life beyond the death of the body. God's punishments, then, can also include those applied in the after-life.

To the second basic question answered by every moral theory, "What obligation, if any, do I have to help others as I seek my own life's fulfillment?", the Hebrew Bible reflects a variety of views. To the stranger who dwells among your people, kindness and hospitality are prescribed. One of the Ten Commandments holds "You shall not kill," and Leviticus 19:18 commands that "you should love your neighbor as yourself." On the other hand, a variety of punishments, including death by stoning, are enjoined for those who break significant laws. Special concern is to be shown to the neighbor defined as all those within your own clan, tribe or community. Persons outside the community are treated with less compassion. For example, in Deuteronomy 7:16, God commands that "you shall destroy all the peoples that the Lord your God will give over to you, your eye shall not pity them." Ethnic cleansing was theologically justified. In the stories of the Exodus and the conquest of Palestine, Yahweh is portrayed largely as a tribal god in competition with the gods of foreigners. Later prophets, as Isaiah, dismissed the gods of other nations as mere fictions and proclaimed Yahweh as the universal God over all peoples and nations.

While the Hebrew prophets provided foundations for the three major monotheisms of the West, Greek traditions offered strikingly different views of the human situation. Instead of prophets, the Greeks had poets and, later, philosophers. The poets sung from a context of myth, while the <u>philosophers introduced critical analysis and theoretical speculation.</u>

Two competing themes in the early Greek poets reflect issues that remain in much future philosophical reflection. Homer's epics (c. eighth century, BCE) provided one theme through the development of the great hero model. "Always be first and best and superior to the others," is the advice Achilles receives from his father in Homer's *Iliad*. From this angle of vision, the truly fulfilling human life was to be found in endurance, cunning and self-assertion. On the other hand, the poetry of the later Hesiod (c. eighth century BCE) emphasizes the role of justice administered by Zeus. This justice brings disaster to the man who commits wrongdoing or expresses overweening pride, but promises rewards for those pursuing the difficult, uphill road of justice. The focus of interest in these poets is not so much on moral behavior, as we might think of it, but upon what it means to be an excellent human being. Such human excellence, as presented either by Homer's heroes or the alternative excellence as portrayed by Hesiod, always brings with it the promise of human fulfillment--as each author envisions fulfillment. An element of tension between these two themes is later expressed by Solon the lawgiver who sought for fame and prosperity but did not want to acquire these in unjust ways; for such injustice, he thought, always brought punishment. Later thinkers transformed the idea of the justice of Zeus into a general principle of natural law expressed not only in the world of nature but also in human conduct and its consequences.

Individual Moral Philosophers: A Survey

The following discussions will not attempt to provide comprehensive views of the philosophical or moral theories of these thinkers. The reader should turn to standard sources for more developed analyses. Instead, the focus will be on the way belief or non-belief in God helps to shape beliefs about the truly fulfilling human life and also the nature of responsibilities toward others.

Protagoras (c. 490-c.421 BCE)

Plato's dialogues, the major source for our knowledge of Protagoras, represents Protagoras as saying "man is the measure of all things: of the things that are, that they are, and of the things that are not, that they are not."[3] While that saying may strike us as obscure, it expresses a form of ethical relativism. By the time of Protagoras, the Greeks were familiar with the varying traditions, customs and moral values to be found throughout the ancient world and were, no doubt, intrigued by the question of just which moral judgments constituted the correct ones. The ethical relativism of Protagoras answered that question by holding that the correct moral judgments for any particular culture are precisely the judgments generally accepted in that culture. This view implies that no objectively or universally correct set of moral judgments can be discerned; neither is there a "natural law" which can be used to evaluate those of a particular culture.

While we cannot reconstruct the complete worldview held by Protagoras, even if his modest view of human knowledge would have allowed him to attempt to construct one, it is clear that he put little store in things religious. He asserted that he was not able to know whether or not gods exist, and what they might be like if they did exist. We would expect his ethical theory, then, to be strikingly different from the divine command theory held by the ancient Hebrew prophets.

Protagoras, however, did not hold the theory of *individual* ethical relativism that maintains that the correct moral values for any particular person are precisely those held by that person. The general opinion held in a community or city is the correct moral norm, for Protagoras, not the individual beliefs of a person within that community. Thus, any individual's moral judgments are wrong, according to Protagoras, when they differ from the general opinions held by the community. In a practical way, his ethical theory tended to lead to conservative conclusions since anyone who claimed to be a moral reformer would necessarily be morally mistaken since such a reformer would be challenging the moral norms of his or her community.

This conservative position is also reflected in his claim to be a teacher of human virtue defined as the ability to reason well not only about one's own affairs but also the affairs of the community to which one belongs. In the long run, the aim of his reasoning was practical for he asserted that the youth should be taught to support the traditions of their society because this helps create a stable society. His approach to worship of the gods was also highly practical, for he held that even if people cannot know if any gods exist or what they are like, nevertheless, this lack of knowledge need not prevent one from participating in the religious ceremonies of their community.

Most human beings, however, have a deep desire to *know*, as Aristotle claimed some time after Protagoras, and the relativism of Protagoras made it impossible to make a claim to knowledge as "true, justified belief." Socrates and Plato brought strong criticism to bear on such relativism, and the modern developments of science lead many to believe that, at least in some areas, we can genuinely come to know something like universal truths. But perhaps Protagoras would still encourage us to believe what our present culture teaches, not because such teachings can be shown to be true, but because such believing makes for a more stable society. Protagoras, himself, appeared to believe that his own relativistic theory was itself true. But while such inconsistency is often viewed as a philosophical sin of the first order, it is not foreign to the history of philosophy.

The relativism of Protagoras, however, does reflect the major themes I have been pressing. He believed that the moral pathway to be followed within one's own community was the most fulfilling pathway for the individual. While a setting of public peace and stability was important for fulfillment, the precise nature of a fulfilled life must be relative to the views of one's community. Given his agnostic position concerning gods and his denial of anything like a "law of nature" in morality, he evidently would not have argued that we have some responsibility to assist in the fulfillment of others aside from following the norms of the community Slavery, male superiority and class structure would be acceptable as patterns worked out in a city or community. Protagoras certainly provided no basis whatsoever for a program of social revolution or reconstruction, and any concept of moral progress would have been incoherent in principle.

Epicurus (341-271 BCE)

Stepping out of a strict chronological order, Epicurus is presented next in order to model a particular theory that clearly reflects the themes pursued in this work. This Greek philosopher developed perhaps the clearest moral theory ever formulated; furthermore, Epicureanism has had a following throughout history as well as in our modern world. The moral advice he presented followed logically from the views he held about the fundamental nature of reality as well as human nature. Epicurus adopted the view of earlier Greek atomists who held that *every* existing thing is ultimately made up of small uncreated and unbreakable--hence eternal--units of matter which are arranged in space in various ways resulting in such things as trees, clouds and persons. Such atomism was an early form of ontological materialism and formed the basis for the worldview Epicurus expressed. According to this theory, this universe is an expression of the eternally existing and uncreated atoms, with no divine hand guiding the process; therefore, human life is the product of these purely natural processes which have no purpose, goal, or point in themselves.

While Epicurus granted that gods might exist, his worldview was essentially naturalistic. Even if gods existed, they were of no concern to Epicurus since he believed that they were also made up of atoms and had no way of intervening in human life. Furthermore, these gods held no threat to us in life beyond the death of the body since individual human existence ends with death. With such claims, Epicurus attempted to free persons from fear of the gods and of death since the gods cannot now influence our lives and cannot punish us after death since then we are no more.

Epicurus' moral theory was an early form of egoistic hedonism that asserts the good life is made up of pleasure for the self. In this central teaching, he accepted what all moral thinkers assume-- that the aim of the rational and morally appropriate life is that of personal fulfillment. He did not deny the possibility of truly altruistic deeds, but he believed such deeds were irrational. His moral theory, he believed, stemmed logically out of his atomistic materialism in this way: Since we live only as long as our body's atoms hold together, and since there is no life after death, then it follows that the rational individual, while alive, should seek pleasure and avoid pain. Furthermore, Epicurus believed that people have no moral obligation to aid others in their quest for the pleasurable life. They pursue their own route to pleasure. Yet we need to be prudent in our relationships since helping others can sometimes maximize our own pleasure. In giving such help, however, the proper rational motive is the ultimate pursuit of our own interests. Other virtues may also function instrumentally as means of maximizing our own pleasure.

Some find Epicurus' definition of "pleasure" as "the absence of pain in the body and in the mind" to be quite odd, and his view differed from other Greeks who concentrated on bodily pleasures of the moment. Epicurus held that mental pleasure is to be preferred over bodily pleasure since it is longer lasting and has few, if any, painful side-effects. He recognized that an evening of gross physical partying could result, negatively, in pain the following day. Furthermore, he cautioned against marriage, not because sexuality as such was evil, but because marriage normally resulted in more pain than pleasure, more worry and concern than peace. For marriage often involves love of the spouse and the children born of that marriage. But wives and husbands and children are mortal, and to love someone only to lose them to death results in enormous pain. Better to have never loved at all than to love and to lose. The wise person, for Epicurus, lives quietly and enhances his security and happiness by surrounding himself with like-minded friends. The best party would involve philosophical conversation with congenial friends while enjoying light refreshments. He, himself, was known to be a warm friend, gracious host and pleasant companion.

Some would ask whether Epicureanism can be considered a *moral* theory at all, since it seems to run counter to the main strands of moral philosophy in many human cultures. There are, however, several reasons for listing him among thinkers who propound moral theories. He is, after all, discussed in any comprehensive history of ethics. Furthermore, he does address the two major issues faced by all moral theorists--the nature of the fulfilled human life and the question of obligation to others. The fulfilled life, for Epicurus, is to be found through the quest of pleasure for the self; and we have no obligation to help others in their quest for fulfillment, except insofar as such help may be instrumental to our own egoistic aims. For many, his outlook has a familiar and modern resonance and is reflected in the vast majority of commercial advertisements. Epicureanism is, after all, one way of seeking to arbitrate among the vast number of creatures pursuing their WNDs (wants, needs and desires) in a world where not all such desires can be met. It remains, for some, a defensible moral theory from within the context of a naturalistic worldview.

The Epicurean worldview is not limited to Western culture. A parallel is found in Carvaka, a philosophical system in ancient India that rejected the authority of the classical scriptures of India such as the *Vedas* and the *Upanishads*. Carvaka taught there is no meaningful divine or spiritual reality and that all existing things are products of an essentially material world which operates, without goal or intent, on the basis of its own laws. This system taught that human beings, like other creatures, are products of the processes of matter and the death of the body ends the existence of the individual. During life, therefore, the rational person seeks to avoid pain and to achieve pleasure. We live prudently with others, but we have no moral obligation to aid them. Both Carvaka and Epicureanism have been minority positions in their cultural traditions. Yet both represent possible positions that have attracted, intrigued and annoyed many who have pondered the human venture.

Plato (430 to 347 B.C.E)

Often cited as the father of Western philosophy, Plato left an enormous imprint on thought and culture. This influence has resulted not only from the power of his analysis and theory construction, but also from the rich mixture of philosophy, religion and poetry in his dialogues. His thought will be developed more extensively than other philosophers, in part because his moral philosophy must be developed within the context of his broad-ranging philosophical system, and, in part, because the thought forms of the later philosophers will be more familiar to most readers. Standard sources should be consulted for a more complete exposition of Plato's thought.

Like most creative thinkers, Plato developed his views in an historical setting wherein the traditional convictions of the times were being challenged. In Plato's day, the city-state was the basic organization of Greek society. The polytheistic Greek religion at the time was closely linked to the city-state setting where personal religion was rare and nothing like a church existed. The city-state was, in effect, both the government and the religion. Skepticism about old patterns of thought were openly expressed during Plato's time and controversy, the twin of skepticism, gave birth to philosophy.

The city-state society was being undermined at that time by a variety of forces. The naturalistic philosophers, for example, sought to explain matters in natural rather than mythological terms, challenging popular Greek polytheism by arguing that whatever gods there were could not possibly exist in the forms expressed in Homer's writings. Another challenge came from certain mystics, such as the Orphics and the Pythagoreans, whose teachings tended to focus on the salvation of the individual's soul rather than allegiance to the city-state. A final challenge came from the Sophists who tended to undermine the basis of morals by claiming there was no divine authority for morality or for the laws of a state. These Sophists held that right and wrong, wisdom, justice and goodness were only high-sounding names. Since morality and laws were human constructs, according to the Sophists, they could also be unmade or altered by human beings.

In addition to these challenges to the city-state, Plato also faced the universal challenge to all humankind—the problems of finitude and death. The challenge of death, of course, brings with it the challenge to the very meaning and point of life itself. Here Plato would agree with the lines from Euripides: "The cleverness of men is no real wisdom if it means forgetting their mortality." In the face of these various challenges, Plato sought to develop a political, social and moral philosophy, as well as a foundation for knowledge and a solution to the problem of death.

In developing his philosophy, Plato threw his complete support to the ideal of the city-state and attempted to bring reform to this form of government and society. He held that the political side and the religious side of any society must be related; hence, reform in one area called for reform in the other. These themes are worked out in detail in many of his writings, especially his *Republic* and *Laws*. One persistent them in these works is that of respect for the laws and judgments of a city-state. Indeed, if Platonism had a patron saint, it would be Socrates who, even when in prison and condemned by Athenian democracy to execution, refused to escape. His argument, briefly: "Do you think a city can go on existing, and avoid being turned upside-down, if its judgments are to have no force but are to be made null and void by private individuals?"[4] Plato's writings seek to demonstrate just why such laws and judgments should have force.

While Plato developed his own religious philosophy, he rejected traditional Greek mythology, reflected in Homer's poetry, not only as irrational but also as a totally inadequate view of the nature of the gods. On the other hand, he did not formulate anything like the views of the Hebrew prophets with their ethical monotheism and a divine command view of morality. Nor did Plato appeal to revealed truth to support his beliefs. If belief in God is to be held, it should be on the basis of careful reasoning. In his late dialogue, *Laws*, he developed the first attempts in Western philosophy at proofs of the existence of God. All these proofs were aimed to defeat several claims made by others at the time, including: 1) Gods do not exist. 2) Gods, if they exist, do not care about human beings. 3) These gods, if they do exist, can be flattered or bribed to benefit an individual. To successfully maintain a city-state, Plato believed that such opinions must be defeated. Hence, in *Laws* Plato sought to prove that gods do exist, they care about human beings and their behavior, and they cannot be flattered or bribed to benefit an individual.

To approach Plato's beliefs about God (or the gods) we might best begin with his own account of the formation of the world. He refers to this account as "a likely story," reflecting a modesty in recognition of the difficulty of gaining clear knowledge about such "exalted matters." Nevertheless, he considered his account to be as reasonable as the subject matter would allow. His likely story involved a claim that three basic factors existed: 1) Certain chaotic matter of which all sensible things are made; 2) A realm of patterns or forms or "ideas" which are non-material entities known only by mind; 3) A Divine Craftsman (Demiurgos, or "world-maker"). All three of these factors were pre-existent, not derived from or dependent upon any other existing substance or entity. The term "God" will be assigned to that Craftsman throughout this chapter, though Plato's God differs from the theistic God identified with Judaism, Christianity and Islam in significant ways.

Roughly stated, Plato held that the physical world as we experience it came into being through the action of the Divine Craftsman. This God used pre-existent chaotic matter to fabricate various entities by using the Forms (Ideas) for patterns. What we experience as a tree, for instance, is an entity resulting from the basic matter being shaped according to the Form or pattern of "treeness." (So also for cats, salamanders, etc.) Religious philosophers, in the centuries after Plato, transformed his thought into a monotheistic system by making Plato's God into an all-knowing, all-powerful and all-good God who brought all things into being "out of nothing" (*ex nihilo*), while Plato's Forms were transmuted into the contents of God's mind.

Plato assumed that this God meant well in fabricating the world and, being good himself, desired to reflect his own perfection in something outside of himself. Hence he used the unchanging world of eternal Forms or ideas to fashion the changing world of sense experience as far as this was possible. However, just as a highly skilled carpenter cannot build a perfect house out of imperfect materials, so the nature of the fabricated world reveals the imperfection of the basic matter this God had to use. This matter was stubborn and resistant resulting in an imperfect world in spite of the stature of the Divine Craftsman. In this story, Plato absolves God of any responsibility for faults that appear in the world. The imperfections, sufferings and evils of the world are to be laid at the door of this stubborn matter, not the Craftsman. This dualism between spirit (good) and matter (evil) still haunts Western thought today.

Plato's "likely story" also accounts for human souls and lays the foundation for his view of morality. While Plato's God fabricated the material world out of pre-existent stuff, he also created what he called a "World Soul" and the "heavenly race of the gods." The World Soul is characterized by mind and has the function of ruling over the physical body of the world, just as Plato taught that the human soul should rule over the human body. The heavenly race of the gods appears to be the gods of the fixed stars and planets. Plato does not insist on a pure monotheism, in part because he rejects the idea that true piety involves the worship of God or the gods. When Plato speaks of the divine elements in the world he sometimes speaks of "the God" and sometimes of "the gods." Yet "the gods" appear to be creations of "the God" (Craftsman) and exist in order to carry out the will of that Craftsman. Parallels to the realm of angels in Western theism seem clear. In all this, of course, Plato insists that Mind/Reason is the ultimate ground of purpose and direction. The universe, for Plato, is not to be construed as the product of pure randomness and chance.

Plato traces the connections among morality, politics and religious belief in *Laws*, his longest dialogue and the product of his later years. The role of the state was of great importance to Plato because the fulfillment of the individual is bound up with the general health and welfare of the entire community. Since no one is perfect, laws are needed to help bring about the good for the general public as well as for the individual. But respect for and obedience to the laws of the state require a link with the gods. Plato argued that the rule of law in the state is an imitation of divine rule, therefore honor must be given to the gods above everything else. "No one who believes in gods as the law directs ever voluntarily commits an unholy act or lets any lawless word pass his lips."[5] In the end, the moral failure of any person is the result of the failure of that person's reason. The laws of the state cannot make the person good, but they stand, with the gods in the background, as a restraint upon those who fail to be good.

Plato's God plays an important role in morality by dealing with individual human beings through a system of rewards or punishments that can extend to life after death and determine the destiny of individuals. The aim of all this, Plato posits, is to maximize the goodness of the world. While God cares for the individual as part of the whole and for the sake of the whole, Plato does not believe that God loves us as individuals. Neither should human beings love the gods, he maintains. Instead, the gods serve as models to be imitated since they are the source of the natural and moral order. These gods are not only living and intelligent beings, they are also moral beings motivated by goodness as they create and govern the world. Their justice will not be compromised and cannot be flattered or bribed by acts of piety and sacrifices. For Plato, true human piety consists in imitating the rationality and goodness of the gods, not in seeking worldly benefits. Although each person is small in terms of the entire scheme of things, yet he or she should remember that they are taking part in a great enterprise by cooperating with the gods. In this way each person shares in realizing the purpose of the universe.

Belief in God or the gods is, for Plato, an important factor in the human community since the concept of God undergirds an objective morality and also gives a serious dimension to the moral life through a system of sanctions. In the end, Plato doubts that human goodness is possible without some grounding in the concept of God. The laws of the city or nation must somehow reflect divine purposes and are reinforced by a sense of the ultimate Divine justice. Here we find similarities to the Hebrew prophet's proclamation of Yahweh's rule over history and the working out of Karma in Far Eastern thought. For Plato, always the philosopher and never the theologian, all such beliefs must be finally grounded in reason.

The concept of justice is central to Plato's moral and political thought and is discussed in *The Republic*, his most influential work. The English "justice" is the common translation of the Greek "*dikaiosune*," but that Greek term has wider connotations than the English "justice." *Dikaiosune* is sometimes used in Plato's writings to express the idea that people should be treated fairly and can also mean "the disposition to act rightly" in dealing with others—as when we speak of a just man or woman. Thus, the term could also be translated as "morality" since theft, breaking promises, committing adultery and neglecting duties to parents and to the gods are often listed by Plato as typical expressions of injustice.

In his analysis of a person who is just, Plato develops a theory of the human soul. The Greek concept of "soul" (*psyche*) was used to explain just why some entities have life and some do not. Plants, animals and human beings all have souls appropriate to their own nature; while non-living things, such as rocks, do not have souls since they do not have life. Thus "*psyche*" names a life principle involved with living entities. Plato teaches that the human soul is made up of three distinct parts—the "desiring," the "spirited," and the "rational," each with its own appropriate role or function. Appetites for food, drink and sexual satisfaction are expressions of the desiring element of the soul, while the spirited element involves such things as strength of will, anger, shame and conscience. Although animals have souls with both the desiring and spirited elements, human souls differ by having the rational element which animals lack. In this analysis, the Greeks shared the nearly universal human conviction that we differ from animals in highly significant ways.

Reason, for Plato, is that part of the soul that should rule and direct the other two parts. In one of his images, he suggests that reason is like the charioteer guiding the chariot of life which is pulled by two horses, a wild and unruly horse (desiring) and a more disciplined but energetic horse (spirited). If life is to be lived in a truly satisfactory way, the three parts of the soul must work in harmony, and that occurs when reason rules the other two parts by controlling the surging desires and directing the energies of the spirited part of the soul. A just person, for Plato, is one who establishes such a harmony brought about through the use of reason. If reason fails to direct a person's life, that person is dragged down by the drives of the desiring element of the soul to a less satisfactory life experience.

Central to Plato's moral theory is his conviction that the just person is also the happiest person. In this he reflects the nearly universal belief that morality is advantageous—that the good life in the non-moral sense is also the good life in the moral sense. Plato held to a form of psychological egoism since he believed that everyone wants his or her individual happiness, and that any action is chosen *because* people believe the action will help bring about personal well-being. The problem, Plato recognized, is that while the quest for happiness is legitimate and normal, beliefs about just how to achieve such happiness are often mistaken.

Herein lies the significance of human reason that helps develop what Plato considered the art of living. This art, like any art, requires an understanding of the elements involved; therefore, the art of living involves the proper function of the three parts of the soul. Each part has its own corresponding virtue when directed by reason. Temperance is the virtue associated with the *desiring* part of the soul, while courage is the virtue associated with the *spirited* part. The third virtue, wisdom, is associated with the *rational* part of the soul. Finally, for Plato, when reason has performed its proper function and the virtues of temperance, courage and wisdom are in harmony, then the fourth virtue, justice, has been achieved.

The specific content of the moral life lived out by a person who has achieved this harmony would reflect the generally accepted values of community life in Plato's day—truth-telling, honesty, loyalty to one's family, friends and community. But these day-to-day practices do not make a person good. Rather, the person who has become good by way of reason will live out such practices. Some twenty centuries later, Martin Luther expressed much the same position: "Good deeds do not make the good man, but the good man does good deeds."

This quest for the good life through reason is, in Plato's thought, linked closely with the Realm of the Forms—the eternal and non-material realm composed of the great patterns for all things existing in the material world. This Realm includes the Form of Beauty and Truth as well as the Good, which is the highest Form of all. The task of philosophy—"love of wisdom"—is that of comprehending this Realm. In the cultivation of reason, the mind ascends from the objects of the physical world, which are only passing shadows of Reality, to the genuinely real objects, those of the Forms. This intellectual ascent is linked to moral development; for as knowledge grows, so love for Truth, Beauty and Goodness also intensifies and life's true happiness comes into focus. Plato was convinced that true knowledge reveals that some pursuits are trivial and disappointing while others are significant and result in well being and happiness.

Plato reverts to mythological language when he explains the origins of individual human souls. Each pure and rational soul, he posits, was once created by the Divine Craftsman and at one time inhabited a star. But some of these souls developed a desire for the world of sensory experience and became enclosed in a material body as a kind of prison. Plato indulges, here, in a Greek pun by using "*soma*" (body) and "*sema*" (prison). Before its "fall" into a physical body, the soul had direct knowledge of the Forms; but when entering the body, the rational side of the soul becomes confused by the addition of the "desiring" and "spirited" dimensions as well as by sensory experience. Each soul, however, may free itself from its bodily prison and return to its star by overcoming the lower parts of its nature through the proper use of reason. Failing in this, the soul can sink to lower levels and enter into a series of animal bodies as stages in the process of purification. We find, here, the doctrine of the transmigration of souls expressed in the philosophies of India.

There is, in Plato the man, as well as in his thought, a deep yearning for some type of existence beyond the transient, changing, and misleading world of sensory experience. He accounts for this yearning with his doctrine of *eros*. When a human being experiences elements of beauty in the sensory world, this inspires in the soul a yearning for the ideal beauty that the soul contemplated in its pre-existence. It is this higher yearning which leads to the craving for fame, the urge to create art, science, philosophy and, especially, the longing for immortality. In this context, Plato develops a curious argument in support of the concept of immortality. Since this passionate longing for immortality is part of our essential nature, Plato posits, then the fulfillment of that longing must be possible. Hence, this yearning constitutes a proof of the soul's immortality. Centuries later, St. Augustine, reflecting Plato's influence, reformulated this human aspiration for a Realm of Reality beyond the limitations of this physical life in a prayer: "Thou hast made us for thyself, and our hearts are restless until they rest in Thee."

In Chapter Two I maintained that the first question which any moral theory must address is the question of what constitutes the truly fulfilling life. Plato answers from within his own philosophical system by holding that the truly fulfilling life is one directed by reason while the soul is embodied. A life so lived will meet its challenges, Plato warned, since such a person may be abused and ridiculed by the rabble. As with the case of Socrates, the ignorant may even condemn such a person to death. Plato believed that in spite of such challenges the rational person is able to withstand such misdirected abuse and live with a sense of self-respect and assurance of soul. It is as though those who punish the truly good "know not what they do."

Having lived a life of reason, the soul will return to the unchanging realm of the Forms where it can contemplate the beauty of the Forms eternally. In more mythological imagery, Plato at times wrote of the "Isle of the Blessed" where good men go after death. But death also held the possibility of imprisonment in Tartarus where the soul goes through a variety of punishments, depending on the severity of its transgressions while embodied. Apparently, some souls were redeemable and eventually released. On the other hand, incurably evil souls—few in number, Plato believed—seemed destined to suffer forever. Those souls would serve as examples designed to strike fear into the hearts of persons contemplating their destiny. Thus, in Plato, we find the themes of delayed gratification as well as delayed punishment commonly expressed in a variety of world religions.

I turn now to Plato's answer to the second basic question to be answered by any moral theory: What obligation, if any, does one individual have to aid another in their mutual quest for fulfillment? Plato's answer is developed in the context of his political philosophy where he asserts that a just and harmonious city-state is essential for the fulfillment of its citizens. The city-state, then, is a matter of primary concern; therefore, a just citizen will put the security and harmony of the city above her own individualistic aspirations. Though, to be sure, in this commitment the citizen also finds her own fulfillment. Socrates, the Platonist saint, was a model of just such a citizen since he refused to save his own life by escaping from Athens precisely because of his commitment to the laws of the city. Even if these laws led to his execution, they must still be honored. Loyalty to the city and its laws was, for Socrates and his student Plato, a central characteristic of a rational human being. The state, in turn, ought not function for the benefit of a few. A well-governed city does not aim for the happiness of one class, but as far as possible for the city as a whole. How, then, should the "city as a whole" be structured?

In his *Republic*, Plato noted that the just state is analogous to a just soul. As we have seen, the just soul, for Plato, was one in which the rational aspect of the soul directs the desiring and spirited element. When this occurs, the soul is in harmony and the four virtues of courage, temperance, wisdom, and justice are expressed. Plato asserted that the city-state should reflect the same ordering principles, for a city is made up of a variety of people with personal needs and varying capacities and talents. Furthermore, the needs of any city must be met by a variety of skills provided by its citizens--to produce food, shelter, clothing, the arts, defense, and governing authority. To meet these needs successfully, Plato believed that a division of labor is required and that individuals should pursue tasks for which they most fitted. As individuals find their proper place, a city-state will develop into three identifiable classes, each with its own particular role. One class, made up of farmers, traders, and artisans will meet the basic needs such as food, clothing, shelter, etc. This class is analogous to the desiring soul of Plato's tri-partite description of the human soul. The guardians of the state who must repel enemies and keep internal order constitute the next class, representing the spirited soul. Finally, the elite class, the rulers who are chosen from the most highly trained guardians, represents the rational soul. Just as reason must rule the individual soul if it is to be just, so also the most rational of men should rule the city-state. It is this analysis which leads to Plato's duly famous "Philosopher King."

In theory, all persons have the opportunity to reach the level of rulers; nevertheless, each individual would stop at the level of his or her natural aptitudes. In order to get citizens to accept this structure in society and in the city, Plato thought it necessary to develop what he called a "convenient fiction" or a "noble lie." This noble lie would assert that the God who fashioned all humankind included gold in the composition of those who were to rule, silver in the guardians, and iron and brass in the farmers and craftsman. These traits, however, were not strictly inherited since the children of the craftsman might be born with the higher gifts, and those of the rulers with lesser talents. To help ensure that many gifted children would be born into a community, Plato taught that the class of guardians should hold wives in common and that young men who show great promise should be encouraged to mate as a reward and privilege. It was important for the state to recognize the various capacities in a child and make certain that children are trained in ways appropriate to their capacities. Plato's ideal city would develop an extensive education program designed to enable every child to reach its maximum level of skills.

The significance of any person, for Plato, is to be found in the role that person plays within the state. Just as Plato's God may care for humankind in general, but not love individuals, so also the state must care for its citizens in general without specific concern for each individual. The individual citizen's responsibilities toward others are carried out, then, through allegiance to the state and its laws. Furthermore, the rational individual guides her or his interaction with others by controlling the spirited and desiring aspects of their soul, thus demonstrating the virtues of courage, temperance, wisdom and justice.

But people are not equal in the eyes of a properly governed city, and concern for all human beings in general was not part of Plato's vision. Other city-states and foreign powers that threaten your own community are to be resisted with force. Loving your enemy would be highly irrational in Plato's scheme of things, which is ethnocentric and "state-centric" in its thrust. There is little in Plato's thought that would support a broader vision of the human community, such as the later Stoics will develop. For Plato, however, truly rational rulers would find ways to reduce the hostilities often generated between city-states. Harmony is the preferred state of things in the individual soul, the city-state and the wider human community. But woe to the state not prepared to guard its frontiers and interests.

While those in the ruling class appear to be in a position of privilege, their lives are not necessarily free of stress since the welfare of the city-state is paramount. The common source of happiness stemming from marriage and family is denied to the ruling elite in order to reduce their temptations to self-interest and to keep their focus on the welfare of the entire community. The lower class of craftsmen and producers tend to get the rewards that are appropriate to their level of existence and their contribution to the community. Furthermore, Plato, an archconservative in many ways, had no confidence in the ability of the lower classes to make appropriate decisions for themselves or the city-state. His ideal form of government would be an aristocracy of the rationally gifted and trained who can control their appetites and their desire for honor and glory. A purely democratic state, in Plato's eyes would be one destined for severe decline.

Slavery appears to be a natural condition in Plato's analysis, though this would not be slavery rooted in force. Instead, his justification of slavery stems from his view that the rational should, by rights, rule the more irrational aspects of the soul or of the city-state. From this perspective, it seems clear that some persons do not have the capacity to make sound judgments about their own lives. So just as we tend to direct the lives of children, so also adults with inadequate capacities need to be directed by those who appropriately direct and hold power. The same type of analysis tends to be employed by most human beings when they justify the use of animals to serve the needs of the wider community. Horses and hunting dogs are, in this sense, "slaves." It does seem clear that this view of slavery carries with it a guard against cruelty and outright exploitation not to be found in conventions of slavery based on power and force. One aspect of Plato's analysis that moderns tend to reject is his view that penalties for an injury should depend on the status of the victim and the perpetrator. A slave must be more severely punished for injury done to a free man than a similar injury inflicted by a free man. This distinction is rooted in the accepted servile status of the slave that makes an injury inflicted by a slave an expression of mutiny against the city-state itself.

Plato's views about women and their role in society were generally positive. He granted the more or less common-sense view that women are usually less physically strong than men; nevertheless, he believed that women should have all the opportunities to express their strengths and skills that men have. If women have the requisite gifts, they should be allowed to be warriors and rulers. Plato's "noble lie" did not suggest that the gods made distinctions between male and female souls, only that souls have different mixtures of symbolic metals.

In summary, Plato argues that we have the responsibility of aiding others in their quest for a fulfilled life only within the context of the organized community where persons fill out their roles and gain the advantages, or disadvantages, their role implies. The quest for pleasure is certainly not the legitimate aim of a fulfilled/rational life. Instead, each of us, in whatever class, must be committed to living out our lives as workers, guardians or rulers in those ways that enhance the security and general welfare of the community. If we manage to become fully rational, we can hope that our souls, our essential selves, will find a more complete and lasting joyous fulfillment by rejoining the realm of the Forms and contemplating truth and beauty eternally.

Aristotle (384-323 BCE)

At seventeen years of age, Aristotle enrolled in Plato's Academy where he spent twenty years as Plato's student. As a young man he appeared to accept all of Plato's philosophy including the doctrine of the Forms (Ideas), the immortality and transmigration of the soul, and the view that true knowledge is a recollection of knowledge the soul possessed before joining a human body. In the end, however, he rejected Plato's theory of the Forms, developed a less religious and more naturalistic view of the universe, and grounded his moral theory in human nature without Divine sanctions. His impressive range of thought included the invention of logic and major contributions to science.

The role of God in Aristotle's ethical theory differed greatly from Plato's view. Even though Aristotle proposed a number of arguments for the existence of God—some borrowed from Plato—this "God" differed radically from the theism expressed in Judaism, Christianity and Islam. Since Aristotle conceived the universe as uncreated and eternal, he had no need to posit God as either the creator or the fabricator of the universe. Since he believed the world of sensory experience could be explained in terms of basic causes, he did not need the concept of God to explain the workings of nature. And since he based his moral theory on a given human nature, he did not need the concept of God to provide an objective foundation for morality. Nor did he need a God to provide moral rules and punishment for moral failures. Finally, since he denied that individual human souls exist in any meaningful way beyond the death of the body, Aristotle did not need the concept of God or gods to provide for punishment or reward in a life beyond earthly existence. What role, then, did Aristotle's God have in his philosophy and moral theory?

Aristotle used the idea of God, in part, to account for both celestial and terrestrial motion in the universe. Since he assumed, with many in his day, that the natural state of any object was to be at rest, the observable fact of motion needed to be explained in some way. Furthermore, since Aristotle held that the universe was eternal and was eternally in motion, he needed an explanation consistent with those beliefs. His answer was that of the famous "Prime Mover" or "unmoved mover," which is the cause of all motion but is itself without motion. For reasons to be explored later, this God, though a rational entity, had no interest in the universe as we experience it. The universe moves, then, not because God reaches in with a metaphorical hand to induce motion, but because the world soul experiences a yearning, an *eros*, for the beauty of the Prime Mover. It is this yearning in the world soul which induces motion into the world. God, as the supreme object of desire, moves the universe as a beloved moves the lover or as a great work of art moves the person experiencing the art. This is expressed in ordinary language as "love makes the world go round." This motion is first induced into the celestial spheres of Aristotle's universe and eventually produces motion on planet earth. Although Aristotle's thought contributed to the development of science, he clearly reverts to mythology or poetry for some of his explanations.

In a series of logical steps, which will not be traced in this work, Aristotle develops the characteristics of this God. As unmoving, God is perfect since only imperfect things are subject to motion. He is eternal, and incorporeal--without body and nonmaterial. "The essential quality of God is life, the best of all lives lived eternally without fatigue."[6] And since Aristotle held that the highest and truest activity of life is that of thought, the activity of the life of God is eternal thought. Furthermore, since God, as perfect, thinks only perfect thoughts, the object of such thoughts must be perfection. This leads to the conclusion that such thoughts must be solely of the only existing perfect entity—God himself.

> (God) has no impressions, no sensations, no appetites, no will in the sense of desire, no feelings in the sense of passions; he is pure intelligence.... .He is is free from pain and passion, and is supremely happy. He is everything that a philosopher longs to be.[7]

This God, then, represents a type of ideal existence not only for individuals, but also for the entire universe. "God is the unifying and directing principle of the world, the goal towards which all things strive, the principle which accounts for all order, beauty, and life in the universe."[8]

While Plato's moral philosophy included the idea of rewards or punishments for the soul beyond the death of the body, Aristotle excludes such possibilities by altering the concept of soul. For Aristotle, the soul is not something different from and independent of the body; rather, it is that which moves the body and gives the body its structure. But body and soul make up a unity that constitutes a living entity. There is no life without the soul aspect, and no soul without the body. With the exception of Aristotle's God, all life is embodied life.

Different grades or degrees of soul exist, with the human soul being the most complex. This soul not only governs nutrition, growth and reproduction, but it also possesses the ability to perceive, imagine, and remember. It is able to experience pleasure and pain, desire and aversion. Following Plato's teachings, Aristotle claimed that the human soul possesses the faculty of conceptual thought such as the capacity to think about the essence of things. The souls of plants and animals have the capacities needed for growth, nutrition and reproduction; but neither plants nor animals possess the rationality required to reflect on the uniquely human questions about the "whence, why and whither of life." But since soul and body make a unity, this human soul cannot exist beyond the death of the body itself. The aspects of soul related to plant animal life, shared by human beings, clearly cease to exist with the death of the body. Even the rational element of the soul does not exist, as an individual soul of some kind, beyond the death of the body. This rational dimension is a spark of the divine mind that comes into the soul from without and has no personal immortality. Aristotle regarded this rational aspect as a dimension of universal reason or, as some interpreters of Aristotle suggest, an aspect of the mind of God. The quest for a moral life, then, is not connected with some hope of a fulfillment (or punishment) beyond the death of the body. If fulfillment is to be achieved, Aristotle holds, it is to be found in the life we live as physical entities.

Aristotle's moral theory grows out of his belief that everything in nature has within itself some distinctive "end" or function. Thus everything has its *entelechy* in that it has "its own purpose within itself." The acorn has the end of becoming an oak tree, the baby that of becoming an adult. Furthermore, Aristotle begins his *Nicomachean Ethics* with the claim that "every art and every inquiry, and similarly every action and pursuit, is thought to aim at some good." But what, then, is the "end" or "purpose" of the human being? What is the "good" at which human activity aims? To discover this good, Aristotle maintains that we must first discover the distinctive function of human nature, for just as a good hammer is one that functions effectively as a hammer, the good man is one who functions effectively as a man. Aristotle's meaning is more clearly understood if "excellence" is used in the place of "good." Thus there are excellent hammers and excellent men. (The masculine pronoun is used here since it most accurately reflects Aristotle's own view that women are naturally inferior to men and cannot, therefore, attain genuine human excellence.) This distinctive function of man is to be found by understanding the distinctive nature of the human soul; and it will come as no surprise to find that this distinctive nature, for Aristotle, is that of reason. The man who functions effectively as man and who deserves to be called good or excellent is the man whose rational powers control the irrational aspects of his soul. The good life, then, is that life characterized by rational actions which aim at the proper end, and the final and sufficient end for Aristotle is that of *eudaemonia*, a term variously translated as "happiness" or "flourishing." Indeed, Aristotle holds that all men will agree that such happiness is the appropriate end of all human action. But, in contrast to the hedonists who held that pleasure was the highest good, Aristotle allowed that pleasure could be a secondary effect of *eudaemonia* but is not to be equated with it. The excellent man, the man who has attained the highest good, has achieved self-realization. This, however, is not to be interpreted as a life of selfish individualism, but rather a life of true nobility. There is an exalted altruistic element in Aristotle's ethics. The excellent man will act in the interests of others and will serve his people and his country; he would also seek to build a state that exercises justice through institutions that reflect lawfulness and fairness. But such justice, lawfulness and fairness is always expressed within some type of political arrangement. Man is, by nature, a political animal and needs companions for a truly fulfilling life, Aristotle believed. While one function of the state is to preserve the life of its peoples by meeting basic human economic needs, the highest function is to enable citizens to attain excellence as far as possible.

Any adequate presentation of Aristotle's ethics would involve a development of his rich and detailed analysis of the nature of the virtues as well as a discussion of his famous "golden mean." (Courage, for instance, is the mean between foolhardiness and cowardice.) Such an analysis, however, moves beyond the intentions of this work. The aspects of his thought that have been reviewed here can reveal his answers to the two basic questions any moral theory must address: 1) What constitutes a truly fulfilling human life?; and 2) While an individual rationally pursues his or her own fulfillment, does that person have any obligation to aid others in their quest for fulfillment?

For Aristotle, a fulfilled life must be achieved in the mortal, embodied life since there is no fulfillment beyond death. And the truly fulfilling mortal life is that of happiness (*eudaemonia*) attained through the excellence achieved by expressing the highest aspect of our human nature—the exercise of reason. Such human excellence is expressed by one who lives honorably, loyally, and nobly within his community. Modern readers of Aristotle may be disturbed by his frankly elitist point of view. He was an aristocrat who defended aristocracy, and nothing in his worldview would necessarily call for a more egalitarian position. Certain men should be rulers, others are confined to a life of labor. Women are naturally inferior, and some human beings are "slaves by nature." He also noted that while short persons may have well-proportioned bodies, they can never be truly beautiful; furthermore, the truly excellent and appropriately proud man should have a deep voice. Aristotle clearly believed that some human beings are superior to others and that any community should acknowledge fact.[9]

Regarding the second question concerning obligation, Aristotle would reply: While friendship and family life have a significant place in the life of the excellent or fulfilled person, there is no call for a general and egalitarian love for individual human beings as equally deserving of respect and care. Excellent persons who prove themselves to be excellent are to be treated with the honor and respect they rightly deserve. Women, as naturally inferior to men, deserve respect appropriate to their proper role. And those who are slaves "by nature" also receive respect in relation to their role as slaves. Thus persons of less capacity or excellence are to be treated in ways appropriate to their own situation. Equal rights are given to those who are equal and unequal rights to those who are unequal. The truly fulfilled and happy man of reason recognizes such distinctions and addresses each individual in ways appropriate to his status and capacities.

Perhaps no thinker has made a more comprehensive and lasting contribution to the history of Western thought than Aristotle. Even though the religious dimensions of his thought were in sharp contrast to traditional theism, nevertheless, Thomas Aquinas adopted many of Aristotle's major themes and linked them to Catholic Christianity in a way that shaped its traditional theology. Nor has Aristotle's influence been restricted to medieval religious philosophy. A recent philosopher has argued that Aristotle's view of the excellent man is an approach to ethics much superior to the ethics of the major Western religious traditions.[10]

Augustine (354 CE-430 CE)

Born of a pagan father and a Christian mother in Roman North Africa, Augustine shaped Christian thought more than any other non-biblical writer. After searching for a satisfying worldview, he eventually became attracted to Neoplatonic philosophy and fell under the influence of Bishop Ambrose of Milan. After a conversion experience in his early thirties, Augustine was baptized by Ambrose. Like other figures reviewed in this chapter, no attempt will be made to summarize the range of his thought. Instead, the focus will be on how Augustine links his moral teachings to his view of God. Of particular interest will be his worldview that led him to deliver one of the shortest moral precepts ever uttered: "Love, and do what you like."[11] The reader should turn to a standard work on Augustine for an elaboration of just how such love is to be expressed.

The worldview presented as theism earlier in this chapter is clearly reflected in Augustine's thought and will not be repeated here. Indeed, in many ways he was instrumental in its formulation. While accepting the Christian canon of scripture as revealed truth, Augustine borrowed abundantly from the heritage left by Plato and Neoplatonic thinkers in constructing his philosophical theology. While the content of his moral vision differed from those earlier philosophers, Augustine shared with them the conviction that the moral pathway leads to human fulfillment.

Augustine held that human beings are created in such a way that they naturally seek happiness. "All men love happiness... For the sake of driving away unhappiness and obtaining happiness, all men do what they do, good or bad. . ."[12] Not only was the quest for happiness rational and legitimate, it was also, for Augustine, a consequence and sign of the incompleteness and finitude of human beings. It is crucial, however, to seek this happiness in a correct and fruitful way. This way is to be found, for Augustine, in the life of love. He draws on the teachings of Jesus and the writings of St. Paul for this position.

The first and great commandment in the Jewish Law was, for Jesus, to love God; and the second commandment, reflecting the first, was to love the neighbor as oneself.[13] St. Paul reflected this theme in his assertion that "love is the fulfilling of the law."[14] This Pauline focus became central for Augustine as he developed his view of ordered love. There are many possible objects for our love that meet various human needs, he observed. These needs include various objects including things, other persons, and one's own self. All of these, therefore, are potentially legitimate objects or relationships of love. But, most of all, there is the need for God. Indeed, the need to love God is the deepest human need and an essential aspect of human nature. When this deepest need is satisfied, the person is freed from the love of illusory goods and misleading adventures. In loving the Highest, one is released from bondage to the lower. Only by first loving God does one discover how to properly love objects, other persons, and the self. In the common life, properly ordered love finds its expression in service to one's community. Finally, while Augustine sees human evil as the product of an act of free will, the capacity to love is not a product of human freewill but a gift of God's grace. God gives what God commands.

In summary, the truly fulfilling live is, for Augustine, that properly ordered life of love which brings true happiness eventuating in eternal happiness through the resurrection and the final beatific vision of God. As do all moral systems, Augustine's reflects various sanctions for moral failure including a dissatisfied life on earth and eternal Hell for those not elected by God. God is both just and boundlessly merciful, for Augustine, and in his later years he supported the doctrine of double predestination holding that God elects those who will be saved and also selects those who will be damned. A long history of theological debate grew out of Augustine's conclusion of predestination that was adopted by the more cautious Thomas Aquinas in the 13th century as well as both Luther and Calvin in the 16th. Finally, Augustine rejoices in the grace given by God and responds by living out a life of love. In this he reflects the position of I John 4:19, "We love, because he first loved us."

With this vision of a truly fulfilling life, how would Augustine respond to the question of our responsibility to others who also seek the fulfilled life? The answer lies in his focus on the ethic of love involving two central implications. First, his ethic and faith implies a universalism that rejects any form of tribalism exalting one particular group over another. Any and all human beings are to be loved without distinction. Second, such love seeks to care for the basic human needs of others, especially those without wealth or power or voice. And since human needs include the need to love God, bringing others into the faith would be an act of love. Yet those who remain outside the faith are not to be abused or rejected. With what appears to be a proper element of modesty, Augustine leaves the ultimate fate of those outside the faith in the hands of God.

Thomas Aquinas (1225-1271)

While Augustine synthesized theology and philosophy by combining Christian faith with Plato's thought, Aquinas produces his highly influential work by linking faith to Aristotle's philosophy. Influenced by Augustine, Aquinas also drew from many earlier writers, including ancient Greeks, Muslims and Jews. What follows is an explanation of how the concept of God shapes the moral philosophy of Aquinas in terms of the quest for the fulfilled life and the nature of responsibility toward others. The theistic worldview he held was described in chapter one.

Aquinas combines Aristotle's ethics with Biblical faith by accepting Aristotle's contention that human beings naturally and appropriately seek happiness. Furthermore, Aquinas accepts and builds upon Aristotle's claims that morality involves this quest for happiness and that in order to achieve such happiness one must fulfill his or her end as a human being. Both held that human beings, like animals, have appetites, passions and sensations linked to the physical body. Both agreed that human reason ought to control such appetites in order to achieve happiness; and both agreed that the natural virtues of courage, temperance, justice and prudence result when the appetites are properly controlled by reason. But while Aristotle thought only in terms of a natural end for a human being, Aquinas added the dimension of a supernatural end that was, finally, the Beatific Vision of God realized in Heaven. To achieve that end, humankind requires supernatural revelation to become aware not only of that high end but also the supernatural means to attain it. Such revelation comes through the Scriptures. In all his philosophical theology, Aquinas held that faith is not in opposition to reason, but adds to it, just as grace does not oppose nature, but adds to it.

Eternal law, natural law and divine law are central to the moral pathway described by Aquinas. Since God is the creator and sustainor of all things, the entire universe is governed by Divine Reason, which Aquinas identifies as eternal law. Natural law is that aspect of eternal law that provides the basis for moral obligations. This natural law can be rationally discerned by examining the very nature of human life and the world. These laws are linked directly to human nature as created by God and are reflected in a variety of inclinations. For instance, persons have a natural tendency to protect their own life, which implies that suicide would be opposed to the natural law to sustain one's life. Another example relates to sexuality. Aquinas argued that reproduction is a natural human inclination and forms the basis for the moral expression of marriage. Since the propagation of the species is, for Aquinas, the natural aim of sexual union, anything that frustrates that aim, such as artificial means of birth control, would be immoral. This view of natural law has left a major imprint on Roman Catholic thought to this day

If natural law is an aid in the quest for temporal happiness, then divine law is a guide for eternal happiness. Here, Aquinas sharply disagrees with Aristotle who held that human reason provides the basis for moral direction. Aquinas argues that divine law, needed to ensure the supernatural end of human existence, is not the produce of human reason, but is gifted to humankind as an act of God's grace. The theological virtues of faith, hope and love are not achieved by way of human effort or natural abilities, but are "infused" into the person by God's grace. Following Augustine, Aquinas holds that God gives what God requires; consequently, Aquinas asserts a form of predestination by arguing that the Beatific Vision of God results entirely because of God's gift of unmerited grace. Those not so gifted remain eternally condemned. While the major Protestant reformers, Luther and Calvin, followed Augustine and Aquinas on predestination, the official teaching of the Roman Catholic Church held to a major revisions of the doctrine.

Regarding the quest for fulfillment, Aristotle and Aquinas diverged considerably. In spite of the affection that Aquinas had for Aristotle's philosophy, the Christian theism of Aquinas led him, in the end, to a moral vision strikingly different from that of Aristotle's naturalism. True human fulfillment, for Aquinas, was to be found through the pathway of faith and morality that leads, finally, to the Beatific Vision of God in Heaven. For Aristotle, since he held individual existence ended with death, human fulfillment was to be gained by achieving human excellence in earthly life through the application of reason. During the earthly journey, the model of Christian humility and service proposed by Aquinas was in sharp contrast to the "great soul" of Aristotle with its self-sufficiency, independence, and elitist tendency of contempt for lesser human beings.

Since Aristotle and Aquinas agreed that happiness, in some form, is the appropriate aim of the moral pathway, they also agreed that straying from that pathway resulted in certain sanctions. For Aristotle, the sanction for failing to be a truly rational--hence virtuous--human being would be a lack of happiness in this life. This would be so even if the person ignorantly believes his or her life is a happy one. Only the truly rational can discern the difference. The sanctions, for Aquinas, are more serious since eternal sanctions beyond death are part of the scene for Aquinas. The morally corrupt person in this life may well appear to be living the happy life, according to Aquinas. But since all human beings are alienated from God because of original sin, those not gifted with divine grace remain alienated and spend eternity in some form of suffering. For Aquinas, God's grace is irresistible when given, yet God's justice is stern.

Regarding the question of aiding others in their quest for fulfillment, Aquinas took a generally egalitarian position. Love (*caritas*) is to be expressed to all human beings since they all have souls with a divine destiny. This love, however, must be an expression of the natural as well as the divine law since such laws are both descriptive and prescriptive of the pathway of graced faith that leads to the Beatific Vision. The difficulties, here, are in the details which cannot be developed in this brief overview.

Concerning the state, Aquinas understood this institution to be part of the nature of human beings; furthermore, he believed the political sovereign derived his authority from God. The function of the state is primarily the common good of its citizens, which includes the keeping of peace, creating harmony among the citizens, providing resources needed to sustain life, and preventing obstacles to the good life. The state rules its citizens through law, but such rule must reflect the requirements of justice reflected in natural law. Any law enacted by the state that runs counter to the general principles of natural law does not bind the individual's conscience and should not be observed. Aquinas also argued that the state should not always attempt to create a civil law to enforce every natural law since such attempts could result in more harm than good to the human community.

In preventing obstacles to the good life, Aquinas believed that the state must be subordinate to the church in the sphere of the ultimate and supernatural ends of human beings. In practice, this implies that the state must guard against heresies that endanger the eternal destiny of human souls. Indeed, in his *Summa Theologica*, Aquinas asserts "If forgers and malefactors are put to death by the secular power, there is much more reason for excommunicating and even putting to death one convicted of heresy." Here the saint reflects a theological tribalism often reflected in monotheistic traditions. He also echoed the long established tradition of male superiority. Women, he suggests, are naturally defective and are "by nature subordinate to man, because the power of rational discernment is by nature stronger in man. . . . (Women) are not tough enough to withstand their longings."[15]

Thomas Hobbes (1588-1679)

Exhibiting the spirit of the early modern mind, Thomas Hobbes broke with the past, embraced the new natural science represented by Copernicus and Galileo, and developed a thoroughly materialistic and mechanical approach to philosophy. The methods of geometry, he thought, were especially fruitful in the search for truth. Born the year the Spanish Armada was defeated off the coast of England, he mirrors the violence of his age by making the fear of death, especially death by violence, central to his theories of ethics and politics. His view of human nature is starkly presented in his claim that in the "state of nature," where there is no civil government, there would be a perpetual "war of all against all" and life would be "solitary, poor, nasty, brutish and short." Furthermore, in this state of nature, morality would not exist nor would there be any concern about the needs of others. For that matter, even when living in a more established and law-abiding state, human beings would still be primarily concerned about their own survival. For Hobbes, man is "a ferocious animal" driven to enmity, competition and war in the quest for life, riches, honor and power. This belief about human nature is not far from the view of "fallen" humanity held by the Protestant reformers John Calvin and Martin Luther. Hobbes description echoes Luther's observation that fallen man is "turned in upon himself." Clearly a psychological egoist, Hobbes believed that human activity is always motivated by self-centered needs and desires. Thus, when persons exercise their "will," they are merely carrying out the causal effects of their own appetites and aversions. Furthermore, they equate goodness with their own desires. How, then, did God and morality fit into this philosophical scheme of things?

While Hobbes reflected at length on a variety of religious matters, it is difficult to understand precisely just what his own personal convictions might have been. Because of his interest in politics and ethics, he was forced to deal with matters religious since religion was largely inseparable from politics and ethics in his day. He granted that there is a God whose existence can be proven in terms of causes; however, he also claimed that we do not and cannot know *what* this God might be. Any and all religious claims needed to be analyzed and critiqued by reason, Hobbes believed, and such analysis and criticism yielded very little in terms of knowledge. In the end, consistent with his emphasis on the absolute authority of the ruler of the state, he left religious matters largely in the hands of the ruling authority at that time. Furthermore, he made no meaningful connection between religious doctrines and moral behavior, and developed his political philosophy with its ethical implications solely on philosophical grounds.

Nor did Hobbes have much, specifically, to say about morality. His major focus was on political philosophy where he discussed questions about human actions and behavior. His famous defense of the absolute power of the sovereign was grounded in his view of human nature. Fearful of death, pursuing security, power and wealth, and concerned primarily about his or her own welfare, a rational person would, Hobbes believed, "seek peace and pursue it." Such peace would be possible only with a powerful ruling authority, he argued; for without the existence of some ruling power that could control behavior through fear of consequences, everyone has the "natural right" to do what he pleases to whom he pleases. This natural right does not, however, have any corresponding responsibility; thus my natural right to do what I please does not obligate others to grant me the freedom to do so. To have a "right," in this sense, is equivalent to having the power. This is parallel to the right of the lion in the African jungle to do as it pleases. This natural right in the human sphere, Hobbes observed, results in the "war of all against all," a situation no rational person would desire. Through an extended argument, Hobbes shows that the rational and prudential person would be willing to give up this natural right if others did the same. But the citizen sets this natural right aside only if the sovereign power takes on the responsibility of protecting that citizen from others.

This transfer of rights is considered to be a contract and establishes a duty to abide by that contract. The task of the sovereign (the great Leviathan) is to make certain, through the use of power, that such contracts are honored. In the absence of such a power, contracts would be "mere words" with little hope of being respected. And in the absence of such a power, there would be little assurance of either peace or safety. We can appreciate Hobbes' argument if we imagine, for instance, New York City or Chicago without a government and police force even for a few days.

There would be no hope for peace without a sovereign power, Hobbes believed, and neither would there be any meaningful concept of justice. The terms "just" and "unjust" held meaning, for him, only when there is sufficient governmental power to compel persons to abide by various contracts and agreements for fear of punishment. Without the threat of a coercive power, contracts could not be considered valid and the very idea of injustice would be empty of meaning. The forest lion in the state of nature cannot, after all, reasonably be accused of being unjust. Given a powerful sovereign with coercive power, just acts would not be punished while unjust acts would be. For Hobbes, the rational person is always guided by prudence; and with an absolute sovereign enforcing the laws, it would be prudent to be law-abiding.

Hobbes often wrote about "laws of nature," and even "moral laws" and "divine laws"; but in the end he reduced these concepts to rational maxims about how persons can best achieve their own security and aspirations in the generally competitive and hostile human world. Such laws have little meaningful connection to theological convictions or to some essential human nature as Aquinas proposed. Hobbes clearly dismissed the traditional natural law theory, as held by Thomas Aquinas, that claimed certain binding moral laws could be inferred from created nature. For this and other elements of his thought, he became the most frequently attacked philosopher of his day.

In summary, Hobbes has little to say directly about what constitutes a truly fulfilled human life. Even given a society ruled by an all-powerful sovereign, Hobbes held no rosy expectations about human existence. The most we can hope for and work for, he believed, is a condition of peace with others that grants us some possibility to pursue our quest for power, honor and riches. Life would be satisfying to the degree that such desires are satisfied. Hobbes neither hoped for glorious fulfillment in Heaven, nor did he appear to fear punishment in Hell. Given his basic assumption that we are always—and necessarily--motivated by self-concern alone, Hobbes sets aside any claim that we have moral obligations to aid others in their quest for a fulfilled life. Instead, a truly rational person would pursue his or her self-interests and would aid others only when such aid serves self-interest. In the end, Hobbes would have us understand that a human being, always a "ferocious animal," may still, as a rational creature, "seek peace and pursue it."

David Hume (1711-1776)

The philosophical position of David Hume, who was generally praised by his friends as a good and kind but tough-minded gentleman, might be properly illustrated by the closing lines of his *Enquiry Concerning Human Understanding*:

> If we take in our hand any volume; of divinity or school metaphysics, for instance; let us ask, *Does it contain any abstract reasoning concerning quantity or number?* No. *Does it contain any experimental reasoning concerning matter of fact and existence?* No. Commit it then to the flames; for it can contain nothing but sophistry and illusion.[16]

Hume's point, in this summary, is that objects of knowledge are of two kinds: relations of ideas and matters of fact. Abstract reasoning--relations of ideas--involves knowledge that is not derived from sensory experience, as the truths of geometry and mathematics. We may learn, through the aid of sensory experience, that two plus two equals four; but the truth of that proposition is not based on sensory experience. Instead, its truth is based on the very meanings of the words or symbols--relations of ideas. Modern logicians refer to such propositions as analytic, wherein the predicate of the proposition does not tell us anything new about the subject. For example, "A brother is a male sibling." So, also, "Two plus two equals four." Thus analytic propositions do not express "matters of fact" which are derived from sensory experience. Propositions that purport to state a matter of fact are termed "synthetic." In propositions of this sort the predicate *does* tell us something new about the subject, as in "That cat is my cat," or "Some crows are white." The truth of such propositions can be determined only by some relevant sensory experiences—such as seeing a crow that is white. In making his claim, Hume is expressing a consistent empiricist view that factual knowledge about the world is derived solely from sensory experience.

This basic claim about human knowledge yields philosophical fruit—or, perhaps, lack of fruit—when Hume addresses religion and morality. Propositions such as "God exists" are generally considered to be synthetic since they purport to make some factual claim about the world. For Hume, however, "God exists" failed to be a knowledge claim since he believed that no sensory experiences can lead to that conclusion. His *Dialogues on Natural Religion* is noted for its sustained and effective attack on attempts to prove the existence of God. For Hume, belief in God is never a matter of knowledge, but of faith in something like divine revelation. Furthermore, he would not have considered himself to be a man of faith.

Having argued that all propositions about God and related claims are beyond the range of knowledge, Hume levels the same argument at claims to moral knowledge. To assert that some action is "morally good" is not to make some factual statement about that action, Hume argues. He points out that one can examine such an action from every angle and yet perceive nothing that we can label as "good." We may see someone binding a wound, or helping an aged person, or feeding a starving child. But in no way do we see "goodness." To discover the meaning of "goodness," Hume argues, we must examine our feelings, for to call some action "good" reveals that we have a sentiment of approval regarding that action.

Reason does not show us what is good, Hume avers; our feelings are the basis for such judgments. Indeed, reason alone never moves us to action. We act only when we perceive that the action may yield some result that we desire. In this sense, says Hume, "Reason is and ought only to be the slave of the passions."[17] Our reason cannot tell us what we *ought* to want; it can tell us only how to *get* what we want. Thus, no matter of fact, by itself, can ever lead to some moral judgment or conclusion. In this analysis, Hume follows his empiricist position regarding knowledge to its logical conclusions. Since knowledge of fact can be derived only from sensory experience, and since we have no sensory experiences (sight, sound, smell, touch, and taste) which identify "goodness," the judgment of goodness must be the result of our feelings.

All this does not lead Hume to ignore morality or to reject its significance in human relations. Indeed, ethics was a major interest and he hoped to bring clarity to this field, just as Galileo and Newton had done in their scientific fields, by relying on facts and observations. In his *Enquiry Concerning the Principles of Morals*, Hume sought to *explain* the nature of morality rather than give us moral advice. His explanation is finally rooted in claim that the human sentiment of sympathy or fellow feeling is the spring from which moral judgments flow. A virtuous action is not one that reflects obedience to some kind of moral law or rule. He held that the very idea of moral rules as some objective aspect of life "can never be made intelligible." There are, for Hume, no moral laws or virtues expounded by God or inherent in human nature that *reason* can discover. Instead, he defines virtue to be "whatever mental action or quality gives to a spectator the pleasing sentiment of approbation; and vice the contrary."[18]

Hume guards against reducing ethics to purely subjective and relativistic terms, like some matter of taste, by claiming that moral sentiments are a natural part of all human beings. "There is a piece of the dove in every human breast." The sense of sympathy or fellow-feeling is "a principle in human nature beyond which we cannot hope to find any principle more general." Human beings from every age and culture express the same sense of approval for deeds which are brave, generous or noble, even when such deeds may be harmful to our own particular self-interest. A brave deed done by an enemy soldier, though it may harm our cause, is still deemed to be virtuous and worthy of praise. But, Hume continues, we praise certain actions precisely because we see them as useful and agreeable to *someone's* interest. And these interests are not just our own for we approve of certain actions because they are useful to the interests of others.

Hume carefully avoids telling us what we "ought" to do, for that would appear to imply that some moral rule should be honored. Instead, he *describes* how human beings generally feel about actions that are useful and agreeable. Furthermore, given his claim that no fact, by itself, can ever entail a value or a motive, he cannot logically claim to give us moral advice. For even if the claim that human beings generally experience sympathy or fellow feeling for others is some kind of *fact*, that fact, in itself, cannot yield some value or moral advice. Hume never argues: "Since human beings generally have feelings of sympathy for others, therefore we *should* act sympathetically toward others." Just as he would not argue that since human beings generally feel hostile toward others who abuse them, they "ought" to take revenge on that other. Natural inclinations, pro or con, do not, in themselves, provide moral guidelines though these inclinations may be part of the cause of our actions. Nor does it follow in some deterministic way that if I feel sympathy toward others I will, therefore, *act* on such feelings. I may honor my enemies wit and bravery, but that fact will not necessarily lead me to act in a benevolent way toward that enemy. I still must decide just how I will act to pursue my own wants, needs and desires that will conflict with those of my enemy. While I may have some sense of sympathy for another person, my own self-interests will be the "passion" which directs my reason.

Hume's emphasis on sympathy and fellow feeling softens the straightforward psychological egoism that Hobbes proposed. Still, the altruistic inclinations Hume describes do not override natural self-interest. The good life may involve altruism, but the most we can reasonably hope for, in Hume's own words, is "confined generosity." This is the language of self-referential altruism. The primary aim of our actions is our own well-being, or the well-being of those we love, or the well-being of those with whom we are linked through some type of identification--clan, faith, nation, ethnicity. In the tussle for the perceived goods of life, we will side with "our own," not the "other." This observation serves to underline the persistent issue in moral philosophy: "Are there ever moral reasons which, at times, properly trump reasons of prudence and self-referential altruism?" Hume did not think so.

Clearly, for Hume, belief in God has no legitimate place in moral reflection. Not only is knowledge of God impossible, religious beliefs that God provides moral guidance and also protects our interest is only a form of baseless infantilism. Hume certainly shows disdain for "celibacy, fasting, penance, mortification, self-denial, humility, silence, solitude, and the whole train of monkish virtues."[19]

The nature of the fulfilled life, as Hume conceived it, reflects a secular approach to a reflective morality with an emphasis on peace and mutual evaluation, not that of "scolding and mutual reproaches." The Calvinists of Hume's day would not be happy with Hume's list of virtues, nor would monks or generals. Furthermore, any fulfillment sought must take place in this life, since Hume rejects any form of personal immortality beyond death. But the fulfilled life is linked to virtuous living. His list of virtues generally accepted by human beings include good sense, knowledge, wit, eloquence, humanity, fidelity, truth, temperance, dignity of mind. He would also include justice, honesty, good nature, mercy, gratitude, kindness, tenderness, generosity, sobriety, patience, forethought and a proud spirit.[20] Since death ends all experience, any sanctions for moral failure must also take place in this life. The disadvantages, for Hume, for failing to express virtuous living would be a lower level of life's joys and satisfactions.

In spite of his skepticism, his friends found in him many of the virtues he listed. Hume carried his convictions to the grave. In his account of a conversation with the dying Hume, the pious Boswell did not find the repentance he had hoped for from this great skeptic. Hume died peacefully, "remaining immune to the consolations of either theism or immortality."[21]

Immanuel Kant (1724-1804)

"Two things fill the mind with ever new and increasing admiration and awe... the starry heavens above and the moral law within." This famous passage from Immanuel Kant suggests his philosophical concerns about the nature of scientific knowledge and the nature of morality. Hume's writings not only awakened Kant from his "dogmatic slumber" but also threatened to undercut scientific as well as moral knowledge. Kant set out to rescue both from Hume's assault by analyzing how reason itself thinks about the world and about morality. For him, reason had both a theoretical and practical function. Theoretical reason discovers what is true about the world, while practical reason provides moral guidance.

In the realm of science, Kant argued that human reason (mind) has certain structures which impose order on the sensory experiences that come from the world "out there." The mind organizes these experiences. This is in sharp contrast to the common view that assumes our minds conform to the order of the world experienced. For Kant, we *do not* know what the tree "out there" is "in itself." What we *do* know is the result of how the mind orders the experiences resulting from sensory contact with that tree. He assumes that the tree is really "out there," not merely a construction of consciousness; but all we can know of that tree is our "inner" experience of how our mind orders sensory experience. In a related way, Kant, with Hume, held that sensory experience does not show us cause-effect relationships in the world. What we observe is that some event X happens, followed by Y in a time sequence. What we do not observe is that "X *causes* Y." For Kant, the conclusion that X causes Y is supplied by the mind that orders thought in terms of cause-effect relations. Cause-effect is a "category of the mind," not something perceived through the senses. So, also with time and space, which are "forms of intuition" employed by the mind, not actualities observed through the senses.

For Kant, mind also played a significant role in his analysis of morality and its possible relationship with the idea of God. With Hume, Kant believed that the existence of God cannot be proven by reason, nor are such things as virtues and goodness discovered by way of sensory experience. But while Hume linked judgments about virtues to our feelings or passions, Kant anchored such judgments in the rational structure of the mind itself. Since he argued that we cannot *know* that God exists, Kant concluded that genuine moral knowledge cannot be based on religious claims. Given that approach, some find it odd that Kant eventually argued that we need to posit something like God in order to make sense out of morality. Kant's enormous influence and his curious use of the idea of God make Kant's philosophy one of particular interest to the argument pursued in this work.

Central to Kant's analysis of morality is his claim that a morally good action must not only *accord* with duty, but must also be done with duty as its *motive*. The will is good if and only if it does its duty for duty's sake alone. Telling the truth, for instance, is in accord with duty, but if one's motive for doing so is to escape punishment, then that act has no truly moral quality. Prudential acts, while not necessarily immoral, have no moral status. Telling the truth solely because it is one's *duty* to tell the truth, in spite of consequences, would constitute a truly moral act. Implied in this analysis is a clear distinction between what is done on the basis of inclination or feeling and what is done on the basis of duty. True morality does not spring from our inclinations; indeed, morality may often be in conflict with them. We act morally only when we pursue duty as recognized by reason. Kant clearly has fundamental disagreements with Hume.

But how, then, do we recognize what constitutes a duty? In pursuing his answer, Kant developed a rigorous philosophical pathway involving a careful analysis of how we think about morality and how we feel about moral obligations. We ask not only "What shall I do?" but also "What *ought* I do?" Furthermore, when we think clearly, we realize that what is considered morally right is often quite distinct from our own interests and desires. Conscience, remorse and the basic awareness of duty attest to the innate claim morality has upon us. For Kant, reason's awareness of duty can properly be called the recognition of a moral law. He argues that the very idea of law involves unconditional, not hypothetical, obedience. That is, law does not provide some type of hypothetical claim which states "If you want X, then do Y." Rather, law orders "Do Y" because it is your duty so to do. The very idea of law, Kant asserts, also implies universality. If law is truly law, it applies to all, everywhere, and at all times. Law is never qualified by a particular set of circumstances or by the special interests of an individual. If the law is law, it applies to all others and to myself; I cannot make modify law to fit my own particular circumstances.

Pressing this analysis, Kant finally arrives at his duly famous categorical imperative: "Act only according to that maxim whereby you can at the same time will that it should become a universal law."[22] This rule is categorical in that it applies universally to all rational beings; it is imperative in that it states a principle upon which we ought to act. A maxim, for Kant, is any general rule of action. Hence, the categorical imperative asserts that if we act according to some maxim, we must be willing to make that maxim into a universal law that everyone ought to follow. If we are unwilling to will the universality of a rule or maxim, then that rule falls short of being moral. Consider, for instance, the practice of making promises. If I am tempted to break a promise I have made, I could formulate the maxim: "I may break a promise when it benefits me." But, Kant asserts, I could not will to make that maxim a universal law that would order all persons to break a promise when it redounds to their benefit. Clearly, if such a law became universal, promises would be stripped of their meaning and no one would trust promises made. Hence, Kant, concludes, reason shows that promising is possible only if promises are honored. While the plain man may not be able to follow Kant's argument here, Kant is certain that this same plain man understands in his very being that promises are to be kept.

Another example of Kant's rigorous application of moral duty is his illustration regarding lying. For Kant, lying is always wrong. If some deranged man comes to your door waving a handgun and asks if your son is at home, the inclination to lie to that gunman would be exceedingly strong. Nevertheless, Kant maintains that lying to that gunman cannot be morally justified. For in lying to the gunman you would be acting on the maxim: "Lie to someone when it redounds to your benefit." But, Kant would argue, that maxim could not be made into a universal law since such a law would undercut the very meaning and function of communication. You would never have grounds for believing what others say.

How, then, does the idea of God fit into Kant's moral philosophy when he maintains that we cannot know that God exists or that some Divine Law has been revealed to us? For Kant, the moral law is "within" as an expression of our nature as rational creatures. Rational creatures think about morality in just the way Kant describes. Yet the concept of God becomes an important one for him since the very way we think about morality leads us to the existence of God as a "postulate of practical reason." He sought to demonstrate that there is a fundamental connection between virtue and happiness, and God's existence must be posited to make such a connection.

Kant maintains that an analysis of the way we think about morality yields several insights. First, if we are to be morally responsible we must be free either to do our duty or to refuse. While this freedom of the will cannot be proven by reason, such a freedom must be a "postulate of practical reason" in order to make sense of morality. If the call of duty is to make sense, we must possess freedom of the will. Second, even though the quest for happiness must not be the *motive* for doing our duty, nevertheless, the very idea of morality implies that a truly moral person *ought* to be rewarded with true happiness. Practical reason, therefore, posits that virtue leads to true happiness. Third, since the moral quality of an action depends on the purity of the *motive* that prompts the action (willing the act on the basis of duty), our moral rewards depend on our *motives*. Fourth, since reason tells us that virtue and happiness are necessarily linked and that truly moral persons are not always rewarded in this earthly life, it follows that the necessary reward of happiness must be found in the life beyond. Furthermore, this soul as a rational moral entity seeks the perfect good, the complete conformity of the will to the call of duty. Since such perfect goodness cannot be attained in this earthly life, it follows that there must be an unending duration of the existence of this rational being. In this way, the immortality of the soul is posited. Given those evident truths linked to morality, the existence of God must be assumed in order to conceive of a universe compatible with such truths. For in order for morality to be as reason understands it, there must be some Power which: 1) accurately knows our motives in order to link our virtue to our happiness; 2) has the power and wisdom to construct a universe in which virtue and happiness are combined; and, 3) has the power and wisdom to provide the scene for an immortal soul to seek its moral perfection. Morality, as Kant conceives of it, would be an absurd enterprise from the standpoint of a purely naturalistic worldview.

The union of virtue with happiness, in Kant's thought, reveals his vision of the truly fulfilled life. As rational beings, he believed, we are fully satisfied only when this union between virtue and happiness is achieved. While Kant expresses a moral rigorism, he despised an asceticism that passed itself off as morality. Happiness has its proper place, for the complete or highest good, the *summum bonum*, must include both virtue and happiness. But while happiness is pleasant to the possessor of it, morally right behavior is always a necessary condition for it.

Kant argues that it is not possible to express a truly moral will in this world where the struggle between inclination and duty continues. Nevertheless, morality demands that a truly moral will ought to be achieved and is to be understood as the holiness which God's justice requires. The call to moral duty continues. Yet the immortality of the soul as a postulate of practical reason makes possible a comforting hope for a blessed future.[23] While Kant is spare about the details of such a "blessed future," it is clear that true human fulfillment is not to be attained in this life.

> Although Kant refers to the "Infinite Being" who imputes to a person perfect virtue even if he has only made progress toward it, there is no mention of fellowship with God or other persons as a source of joy. Happiness is regarded as having its source solely in one's virtue.[24]

John Stuart Mill (1806-1874)

One of the founders of utilitarianism, J. S. Mill caught the interest not only of professional philosophers but also of politicians and ordinary citizens. With its general simplicity and its compatibility with what many people already believe, utilitarianism helped to bring about social and political reform in England and remains an influential moral theory to this day. Mill was deeply influenced by Jeremy Bentham, fifty-eight years Mill's senior. Bentham, himself influenced by Hume's emphasis on empirical method and psychological analysis of human motives, intended to make morality into a science as much as possible. The opening lines of Bentham's *Introduction to the Principles of Morals and Legislation* states his basic claim:

> Nature has placed mankind under the governance of two sovereign masters, pain and pleasure. It is for them alone to point out what we ought to do, as well as to determine what we shall do. On the one hand the standard of right and wrong, on the other the chain of causes and effects, are fastened to their throne. They govern us in all we do, in all we say, in all with think...[25]

These lines carry an open endorsement of psychological hedonism, the theory that people *necessarily* act in ways which promise to bring them pleasure and to avoid pain. Psychological hedonism is a *descriptive* theory in that it purports to describe *how* persons *do* act, but does not describe how they *ought* to act. But Bentham's argument moves from the psychological theory to his principle of utility. From the fact that we *desire* pleasure, we can conclude that we *ought* to pursue pleasure. While Kant argued "I ought, therefore I can," Bentham appears to conclude, "I ought since I can do no other." Although Bentham subscribes to psychological hedonism, he does not endorse an ethic of selfishness. His emphasis was on self-interest, not selfishness, for he was convinced that our own happiness is best achieved by pursuing the general happiness of others. It is in our own self-interest, Bentham believed, to pursue this general happiness.

Bentham's principle of utility—"the greatest good for the greatest number"—was formulated as his primary moral principle. And "good" is to be understood in terms of happiness or pleasure. Bentham was aware that he was not able to prove in some empirical or deductive way that happiness is the basis of what is good and right. Nevertheless, he claimed that all other moral principles would, when closely analyzed, reduce to the principle of utility. For instance, religiously based moral rules would reduce to his principle since God's reasons for providing such rules would be that of producing the greatest happiness for the greatest number. But Bentham finally sets the problem of proving the principle of utility aside by asserting:

> Is it susceptible to any proof? It should seem not; for that which is used to prove every thing else, cannot itself be proved: a chain of proofs must have their commencement somewhere. To give such a proof is as impossible as it is needless.[26]

In his *Utilitarianism*, J. S. Mill seeks to defend the principle of utility expressed by Bentham; but while Mill accepted Bentham's premise of psychological hedonism, his own formulation of Utilitarianism differs from Bentham's in several ways. Building on his claim that pain and pleasure are the causes of human actions, Bentham argued that a number of sanctions or forms of punishment help shape human behavior. These sanctions include the physical, political, moral, and religious. Burning my finger on a candle flame is a physical sanction that teaches me to avoid such contact. A jail sentence given to me by a magistrate is a political sanction that teaches me to avoid the life of crime. My neighbor's refusal to assist me because of his or her dislike of my moral character is a moral sanction that may alter my future behavior. Finally, God's punishment for a sin I committed represents the religious sanction. To these basic sanctions, Mill adds the internal sanction of conscience, the general sense of duty that exists as a subjective aspect of our nature and influences our actions. He links this to the principle of utility by maintaining that genuine happiness must include that sense of personal affirmation felt by everyone when honoring duty. This is not, however, "duty for duty's sake." Rather, it is duty for the sake of our own happiness. The pursuit of duty, Mill believed, is a fundamental element in our natural and legitimate quest for happiness. It was this emphasis on the satisfaction derived from duty that led Mill to claim that his utilitarian position was basically a restatement of the teaching of Jesus on love of neighbor. To pursue "the greatest happiness for the greatest number" is the practical equivalent of such love. But Mill's principle of utility is not grounded in some revealed truth; instead, he claims it is a logical consequence of the natural human desire for happiness.

Mill followed Bentham in generally equating happiness with pleasure, but he introduced a qualitative distinction between pleasures which Bentham denied. The charge of "pig philosophy" had been leveled at Bentham's utilitarianism since Bentham had argued that all pleasures are equal, that "pushpin is as good as poetry" if it results in pleasure. All pleasure, as pleasure, is a good. Bentham's critics suggested that a pig happy in a mud puddle would be an ideal utilitarian. Mill, on the other hand, argued that qualitative distinctions between pleasures could and should be made, and that "it is better to be a human being dissatisfied than a pig satisfied." While a pig may have pleasures of mere sensation, human beings have the capacity for pleasures derived from imagination, feelings and intellect. Who, then, is in position to decide which pleasures are preferable? Mill's response was that only a person who had experienced both pleasure X and Y was in position to judge which is preferable; and he was convinced that the higher pleasures of human experience are qualitatively superior to mere animal sensations. This distinction resulted in some philosophical difficulties for Mill, but such criticisms run beyond the intention of this book.

The role of belief in God is marginal, at best, in Mill's moral theory. He granted that belief in the supernatural may have once helped to support public and private morality, but he concluded that belief in God was no longer needed. Nor did he believe that belief in God was effective in producing moral persons. Furthermore, evidence or argument could not support belief in

God. Mill thought the only interesting argument for God's existence is the argument from design. But that argument gives us "no more than a probability" that a God exists and gives us no information about the nature of such a God. Indeed, the general suffering of human beings and other creatures makes it impossible to believe that such a God can be at once all-powerful and benevolent. Mill concluded that while one can believe in a benevolent God, this God must be severely limited in power. If all-good, this God cannot be all-powerful given the amount of innocent suffering in the world. Human beings, by their ideals and actions, can help such a deity bring about more satisfactory conditions for human life. In that way, figures such as Christ could serve as pictures of moral excellence and could aid in establishing a Religion of Humanity, or a Religion of Duty.

While he believed there is no evidence for the immortality of the soul or for miracles, Mill granted that there are no arguments that stand strongly against such claims. Some basis for hope seemed important to him, and such beliefs tend to leave room for hope. Religion, in this way, could have a certain social utility. During his life, Mill generally avoided public comment on religious subjects. But after his posthumously published *Three Essays on Religion*, Mill's non-religious admirers were disturbed because Mill did not totally discard religious aspirations and views. Meanwhile, Mill's religious critics claimed that his philosophy had resulted in both intellectual bankruptcy and moral collapse.

While the role of God in Mill's philosophy was marginal, at best, he still held to an egalitarian view of a good and just society. There may be distinctions in the pleasures experienced by human beings, but Mill maintained that one person's happiness is never more important than another's. He agreed with Bentham's dictum: "Everybody to count for one, nobody for more than one." In Mill's words, the "ideal perfection of utilitarian morality" is "to do as one would be done by, and to love one's neighbor as oneself." In this claim, of course, lies the issue of just how one defines "neighbor." Mill would clearly apply that term to all of those who shared his English nationality and heritage. It is not, however, entirely clear that he would extend that term, with all of its utilitarian meanings to, say, the French, the Germans and the Russians. The question of just who belongs to my "tribe" remains.

Of all the philosophers reviewed in this chapter, J. S. Mill comes closest to maintaining that traditional Christian moral principles can be sustained on non-religious grounds. His position, therefore, represents a challenge to a major claim of this book. An extended critique of Mill's utilitarianism will not be pursued here. He reflected much of the optimism of Enlightenment thinkers in his claim that if we all thoughtfully pursue our own self-interests then all who share life's journey with us will also benefit. After the bloody twentieth century, such optimism may not seem warranted.

Karl Marx (1818-1883)

"The philosophers have only *interpreted* the world differently: the point is, however, to *change* it." When Karl Marx made this observation, he was witness to the miserable social conditions resulting from an unregulated and rampant capitalist economic system. He was determined to change the world. Many of his ideas came from a variety of earlier economists and philosophers. Ricardo, for example, had developed the labor theory of value; Saint-Simon had declared that history is shaped by conflicts between social classes; Hegel had described the dialectical processes of history; and Feuerbach had revived philosophical materialism with its open atheism. Borrowing from these thinkers, Marx constructed a system of thought that, at one point in the twentieth century, was the official philosophy controlling nearly a third of the people on earth.

Marx adopted a thoroughly materialistic and deterministic view of both the physical and the social world. His materialism was ontological in that he believed all reality, including human thought, is an expression of some form of matter; that is, nothing exists outside of or other than material entities. There is no God or transcendent reality. Marx's "historical materialism" claimed that "the mode of production of the material means of existence" shapes the historical development and structure of any society. For example, a hunter-gatherer economic system will have a social structure quite different from that of a society with an agricultural base or one based on industrial production. He did not hold, however, to "ethical materialism" that maintains the material things of life are the good things to be pursued.

His determinism claimed that all events, natural and social, are caused by antecedent circumstances. The laws of chemistry and physics involve a mechanical determinism, while the forces of history and social life, though deterministic, are subtler and less open to precise predictions. With such explanations in place, religious ideas are no longer taken seriously but can be themselves, explained in terms of this materialistic determinism. The idea of God is a creation of human thought, he maintained, and played a role in the development of human history. As the "opium of the people," religion is a means by which "oppressed creatures" seek to ease their pain. When this pain is relieved through changes in economic systems, such an opiate will no longer be necessary.

Marx did not set out to create a moral philosophy that would inform persons about what is good and how to act rightly. Instead, he intended to explain how morality develops out of the economic structures of a society. As a scientist, Marx claimed to be purely descriptive, not prescriptive. He believed not only that morality is always linked to the wants and needs of human beings but also that such wants and needs are shaped by the circumstances in which persons live. Fundamental to such circumstances is the economic system dominating the society His aim was to describe the dynamics of history, especially in terms of the impact that economic systems had on any society. Moral systems, he believed, always reflect the economic systems in place at any time in history; therefore, an ideal moral system can develop only when people live in an economic system that frees them and enables them to be good. In contrast to the pessimism about human nature reflected in thinkers such as Hobbes, Marx optimistically believed that human nature is pliable and can be molded by changes in social and economic systems. Nurture is stronger than nature.

Marx argued that t he prevailing economic system, at any stage of history, shaped the ideas, values and moral convictions of those living at that time. In a capitalist economic system, morality will reflect the competitive economic setting and the "class struggle" between those who own the means of production and those who do the productive work. Given this analysis, Marx does not consider the capitalist who "exploits" labor to be morally blameworthy, because the capitalist merely reflects the nature of the capitalist system. Nor would Marx fault workers who sought to develop labor organizations that could yield some power serving their own interests. The capitalist system necessitates such self-interested activities and, consequently, those living under that system are not free to be good.

An ideal moral system can develop only when a just economic system is in place and the long historical struggle between classes has been overcome. This occurs when those who worked on the means of production also owned those means. The class system would then cease to exist. History, Marx believed, was moving inexorably toward such an ideal community. While the Kingdom of Heaven is no longer awaiting mankind, the kingdom of the classless society is promised. In this classless society, the long struggle between the classes will necessarily cease bringing peace and prosperity for all. In the meantime, all within a capitalistic system are members of either the owner or the worker class, or like lawyers and physicians, have "class interests." Lawyers, for instance, seldom find their interests linked with the poorer, working class.

The revolutionaries who understand the historical processes will, Marx believed, work toward the ultimate revolution that will bring in the classless society. In such a society, the state would wither away because competing class interests that needed to be defended would no longer exist. These new human and economic relationships would make it possible for all to live out the motto "To each according to their need; from each according to their abilities." The specifics of the moral relationships that would develop in that ideal society could not be predicted with precision, Marx believed. Nevertheless, with the classless society in place, human relationships would reflect communal interests and the specifics of morality would develop naturally to meet the basic needs of the people. The dynamics of history have replaced the will of God.

Friedrich Nietzsche (1844-1900)

The son and grandson of Lutheran ministers, Friedrich Nietzsche became a passionate opponent of the Christian faith and its attendant morality. Although his last decade was marked by hopeless insanity, his writings bear the mark of a brilliant and searching mind. Though capable of subtle arguments, much of the power of his writing lies in his use of striking aphorisms and metaphors. The major themes he pursued include the death of God and the consequent revaluation of all values. He produced no formal system of philosophy, largely because he believed that all such systems build on self-evident truths that must, themselves, be challenged. He did not seek to be, as he put it, an "unriddler of the universe." However, if his aim was to provoke serious thought, he most certainly succeeded.

Most widely known for his proclamation that "God is dead," Nietzsche regarded this pronouncement with misgivings as well as hope. If Darwin's theory of evolution and the implications of the collapse of religious faith came to be widely understood, Nietzsche believed that catastrophic wars could be part of the future. Much of his attention is given to the question of human values in a world where belief in God can no longer be taken seriously. With God no longer on the human horizon, "the sea, *our* sea, lies open before us. Perhaps there has never been so open a sea." I will briefly explore the "open sea" of values he posits and show how these values are the related to the demise of God. Standard works on Nietzsche should be consulted for a comprehensive view of this brilliant and disturbing philosopher.

Central to Nietzsche's approach to values was his conviction that the "will to power" exists as an elemental force in all life. In people, this is an inner drive to express more than simply the will to live; it expresses the desire to affirm all human powers—physical, intellectual, emotional, psychical, and creative. More than "a miserable struggle for existence," the will to power is "a Will to War. A Will to Power, a Will to Overpower!" Any attempt, then, to formulate some universal moral rule for all to follow is, for Nietzsche, a fundamental error that robs the human being of the vitality of life. Here Christianity and Judaism are major offenders since the Judeo-Christian ethic of love and compassion is so contrary to basic human nature that it produces only "botched and bungled lives." He had equal disdain for utilitarians, like Bentham and Mill, who believed that people are basically motivated by the desire for pleasure.

Even the Christian ethic, Nietzsche observed, expresses the "will to power" by developing a "slave morality" promoted by the weak in order to restrain the powerful who expressed a "master morality." In the master morality, "good" is the term of approval used for those who are noble, those who directly express their will to power, those who are not ashamed to glorify themselves, and those who take pleasure in what is severe and difficult. Nietzsche would approve of the pleasure attendant to the feeling of increased power; but honest persons recognize that they desire power, not pleasure.

The contrasting slave morality arises from those who are weak and oppressed and who lack the courage of bold self-affirmation. In contrast to the values of master morality, slave morality exalts such qualities as "sympathy, the kind helping hand, the warm heart, patience, diligence, humility and friendliness." This is the morality of "the herd," those who fear the strong and the noble. This is the morality that springs from resentment and seeks revenge upon the strong by redefining the aristocratic virtues of power and pride as forms of evil. In this way, Nietzsche believed, Christian morality subverts true humanity. "I regard Christianity as the most fatal and seductive lie that has ever yet existed—as the greatest and most *impious* lie . . ." It was a great piece of historical irony, he once remarked, that the Greek ideal of "virtue," as the noble, powerful and assertive man, became a term applied to the sexual purity of women.

In Nietzsche's thought, the connection between an ontology and morality is clearly demonstrated. His boldly naturalistic worldview dismisses the idea of God; and he maintains that with the "death of God" the traditional moral values linked to belief in

God must also collapse. Nietzsche's vision of what constitutes a fulfilling life would be an example of Kierkegaard's aesthetic stage. The meaning of life is not to be found in religious faith, nor in the commitment to community moral values; rather it is found in expressing the passionate vitality of life found in a joyous expression of the various forms of human power. This life would include elements of the mood expressed in the Greek worship of Dionysus, who represented those vital aspects of life that acknowledge no restraints or boundaries—symbolized in the drunken frenzy of Dionysian worship.

On the other hand, Nietzsche maintained, there is another side of human nature that must also be honored—that of the cool and controlling rational side symbolized by the god Apollo. The dark powers of the soul, symbolized by Dionysus, must be controlled and directed into the creative acts of life through the use of Apollonian reason. But in the end, this human life of flesh and blood is to be celebrated, not condemned and rejected in some display of humility and asceticism. For Nietzsche, the religious ideal of "holiness" is "merely a series of symptoms of an impoverished, unnerved, incurably corrupted body."

With the collapse of religious belief and traditional moral values, Nietzsche would deny that persons have any particular responsibility to be concerned about the fulfillment of others. His quest was for a life "beyond good and evil" that reflected higher values expressed in vitality and courage. Human beings vary, he held. The strong and vigorous pursue their power, while the "herd men," like sheep, take refuge in conforming to the common triviality of day to day life. But the truly strong have no need to be bullies; they rejoice primarily in contests with others who are also strong. Neither a great athlete nor a great intellect finds joy in competing with a weak opponent.

For Nietzsche, there are no external sanctions on the activities of the strong, no divine judge or judgment, no problematic conscience. Yet the individual does have a price to pay, a sanction of sorts, in failing to pursue the "open sea" in the celebration of life that constitutes the higher morality. Failure to pursue this higher pathway brings with it the repression of the will to power resulting in the drudgery of conformity, debilitating weakness, resentment toward those who are noble and strong, and belief in a God who will finally protect and reward the weak and humble. Nietzsche was no lover of human beings as they are. He hoped that history would produce a higher kind of man, an *ubermensch* or "superman." This higher man who has won his freedom "tramples ruthlessly upon the contemptible kind of comfort which tea-grocers, Christians, cows, women, Englishmen, and other democrats worship in their dreams."

Jean-Paul Sartre (1905-1980)

While Soren Kierkegaard is often cited as the father of modern existentialism, that philosophical movement is most popularly linked to Jean-Paul Sartre. His novels and plays, perhaps more than his more technical works, helped move existentialism from the obscure recesses of academic philosophy to a broad cultural phenomenon. More than a passing fad, existentialism, with its themes of anxiety, meaninglessness, and radical freedom, deeply influenced art, literature, psychology, and theology

Sartre took atheism seriously. He agreed with Nietzsche's pronouncement that "God is dead," and explored Dostoevsky's claim that "if God did not exist, everything would be permitted." With the demise of God, according to Sartre, we are left with the responsibility to invent or construct our own meanings and values. This is, he asserts, a "terrible freedom." Since there is no God who created a specific human nature or essence, the individual is left to define and create his or her own essence through free choices and projects. There is no divine realm that can reveal to us what we should be and what we ought to do; nor can human reason discover or define a human nature or provide objective moral rules. Neither can there be a true science of humanity, since human freedom cannot be understood or contained within the causal structures that science attempts to discover. "Existence precedes essence" for human beings. We are what we make ourselves to be. Since no pattern exists for us to emulate or pursue, we are "condemned to be free" and must make those choices that define us as individuals. All this results in a human condition characterized by anguish, forlorness, loneliness, and a sense of abandonment. While Sartre repudiates a religious theory as a basis for morality, he ends up by constructing a theory about human nature—that of a free being conscious of its freedom—to serve as the basis for his own perspective on morality.

Sartre had no moral advice to give; he asserted only that we must choose and then bear the burden of our inevitably free choices. Such choices can never be justified in some objective way because no basis for justification exists; there are no divine laws revealed, no basic human nature to be found, and no "categorical imperative" discovered by human reason. Any attempt to justify moral choices on the basis of some objective reality such as God or reason, constitutes, for Sartre, a matter of self-deception--a lack of honesty about the human situation. In his more mature years, Sartre moved away from the severe individualism of his earlier works and recognized that individual freedom is curtailed by a capitalist society that exploits persons. While he came to accept aspects of a Marxist analysis of economic and social dynamics, he never accepted the materialism and determinism of orthodox Marxism.

Instead of concern about a fulfilling life, Sartre preferred to use the language of "authentic existence." Such existence would involve overcoming self-deception by recognizing our freedom and the burden of choice. The authentic person refuses to play a role or to take on some kind of objective identity. The authentic person does not "play" at being a waiter, or clergyperson, or an existentialist philosopher. The inauthentic life is that of disguise, of playing roles, of excusing ourselves because of fate or circumstances. For the inauthentic person, image is everything.

Regarding moral responsibility toward others, Sartre denied that such an objective responsibility could exist. While others are "mostly in our way," he was convinced that an honest and authentic human being would recognize the freedom of others. He, himself, chose to work in the French underground during the period of Nazi occupation. But his choice to be part of the resistance to the Nazis was his free choice; he did not claim that such action was morally required of others. In terms of Kierkegaard's "stages," Sartre would reject both the moral and the religious stages since neither have a foundation and both would constitute a rejection of human freedom as well as a form of self-deception. This leaves the aesthetic stage as Sartre's approach to the meaning of human life—assuming that Kierkegaard's three stages exhaust the options. The meaning of existence for the free individual, then, would consist of the full and honest recognition of freedom and the pursuit of those life projects by which we make ourselves into what we are. Finally, Sartre would advise us that human existence is absurd, and that the only meaning we can have is that which we affirm by pursuing our own commitments.

Alfred Jules Ayer (1910-1989)

A highly debated but influential view of ethics involved a number of philosophers around the middle of the twentieth century. Sometimes called the "emotivist view" of morality, it was put in a lively and clear form by A. J. Ayer in his *Language, Truth and Logic*. While his own development of the emotivist view was among the more radical, his position is developed here not only because of its clarity but also because of the challenges it presented to other philosophers.

Influenced by logical positivism, Ayer argued that moral claims cannot be matters of fact, but are, instead, expressions of emotions. Philosophers had come to realize that language has a variety of functions including the informative, the interrogative, the directive, and the emotive. When language performs the informative function, it purports to state some kind of fact, such as, "An ice cube will float in water." When a question is asked, the interrogative function is present, as in "Are you going to the play this evening?" When language is used to bring about some behavior in another person, the directive function is illustrated, as in "Bring me a cup of coffee." The emotive function takes place when language is used to express some emotion, such as "Phooey on broccoli." Note that the utterance, "I hate broccoli" would be informative in its form, though it implies an emotional attitude. Notice, also, that a sentence may be informative in form but carry the directive function. For instance, I may tell a waiter, "I would like a medium rare steak." While I am stating a fact about my tastes in steak, nevertheless, I expect the waiter to understand my utterance as a directive or command. I would not expect the waiter to respond, "I appreciate your taste in steaks, but have you decided what to order?" An important distinction between these four functions is that only the informative function involves statements that can be true or false. Questions, orders, and emotive expressions may be appropriate or odd or rude, but they are never true or false.

All this links to A. J. Ayer's claim that moral utterances are emotive expressions not informative utterances. Most people believe they are stating some kind of fact when they make a moral judgment such as "Killing innocent persons is wrong." According to Ayer, however, if I state, "Killing innocent persons is wrong," I am actually uttering something like "Phooey on killing innocent persons." With this emotive interpretation of moral claims, it becomes clear that such claims are never true or false since they have no informative content. "Phooey on killing innocent persons" may express my feelings, but the utterance is neither true nor false.

This view of moral language is tied to a distinction made between sentences that have cognitive meaning and those that do not. A sentence has cognitive meaning if and only if it is either true or false. Note that a sentence such as, "There is sentient life in outer space" can have cognitive meaning even though we do know actually *know* whether it is true or false. A sentence that does not have cognitive meaning (noncognitive) can be neither true nor false; yet such a sentence could have *emotive* meaning if it expresses an emotion, such as "Phooey on broccoli." In order to make a clear distinction between cognitive and noncognitive sentences, the verifiability principle of cognitive meaning was proposed by some philosophers. This principle held that a sentence has cognitive meaning if and only if it can be verified through some sensory experience—some empirical observation. Compare the sentence (1) "An ice cube will float in water" with (2) "Stealing is morally wrong" and (3) "God knows your innermost thoughts." Sentence (1) can be verified by placing an ice cube in water and watching to see whether or not it floats. (A very simple application of scientific method.) But sentences (2) and (3) cannot be shown to be either true or false by some empirical observation. If so, just what observations could verify either of them? Hence, Ayer maintained that sentences like (2) and (3) are without cognitive meaning. Since both are devoid of related sensory experiences, he labeled them as "senseless."

In a curious way, Ayer's position reflects my own claim that the metaphysical position held by a philosopher will influence that philosopher's view of the nature of morality. Ayer jettisons both metaphysics and morality as matters of cognitive status. In one stroke, the verifiability principle of meaning strikes both moral and religious utterances from the realm of cognitive meaning. The proper task of philosophy, for Ayer, is that of clarifying concepts, not giving advice. The quest for propositions that can be either true or false should be left to the sciences. Much like David Hume, Ayer holds that neither philosophy nor science can give us anything like universal moral truths or directions. Nevertheless, Ayer had to make decisions that were "moral" as defined early in this work. He no doubt made regular decisions about what constitutes human fulfillment and who gets it--whose wants, needs and desires end up being honored. Following Hume's dictum that "Reason is and only can be the slave of the passions," Ayer evidently used his reason to get what he wanted. Like Sartre, the existentialist, Ayer leaves ethics in the realm of pure subjectivity but without any of the overtones of anguish reflected in Sartre's philosophy. Ayer appeared to be utterly at home in the world without any need for moral or metaphysical truths or religious consolations. He was one type of a thoroughly modern man.

CHAPTER FOUR

RELIGION-BASED MORALITY: AN OVERVIEW

> *The religious perspective... is the conviction that the values one holds are grounded in the inherent structure of reality, that between the way one ought to live and the way things really are there is an unbreakable inner connection. What sacred symbols do for those to whom they are sacred is to formulate an image of the world's construction and a program for human conduct that are mere reflexes of one another.*
>
> Clifford Geertz [1]

An overview of the dynamics and nature of religion-based morality will assist in understanding just how the concept of God may be related to morality. Such an overview acknowledges that the influential moral patterns of most cultures have, for good or ill, developed out of the religious traditions that shaped those cultures. In Western civilization, Judaism, Christianity, and Islam have been widely influential. All three are forms of ethical monotheism; hence, they are grounded in the conviction that God exists. Traditions in the Far East seldom reflect a clear parallel to Western monotheism; nevertheless, Hinduism, Buddhism, and Taoism each provide concepts that shape the moral patterns of their own distinct belief system. This chapter seeks to describe the major patterns of moral views rooted in various religious, but will not attempt to justify or critique any of those represented.[2]

A preliminary question must first be raised: What possible relationships are there between religion and morality? Clearly, religion and morality have often been inescapably linked not only in the popular mind but also by persons of philosophical distinction. For instance, in the 19th century, the passionately religious Fyodor Dostoevsky asserted through a character in one of his novels that if God is dead, anything is permissible; and in the 20th century the equally passionate atheist, Jean Paul Sartre, believed that with the demise of God there is no longer any objective basis for morality. With no objective answers for our moral quest, Sartre concluded that one must freely choose with no hope for a rational justification of that choice. The influential 17th century British empiricist, John Locke, believed that religious convictions were an important aspect of personal morality and that we have no good grounds for trusting an atheist; while a century later, Immanuel Kant argued that a careful analysis of the very idea of morality necessarily leads one to posit the existence of God. On the other hand, some influential thinkers have maintained that moral traditions rooted in religious systems are irrational or morally corrupt in that such systems are often cruel, divisive and vindictive. This and other objections to a religion-based morality will be explored in Chapter Ten.

At this point, three claims regarding the relationship between morality and religion will be made without any extended attempt to defend the claims. 1) There appears to be no direct correlation between atheism and immorality. In our culture, atheists and religious believers can and often do hold and practice the same general moral values. Yet this in itself is not an interesting philosophical point since most of us, whether religious or not, absorb our moral values quite uncritically from our cultural setting. Hence, an atheist may hold rather traditional moral values even though these values are historically rooted in a religious worldview. 2) Systems of morality can be developed on purely naturalistic (non-religious) grounds. History is replete with such examples from Aristotle and Epicurus to contemporary thinkers. These moral beliefs, however, do differ in significant ways from morality grounded in religious beliefs. 3) The moral patterns of classical theistic traditions of the West cannot be rationally defended apart from the theological beliefs in which they are rooted This last claim is, of course, a central theme in this work.

Before describing some of the elements of religious morality as developed in various traditions, we must first recognize that being moral is not synonymous with being religious. It is true that all major religions include a moral pathway, yet these same religions serve their followers in ways that reach far beyond moral issues. These religions also provide believers with a basic set of concepts, symbols and rites through which they come to understand not only the nature of the universe but also the meaning of their personal venture through life. Religions deal not only with the question, "What ought I to do?," they deal also with such questions as: "Why am I here? Where am I going? What does it all mean?" As the epigraph at the beginning of this chapter indicates, religions seek to be grand conceptual schemes that represent attempts to make sense out of the human venture as well as the cosmos in which persons find themselves. As religions attempt to explain the nature of things, their language is that of symbol, myth and legend; but their goal is to provide a way of walking, with some sense of confidence, hope, and inner peace, through a world too often full of pain and suffering. When a religion fails to bring this vision into place for a believer, then he or she must look elsewhere for answers to these crucial questions.

To understand a religion-based morality, one must examine the worldview in which it is grounded. All religious worldviews share two convictions about the human experience. First, they reflect an initial pessimism in that they believe human life is broken, painful and difficult. The Buddha, for example, held that the first "noble truth" is simply this: "To live is to suffer." Religious language employed to describe the human situation includes a variety of terms such as "lost," "fallen," "sinful," "blind," or "ignorant." Thus, on the one hand, human beings find themselves in need of enlightenment or release or redemption or salvation. On the other hand, the major world religions reflect an optimism about the human situation which runs beyond that of most naturalistic philosophies. Every major living religion teaches that, ultimately, there is a totally fulfilling answer to the problem of the human situation. Release (enlightenment, redemption, salvation) is possible. Such release always involves a moral dimension; but more than morality is involved. From the eye of religious belief, the moral pathway is always seen as fulfilling. Morality is not a burden to be tolerated, it is an integral part of the path toward the highest human fulfillment. To be sure, the moral pathway during life calls for courage and discipline in the face of suffering; yet, in the end, the promise of fulfillment is there. Most religions, in this sense, have a highly extended sense of delayed gratification. Heaven, for example, must wait until life's earthly journey is over.

Since religions express a basic quest for salvation (Western monotheism), Nirvana (Buddhism), or release (Hinduism), an analysis of the role that God or some alternative Reality plays in such a quest would be fruitful. Views of the relationship between the salvation sought, the moral pathway to be traversed, and the activities of the Divine can be illustrated by three models of interaction between mothers and their offspring.[3] In each model, the mother symbolizes God's role in the saving process, while the child represents the human being in need of salvation. The major issue in each model is whether one is saved through good works alone, by God's grace alone, or a combination of good works and grace. The terms "salvation" and "saved" are Western in mood, but can be interchanged with the language of other traditions. The following descriptions explain the various understandings of the "saving" process with no implied criticism of any particular model. However, major theological debates often grow out of differences among the models represented.[4]

The "sea turtle model," represents the view that salvation is achieved "by works alone." There is no Divine assistance involved. In nature, the sea turtle buries her eggs in the sand on an ocean beach and then returns to the sea completely ignoring her potential offspring. As the baby sea turtles hatch and make their way to the surface of the beach, they get no assistance from mother. Furthermore, they are often threatened by a variety of predators waiting for a meal of tender turtle. Instinctively, the baby turtles make their way frantically to the safety (salvation, release) of the sea; but they are totally on their own since mother is not present to help or "grace" her child's journey. Hence, the model represents "salvation by works alone." In religious terms, one is saved only by being obedient to the given moral structures, such as the Law of Karma in Eastern religions. Western monotheisms have never reflected this model since they always subscribe to God's graciousness in some form, while most forms of Hinduism, Jainism and early Buddhism do reflect this model. Yet, in all these faiths, the moral pathway is always perceived as the fulfilling pathway.

The second or "monkey-hold" model represents salvation through works in *cooperation* with grace. In this model, while the mother monkey (God) watches her child (the human person) play on the jungle floor, she is aware that a leopard is creeping toward her child. The child, itself, is initially unaware of the danger. The mother monkey leaps to the floor of the jungle, lifts the child and clasps it to her breast as she bounds to the safety of a tree. In this model, the initial action of the mother is crucial; but the cooperation of the child is also required for the child must cling to the mother to attain salvation. If the child fails to cooperate, it will fall again to the jungle floor and face destruction. Thus, salvation is initiated by a gracious act of God; but the believer must then cooperate with this gracious act by being obedient to the moral law as known. This second model represents the traditional Roman Catholic view of the relationship between God's saving grace available through the Church and the requirements of right belief and right moral actions on the part of the believer. The repentant sinner can be forgiven by God, through the sacraments of the Church, but the forgiven sinner always risks alienation from God through further sinful acts. The believer must exercise her part in the saving process through faithful obedience. Traditional Judaism and Islam reflect this model as well since both view the gift of the Divine Law (Torah, Shari'a) as a gracious act of a compassionate God. But in both faiths the Law must be followed if salvation is to be achieved.

The third or "cat-hold" model of salvation represents the position of "by grace alone." When mother cat (God) sees that her child is in danger, she picks it up by the nape of the neck and carries it to safety. The kitten does nothing to contribute to this process, but merely curls up and trusts in the mother. This model represents classical Protestantism where salvation is by "grace alone through faith," and neither the believer's good works nor correct beliefs contribute to the saving process. One "has faith" (trusts) only in God. And this faith is, itself, understood as a gift from God—a position also held by Roman Catholicism. Of course one who truly trusts in God will also seek to live by the Divine will; but this obedience is not seen in any way as a *means* of being saved. Instead, having discovered and experienced the nature of God's saving love, the individual rejoices in that great gift and is transformed in her inner being. She then does the will of God, not because she must, but because the will of God now reflects her own loves and desires. She is secure in her faith believing that since she is elected, saved, by Divine grace, she will be eternally held in that grace. God will never abandon her.

The logic of this third model led both Luther and Calvin, the two primary figures of the Protestant Reformation, to embrace predestination. In this they followed both Augustine and Aquinas. This doctrine asserts that only those whom God freely elects will attain Heaven and that no human being can ever merit Heaven on the basis of his or her good works. It should be noted that this doctrine of predestination is not to be confused with a view often called fatalism or predeterminism. Both of the latter concepts hold that human choices cannot alter the future since all events are willed by God. "What will be, will be." Both Calvin and Luther, however, believed that our choices can and do alter certain aspects of the future; their doctrine of predestination held only that human choices and actions cannot alter one's ultimate destiny, that of Heaven or Hell. While this cat-hold model reflects what I call Classical Protestantism, a variety of Protestant groups have taken positions more akin to the monkey-hold model.

Since in all major religions the path of salvation (moksha, nirvana) always involves a moral dimension, religious traditions are necessarily concerned about properly discerning such moral dimensions as reflected in the will of the Divine. How does the believer come to know God's will or the rules of the proper moral pathway? One widely held position maintains that human reason can correctly discern proper moral rules and principles, in part, without the aid of Divine revelation. There is, according to this view, a "Natural Law" (natural laws regarding morality, not "laws of nature" in the scientific sense) which exists in the nature of the created world and can be discerned and understood by the human mind quite apart from any revealed scripture to which one might appeal. The traditional Roman Catholic view regarding artificial means of birth control grows out of this Natural Law approach. The reasoning goes as follows: A rational examination of the phenomenon of sexuality in nature reveals that the primary purpose and end of sexuality is the procreation of children. Given this primary purpose within nature, it follows that any sexual act which deliberately and artificially frustrates this primary natural purpose is an immoral act. Since artificial means of birth control involve the thwarting of this natural scheme of things, the use of such means is an act against God's will as expressed in created nature. Another example of natural truths of justice or morality in a different context is expressed in the Declaration of Independence. This document holds that there are "self-evident" truths such as, "all men are created equal, that they are endowed by their Creator with certain unalienable Rights, that among these are Life, Liberty and the pursuit of Happiness." It should be noted that philosophical criticisms of Natural Law Theory have weakened if not mortally wounded the theory.

Some religious traditions have held that human reason is unable, left to its own devices, to either understand the moral law or to live by it. Indeed, in their natural state of alienation from God, human beings are blind not only to the moral law, but also to their own greatest good. So apart from the gracious saving work of God, including the revelation of the Divine will, human beings can neither know the moral law nor live by it. This position, of course, goes on to assert that God has, in fact, revealed the moral law to the human scene through some Holy Book and/or through some special persons. Conservative Protestants, Orthodox Jews and Muslims reflect forms of this view. These groups hold that their scriptures (the *Bible*, the *Torah*, the *Qur'an*) are infallible by nature. Thus, to learn God's will the believer turns to the Holy Book taken to be revealed by God (Yahweh, Allah). All of these traditions also involve learned commentaries on their scriptures that help in understanding and applying the Divine will. Less conservative groups within these traditions may not consider their scriptures to be wholly infallible, since some parts of the scripture may reflect old views of nature and science which we now know to be mistaken. Nevertheless, they believe that the central moral truths are to be found in the writings or in the history of the people recorded in the writings.

An examination of religious ethics requires that a distinction be made between Rule Absolutists and Principle Absolutists. Both positions are absolutist since both hold that moral rules or principles exist that properly apply to all human beings in any time or place. Neither claim that all human beings *know* these rules or principles; nor do they claim that human beings follow the rules or principles even if they do know of them. They claim only that such rules or principles exist and that human beings would benefit from knowing and obeying them.

A Rule Absolutist would claim that the Divine moral law consists of a series of specific rules which identify specific actions that one should perform as well as specific actions one should avoid. These rules are absolute in that they would correctly apply to any person at any time in any culture. Several of the traditional Ten Commandments would represent such a position, such as the prohibitions against stealing, killing and adultery. According to some Rule Absolutists, lying is always wrong since it breaks a specific and absolute rule. Some Rule Absolutists would oppose all abortions, for instance, since they understand abortion as the killing of an innocent human being.

A Principle Absolutist, on the other hand, holds there is one absolute general principle that properly applies to all persons at all times and in all places, while specific rules may not properly apply in all settings. This approach is reflected in what some refer to as "situation ethics" in that the application of the one general moral principle has to be worked out within the context of a particular situation. Some Principle Absolutists, drawing on the teachings of Jesus and the writings of St. Paul, hold that the one absolute general principle is the Law of Love and that all basic morality is summed up in this law. As St. Paul wrote, "Love does no wrong to a neighbor; therefore, love is the fulfilling of the law."[5] This, of course, implies that one must decide just how to love someone properly in certain situations and under certain conditions since no specific actions are identified in the Law of Love. For instance, in some situations the loving act may include the telling of a lie, while in another situation the loving act may necessitate the telling of the truth. To use a common illustration, if you were concealing Jewish friends from the Nazis during World War II, should you tell the truth to the Nazi military police if they knocked on your door and asked if you were concealing Jews? Would lying to the Nazis be morally wrong? A Principle Absolutist could argue that the ultimate moral principle is the Law of Love, and that one is thereby required to lie to the Nazis to honor that law. In that situation, lying may be morally required. On the whole, however, the Principle Absolutist would maintain that the truly loving thing to do in the vast majority of situations is to tell the truth.

Some religious defenders of abortion rights use an argument parallel to the question of lying. They may admit that while abortion is always a sad and a difficult alternative, nevertheless, there may be times when allowing an abortion is the most loving thing to do in the given circumstances. If a woman's mental or physical health is at stake, or if she has been raped or has been the victim of incest, perhaps the loving thing to do in that situation is to allow an abortion. On the other hand, few, if any, Principle Absolutists would see abortion as a general means for birth control as a legitimate expression of the Law of Love. I note, again, that neither Rule Absolutists nor the Principle Absolutists necessarily believe that all people actually know of these rules or principles. Rather, they hold that such rules exist as objective moral truths and that people should seek to know and obey them.

Another important distinction made in various formulations of religious ethics has to do with the function or purpose of the

Divine Law. The following four functions have been identified, though not all theologians would affirm the legitimacy of all four: 1) the saving function, 2) the civil function, 3) the normative function, and 4) the theological function.

The Divine Law exhibits a saving function when obedience to that Law becomes the *means* to salvation. The person is saved or put in right relationship with God only by being obedient to the Law. Traditional Judaism and Islam hold this view of the Law, though both of these traditions have a strong sense of God's compassion and forgiveness. The Law of Karma, or the moral law of cause and effect in traditions of the Far East, represent much the same view. Classical Christianity has generally rejected this saving function of the Law in part because Christianity has a more pessimistic view of human nature linked to the doctrines of the Fall and Original Sin, and because of the meaning given to the crucifixion of Jesus. Christians have generally held the view that human beings tend, by their fallen nature, to be sinners—to be self-centered and anxiety driven. Furthermore, persons are not able to lift themselves by their own moral bootstraps, nor are they able to earn God's forgiving and accepting love. Such forgiving love is, ultimately, a gift. To be sure, traditional Roman Catholicism and some Protestants have taught that if one is disobedient to the Divine Law, then one is in danger of alienation from God and threatened by eternal rejection. Nevertheless, Catholicism has never taught that salvation can be attained only by being obedient to this Law. Instead, one is saved through and by the grace of God conferred through the various sacraments of the Church. Infant baptism, which removes original sin, exemplifies this initial act of saving grace without which, according to traditional Catholicism, the individual cannot be saved.

The civil function of the Divine Law is exercised when this Law is used as a model for civil laws that are instituted by states or nations. Here, the Law is used to keep order and to seek to establish justice. Civil laws against murder represent such a use of the Law. Such laws are intended to restrain persons from doing evil deeds, not to provide a path to salvation. Nations or states seldom attempt to put all aspects of the Divine Law into forms of national or state laws, though some who think of themselves as theocracies approach this pattern.

The normative function of the Divine Law is expressed when this law is taken as a basic guide for the living of one's life. Thus, while a person does not believe that she is saved or put right with God through obeying the Law, she nevertheless believes that a devout person accepts the Law as the moral guideline for life. The believer obeys, not as a way of saving herself or earning God's forgiveness and acceptance, but out of loyalty to God and as part of the quest for the fulfilling and significant life. The Calvinist tradition in Protestantism most clearly reflects this normative function of the Divine Law, though this tradition accepts the civil function and the theological function as well.

The idea of the theological function of the Divine Law is drawn largely from the writings of St. Paul. Here the Law's main function is to show persons just how badly they err and how much they are in need of God's grace and help. The premise, here, is that no one is able to reach the high moral standards of, say, the Sermon on the Mount. To take that sermon seriously as a moral guideline would lead the believer to guilt and despair. The Law crushes human presumption and shows persons their need of grace. As Luther put it, God wounds in order to heal. This view of the Law holds that all persons stand guilty and condemned under the Law, and only by trust in the gracious love of God can one live without despair. But, these theologians continue, the discovery of this gracious love of God can change one's heart and turn one to a new direction in life. Now one lives, as far as one is able, by the Divine Law of love. But one now lives by the Law, not in an attempt to earn God's love, but out of a joyous response to the Divine Love that has already been freely bestowed. The well-known folk hymn, *Amazing Grace*, reflects the mood of this theological function of the law.

Finally, a psychological analysis of human reactions to the Divine Law is offered by various religions as they address the question of why human beings seem to rebel against or fail to understand the very pathway that promises to lead to their joy and fulfillment. The answers offered by religious traditions usually involve some view of human ignorance, blindness, or willful rebellion.

Buddhism teaches that our basic problem is that of ignorance. After all, we start out in life with nothing that can be called knowledge. Presumably, we learn as we grow older; but we learn by accepting, quite uncritically, what is told to us by our family, our culture, our peer group or our gang. So we *believe* that we know when we do not really *know* at all. We believe that what the people around us value is really valuable; we believe that we really know what is good. But the Buddha thought otherwise. He taught that we are victimized by "ignorant craving" which leads us to pursue things which are not truly desirable but, instead, bring us suffering. The evil deeds which persons do—theft, cheating, murder, rape, war, violence—all result from ignorant craving. The Buddha aimed to bring "enlightenment" so that his followers could, in properly understanding the nature of the human situation, overcome their ignorant cravings and find ultimate peace of Nirvana.

St. Augustine, in the Christian tradition, suggested a psychological explanation of human resistance to Divine Law. As he reflected on his days as a youth in North Africa, he thought of the night when he and his friends raided someone's garden, gleefully picked all the unripe pears off a tree and threw them to pigs nearby.[6] As a man in his forties, he wondered why he and his friends *enjoyed* doing what they did that night. He concluded that they enjoyed doing it precisely because they *knew* it was wrong. For Augustine, then, evil was not a matter of ignorance. It is not that our minds fail us; the problem is that our hearts are corrupt. Evil is an expression of our fallen and sinful state; we love what we know we ought not to love, according to Augustine's analysis.

Paul Tillich, a twentieth century theologian, put the matter in a different way by analyzing the situation in terms of autonomy (self-law), heteronomy (other-law) and theonomy (Divine-Law).[7] Tillich suggests that we all desire to live by our own individual judgments of what is right and wrong. We want to be "autonomous." Furthermore, this desire is both normal and appropriate. For to be a genuine individual, to be authentic, we must live by our own judgments, not those of someone else. But when we are confronted by the Divine Law in some form, we tend to experience such law as "over-against us." These laws appear to be "heteronomous," or laws that are "other" and not part of our own being. We experience those laws as irritating and inappropriate rules; we deeply resent them and may express this resentment through open or hidden rebellion. An analogous situation exists when youngsters come to the point of resenting the "laws" or "rules" laid down for them by parents and others. The young person sees those laws as "other," as not part of their own choosing or being. This youthful rebellion is an example of "the rebellion of autonomy against heteronomy." Finally, Tillich suggests that religious believers come to see that the Divine Law that first appeared to be foreign or *other* is, in reality, an expression of their own essential being and not *against* them at all. This, then, is the state of "theonomy," whereby one comes to realize that the Divine Law is truly an expression of one's own essential nature and is, therefore, a means of being truly fulfilled.

This chapter has attempted to describe some of the major facets of morality rooted in religious belief systems. These descriptions have, of course, been brief and have not expressed some of the finer nuances of these traditions. Furthermore, this chapter has been *descriptive*. No attempt has been made to defend the truth of any of the positions or to criticize them. It would appear that they cannot all be true since they often hold contradictory positions. It may be that all of them are, in fact, false. On the other hand, perhaps one of them is close to the truth.

CHAPTER FIVE

HOW "GOD" MAKES A DIFFERENCE

... if (the) theistic position were not only coherent but also correct, it could make a significant difference to moral philosophy. . . . the good for man might be more determinate, more unitary. . . .It therefore matters a lot for moral philosophy whether any such theistic view is correct: the theological frontier of ethics remains open.
J. L. Mackie[1]

The modern age, more or less repudiating the idea of a divine lawgiver, has nevertheless tried to retain the ideas of moral right and wrong, not noticing that, in casting God aside, they have also abolished the conditions of meaningfulness for moral right and wrong as well.
Richard Taylor[2]

The intent of this chapter is purely descriptive and will make no judgments about the adequacy or inadequacy of a religiously-based morality. While I will claim that a theistic worldview can support a moral perspective that cannot be justified on non-theistic grounds, this claim in no way implies that the moral perspective held by a theist is either superior or inferior to a morality grounded in naturalism. I will show *that* "God" makes a difference, for good or ill, in the practice of morality. I will also show just *why* that is the case. Many theists and non-theists will not find my claim to be either new or challenging since they, themselves, have long held such a position. My theory will be a challenge only to those who believe that the central elements of theistic morality can be justified in the context of a naturalistic worldview.

While the loss of God from a worldview will, I suggest, require some restructuring of the moral content of that worldview, there are certain implications which will not necessarily follow. For instance, it does not necessarily follow that a person's morality will collapse if his or her religious beliefs collapse. Empirical evidence indicates that atheists can and do hold to moral principles affirmed also by theists, and that an atheist can act as morally, in traditional terms, as a theist. Indeed, an atheist may often best the theist's behavior even in terms of the theist's own moral principles. Hence, if Joe ceases to believe in God he does not necessarily become immoral or find himself devoid of moral convictions. But in many ways this is not an interesting philosophical point since most of us gain our moral values from the culture that shapes and sustains us. We tend to imbibe traditional Western moral values with our mother's milk—and through various educational processes. Furthermore, most human beings learn that prudence is a habit worth cultivating. If God is dead, everything may be permissible in a certain theoretical sense, but not necessarily prudent. Our behavior tends to reflect the general norms of our community and our own rational self-interest as part of that community. The origins of our moral convictions may be largely a matter of psychology and sociology. However, my interest in this text is philosophical in that I seek to demonstrate how moral issues are raised, articulated and rationally defended within the conceptual maps or worldviews that human beings generate.

The particular philosophical question raised in this work is whether or not one can defend or justify traditional religious moral principles without grounding them in a religious worldview. The epigraphs from J. L. Mackie and Richard Taylor at the beginning of this chapter directly reflect this question. We note that neither of them cross the "theological frontier of ethics" since both hold that theism is devoid of any supporting arguments and seems utterly implausible in the light of scientific knowledge. Mackie's position yields a rather positive view of theological

Ethics—if a religious worldview were coherent. Taylor, on the other hand, reflects a general disdain for the moral patterns which grew out of the Biblical traditions when he writes:

> We have been taught that meekness is a virtue, that ignorance and stupidity are not moral faults, that the gods look upon the vulgar with the same favor as upon the wise. As a result our morality has become a kind of petty clockwork of behaving, the point of which appears to be nothing nobler than innocence. We have been so conditioned and enervated by the Beatitudes that we are hardly capable any longer of understanding, much less appreciating, the truth that was so obvious to the pagan moralists: that what is worth having (or being) is not the common, but the uncommonly good . . . all of the moralists of classical antiquity called it virtue. . . strength, superiority.[3]

This chapter will reflect Mackie's and Taylor's positions by showing *how* the existence of God would impinge on the nature and rational justification of morality. In pursuing this analysis, however, the questions of whether God exists and whether a religion-based morality is adequate are left open.

In Chapter Two, I argued that the point of morality is to find some way to *appropriately arbitrate* among the multitude of conflicting and competitive wants, needs and desires (WNDs) experienced by sentient creatures. I also asserted that two basic issues must be addressed in the process of finding such an appropriate arbitration. The first issue is that of determining just what a genuinely fulfilled human life might be and how best to attain it. The second issue is that of determining whether or not we have any obligation to support other creatures in their quest for fulfillment even as we pursue our own. Any fully developed moral philosophy must address both issues. This chapter will explore how the idea of God can shape the answer to the question of the fulfilled life. The following chapter will examine the question of just how the idea of God links one's own quest for fulfillment to the lives and experiences of other creatures—both human and non-human.

While the very idea of a fulfilled life is complex, philosophers have generally argued that rational persons seek such a life as they, themselves, understand it. Following chapters will demonstrate that this rational quest for a fulfilled life does not necessarily imply selfishness, since our own fulfillment is often closely linked to that of those we love. Nevertheless, a rational morality will involve a "self-referential" dimension in that the fulfillment of those we love contributes to our own. This chapter will examine the idea of a fulfilled life by analyzing two issues which make up the core of any concept of such a life. A) What is the meaning or point of our human life, if any? B) In the face of finitude and mortality, what basis is there for the significance of the individual person? While these two issues are often interrelated, they can be separated for our present purposes.

A. What is the Meaning or Point of Human Life?

A person's quest for fulfillment necessarily hinges on what that person understands to be the point of the human venture from birth to death--and perhaps beyond. Many of our day-to-day actions, and certainly our long range plans and aspirations, will reflect our convictions about the meaning of the human venture. The possible views held by human beings about the meaning of life are manifold, but most can be seen as variant forms of one of three basic views: nihilism, cosmic meaning and temporal meaning.[4]

Before examining these alternatives, it may prove fruitful to explore just what we are asking about when we inquire about the meaning of life. Richard Taylor has suggested that the question of life's meaning might best be explored by first constructing what might be thought of as a totally meaningless existence.[5] To do so, he analyzed the ancient Greek myth of Sisyphus. Sisyphus had angered the gods who condemned him to the eternal labor of rolling a large boulder up a hill. But each time he would almost reach the summit of the hill, the rock would slip from his grip and roll to the bottom. He would then return to the bottom of the hill and begin, again, to roll the rock toward the summit—knowing full well he would never get it to the top. Taylor suggests that this is a picture of an utterly meaningless existence. Like all great myths, of course, the story of Sisyphus is not just about some unfortunate figure who met a sad fate; it is, instead, the story of all human beings. Each day as we arise, we begin to roll some kind of "rock," whatever our chosen work may be. And each day we retire, only to rise again the next day facing the same activity. The myth asks of us, "Toward what end or for what purpose do we live?"

There are those who would answer that our fate, as that of Sisyphus, is a life without any meaning. Call these the Nihilists. Rejecting a religious interpretation of life, nihilism holds that just as there is no essential purpose or meaning to the universe, even so there is no essential purpose or meaning to the human lives cast up randomly by this universe. Our day-to-day labors have no point or purpose. Even our brief experiences of joy appear, upon reflection, to be empty. A striking literary expression of nihilism is found in Ernest Hemingway's short story, "A Clean Well-Lighted Place," where, near the end of the story, the main character utters a nihilistic revision of elements of Christian liturgy by substituting *nada* (nothing) for a number of key words in the Lord's Prayer and the Hail Mary.[6] While nihilism is a minority view, historically, nevertheless it is reflected by some people in almost every age.

In sharp contrast to nihilism, cosmic meaning is rooted in religious belief and thus is not an option for a worldview without God. This view is most clearly expressed in, though not limited to, the sister theisms of Judaism, Christianity, and Islam in their traditional forms. Each of these would revise the Myth of Sisyphus by allowing him to live day by day while trusting that his life's venture will lead him to a joyous fulfillment after his death. En route, his rock rolling would include caring for his loved ones, his community, and humanity in ways revealed by the source book of his individual faith. Though his labors may be difficult, he is saved from emptiness and despair by his beliefs that the cosmos has meaning and purpose since it was brought into existence by God and will come to fulfillment under God's guidance. Human life, then, is part of that universe of meaning and believers trust that their lives are meaningful insofar as they participate positively in the work and will of God.

Cosmic meaning, like nihilism, can be reflected in art or literature. An example would be a prayer recited by a nurse at the close of the day to small orphaned boys in the film, "The Cider House Rules":

> O Lord, support us all the day long in this troublous life, until the shadows lengthen and the evening comes, and the busy world is hushed, and the fever of life is over, and our work is done. Then of Thy mercy grant us a safe lodging, and a holy rest, and peace at the last; through Jesus Christ our Lord. Amen.[7]

The third major view of life's meaning can be called temporal meaning. This view is essentially non-religious. But while temporal meaning holds, with the nihilist, that the universe has no essential point or meaning, nevertheless, human beings can find meaning in the joys and commitments they experience during their lifetime. Temporal meaning could be expressed in the myth of Sisyphus if some alterations were made in the basic plot. For example, if Sisyphus managed to get his rock to the top and add even more rocks so that he could construct a home to provide shelter for himself and for those he loved. On the other hand, as Richard Taylor suggested, Sisyphus could find sufficient meaning if the gods injected a substance into his veins which would make him experience joy and satisfaction in the very rolling of his rock. The meaning would not be in the goal, since there was none, but in the journey.

It appears, then, that temporal meaning can be expressed in many ways. Some may find meaning exclusively in the pleasures they manage to experience; others may find meaning by devoting their energies to the service of other human beings and the protection of planet earth's eco-system. The point, here, is that one's view of the meaning of life is crucially linked to what is deemed to be valuable and worth pursuing in the absence of religious consolations. Bertrand Russell once expressed a view of temporal meaning in vivid prose:

> Brief and powerless is man's life; on him and all his race the slow, sure doom falls pitiless and dark. Blind to good and evil, reckless of destruction, omnipotent matter rolls on its relentless way; for man, condemned today to lose his dearest, tomorrow himself to pass through the gate of darkness, it remains only to cherish, ere yet the blow falls, the lofty thoughts that ennoble his little day; disdaining the coward terrors of the slave of Fate, to worship at the shrine that his own hands have built, undismayed by the empire of chance, to preserve a mind free from the wanton tyranny that rules his outward life; proudly defiant of the irresistible forces that tolerate, for a moment, his knowledge and his condemnation, to sustain alone, a weary but unyielding Atlas, the world that his own ideals have fashioned despite the trampling march of unconscious power. [8]

Another analysis of the question of life's meaning was made by the Danish philosopher, Soren Kierkegaard, who sought to describe alternative attempts to make human life meaningful. He proposed that there are three "stages on life's way": 1) the aesthetic, 2) the ethical, and 3) the religious. These stages do not necessarily represent a chronological sequence in a person's life, nor is it inevitable that a person will experience all of them. According to Kierkegaard, an adult may choose to live in any one of the three; but only one stage at a point in time since the stages are mutually exclusive. Furthermore, the choice is forced; a person must live either as an aesthete, or in the ethical stage, or in the religious stage. In selecting the stage, one selects the meaning of one's life.[9]

We must be content, here, with a brief description of Kierkegaard's stages, though such a description will not do justice to the subtle analyses he pursued. Each stage is characterized by the way a person seeks to find meaning in life. In the aesthetic stage, an individual finds meaning through the immediate experiences that he or she finds interesting and satisfying in some way. Kierkegaard, no doubt, had in mind some of the Romantics of his day. Since such experiences constitute the meaning of life for the aesthete, she must, in principle, deny any constraints on her pursuit of these experiences. This implies the rejection of any moral rules that would inhibit or undercut this quest for experience. On the other hand, boredom is the great enemy of the aesthete, since boredom is precisely the lack of immediate experiences which are interesting and satisfying. Curiously, boredom appears to be a problem only for the aesthete. Those who are at the ethical or the religious stage are seldom, if ever, bored.

The small child represents, for Kierkegaard, a paradigm case of the aesthete's quest for meaning. As long as he or she is comfortable and has some interesting activity at hand, the child is generally happy--and life is experienced as meaningful. But if discomfort enters or the activity at hand no longer interests him, then meaning is threatened and his world collapses. In a child this pattern is accepted as innocent and natural, but innocence disappears for the adult aesthete. The adult aesthete finds that she must constantly generate new activities or interests since most activities become dull upon repetition or as she matures. As an aesthete, the very small child is content for a few moments with her blocks, but blocks seldom satisfy older children. They move on to other experiences—to the tricycle, then to the bicycle, then to the automobile.

According to Kierkegaard's analysis, each step in this sequence has its moments of fascination and interest, yet each has some tendency to become dull and empty. Where does one go when the first car begins to lose its emotional luster? A new model with more power or status? And then what follows? Kierkegaard suggests that the aesthete finds himself continuously threatened by the specter of boredom since he realizes, perhaps only vaguely, that his quest for meaning is a sequence of experiences each of which tends to turn to emptiness and dust. Certain dimensions of the drug scene may be expressions of the aesthetic stage, though the motivation for drug use may be that of an escape from despair as often as it is a quest for a satisfying experience. The aesthete is continually threatened by the question, "Can this be all there is?" There is a constant need to push the envelope.

Another paradigm of the aesthete, for Kierkegaard, is the legendary figure of Don Juan who finds life's meaning in sexual encounters with a series of women. His attendant kept a record of Don Juan's ventures in various lands. But, as the legend suggests, this form of meaning is ultimately undercut since meaning is rooted only in the vitality of the mortal body that eventually disintegrates. When the body fails, this quest for meaning fails.

While the child and the Don Juan figure exemplify the aesthetic stage of life, this stage can also be expressed in a variety of other ways that focus on meaning found through immediate experience. The intellectual aesthete finds meaning through the analysis and discussion of new ideas, new works of art and other creative activities. This stage can also be expressed in a religious mode when religious worship or participation is pursued purely as an experience of beauty or art or of "feeling good." Perhaps the aesthete of the ordinary life finds life's central meaning searching the TV with his remote—or in going shopping. Jean-Baptiste Clamence, the main character in Albert Camus' *The Fall*, is a striking literary representation of the collapse of someone in the aesthetic stage to a state of near despair.[10]

If the aesthete is threatened by despair, she may choose the ethical stage of existence where the core meaning of life is to be found in living out one's sense of moral duty as understood by her community. The person in the ethical stage does not reject pleasant experiences that life can bring such as entertainment, good food, sexuality, art; but the central meaning of life is not found in those experiences. Kierkegaard's paradigm for the moral life is the middle class "pillar of the community" of his Danish heritage. This person lives out his or her duties as parent, spouse, and contributing member of the community. These duties are pursued, not because they always bring satisfying and interesting experiences, but because of his commitment to the responsibilities he has assumed. The aesthete, on the other hand, would find that the satisfactions of marriage and family would eventually wear thin. If the aesthete tires of the duties linked to spouse and family, his remedy would be to withdraw from these commitments, trade in his wife for a "new model"—as he might his car—and live in a yacht off the coast of California, finances permitting.

The ethical stage does not necessarily imply a religious interpretation of life nor of morality as an expression of God's will. Meaning, in this stage, is found in living by the socially established norms and rules of one's community. But the ethical stage of existence exacts its own costs, as Kierkegaard shows when he develops a type of Hegelian dialectic. The person who has chosen the ethical stage cannot, in principle, trivialize morality since the very meaning of life is at stake. The person, therefore, must take moral duty with deep seriousness. But in doing so, can a man be confident that he is the spouse, the parent, the worker, the neighbor, the responsible community member that he, himself, believes he should be? This commitment to moral duty results in a profound sense of inadequacy and guilt for failing to live up to the standards adopted. And if the person who has chosen to find life's meaning through the ethical stage of existence finds that her morality falls short of her aspirations, then the very meaning of her life is threatened. Furthermore, she may come to feel imprisoned by a complex set of moral rules which were not of her making and which undercut any sense of individual personal identity. She finds herself to be merely a reflection of society's ideals and codes. Finally, the specter of death begins to haunt. If life is one long attempt to live out difficult moral commitments and all ends in death, perhaps one fares better by forgoing these commitments and returning to or adopting the aesthetic stage—which always stands as a possible option to be freely choose. Again, despair looms on the horizon.

Given his passionate religious bent, Kierkegaard regards the religious stage as the only one that can ultimately rescue us from despair—the "sickness unto death." The person who chooses the religious stage is no ascetic; she does not forgo life's rich experiences and the joys of embodied living. Nor does she dismiss moral duty as a misguided concept. But the meaning of her life is now centered on her individual relationship with God. All this is grounded in a faith that trusts beyond what she can know or verify through argument and evidence. This faith is a "leap" which is not achieved at one moment in life but by reaffirmation day by day in the face of doubt and even anxiety. Faith does not overcome doubt since true faith is held only in the face of doubt. Faith is "treading water forty fathoms deep." The person in the religious stage realizes that faith is not a form of knowledge verified by argument or fact, but a chosen orientation which could, in principle, be mistaken.

Furthermore, Kierkegaard maintains that the bar tender at the local pub may be existing in the religious stage, while the clergyman may not be. This is so since faith is an intensely interior reality and does not necessarily show itself in outward demeanor or in babbling about matters explicitly religious. But in the stage of faith the person finds that the anxiety of guilt is muted since she finds herself to be accepted, forgiven, even though she fails, at times, to be what she is called to be or desires to be. And in the stage of faith the anxiety of death is overcome by the trust that one is secured by the Infinite, both now and beyond death. Finally, in the stage of faith the anxiety of emptiness and meaninglessness is overcome. Meaning is now rooted in the Eternal, not the ephemeral.[11]

In summary, "God" makes a difference regarding the meaning of life in the following ways: With the existence of God, Cosmic Meaning is a possibility. Without God, the options are either Nihilism or Temporal Meaning. And the category of Temporal Meaning could include both Kierkegaard's aesthetic and ethical stage, since the absence of God does not imply the absence of moral structures. In Kierkegaard's analysis, the existence of God in one's worldview makes the Religious Stage a possibility. Without God, the options are the aesthetic stage or the ethical stage—each with their tendency to be undermined by life's experiences.

Up to this point, the analysis of the meaning of life has been largely philosophical in nature. But one might ask if there is any empirical research that addresses this issue and links it to other dimensions of human experience? Scholars interested in the psychology of religion have developed instruments that attempt to measure whether an individual's level of life's meaning is high or low.[12] One author states, "A person with a high sense of meaning has relatively clear goals, sees reasons for existence, sees himself or herself as responsible, is prepared to die, and perceives life as a mission." Those with a low sense of meaning have opposite characteristics and are described as reflecting an existential vacuum or "frustrated will to meaning." Moreover, other researchers have developed instruments designed to detect the values that people tend to pursue in life. In his "Value Survey," Milton Rokeach listed eighteen "terminal values"—end states pursued--which include the following: a comfortable life, an exciting life, pleasure, a sense of accomplishment, family, security, mature love, salvation, and self-respect. Subjects who took this value survey were asked to rank the eighteen items in order, listing their highest value as number one. Given this research, psychologists began to ask if there were any correlation between the meaning of life indicated with the values preferred. They discovered that only four of the terminal values had any significant relationship to the level of meaning which persons expressed: pleasure, excitement, comfort, and salvation. Of those four values, only salvation was positively related to a sense of purpose or a meaning in life. Those who ranked salvation as a high value tended to have a higher score on a Purpose in Life Test. On the other hand, subjects who ranked pleasure, excitement and comfort high on their values list tended to have low purpose in life scores; and those who ranked those three values low tended to have higher purpose in life scores.

While this data shows some interesting correlation between what is valued and the meaning of life, it in no way proves that some values or meanings are "better" than others. Such science helps to show what might *be* the case but it cannot show us what *ought* to be the case. Those familiar with sociologist Peter Berger's *The Sacred Canopy: Elements of a Sociological Theory of Religion*, would probably expect to find a correlation between "salvation" and a high sense of meaning in life. Berger and other sociologists consistently claim that one of the major functions of religion is just that of helping to supply such meaning. These sociologists would note, however, that even if religion does tend to supply meaning to life such a fact does not imply that religious belief is true. Furthermore, a correlation between goals such as pleasure, excitement and comfort with a low sense of life's meaning—a tendency toward despair—would have been fully anticipated by Soren Kierkegaard. Such values would be closely related to the values pursued in the aesthetic stage of life as Kierkegaard described it.

B. Significance in the Face of Finitude and Mortality?

Human beings not only want to *be*, they want to be *significant*. They want to *count* in some way. Ernest Becker shaped this issue clearly when he observed,

> . . . what man really fears is not so much extinction, but extinction with insignificance. Man wants to know that his life has somehow counted, if not for himself, then at least in a larger scheme of things, that it has left a trace, a trace that has meaning."[13]

Thus, the individual's quest for significance is an intimate aspect of the search for fulfillment. The sense of individual significance, however, can be undercut by a variety of circumstances. Unsatisfactory interpersonal relationships can weaken our sense of significance if those who should love us and support us fail in some basic way to do so. Perceived inadequacies and limitations of various kinds—physical attributes, intellectual capacities, even social and creative skills—can threaten our sense of significance.

Many observers of the human scene note that a sense of cosmic insignificance can also threaten us. Pascal once expressed this anxiety:

> When I consider the brief span of my life, absorbed into the eternity before and after, the small space I occupy and which I see swallowed up in the infinite immensity of spaces of which I know nothing and

> which know nothing of me, I take fright and am amazed to see myself here rather than there: there is no reason for me to be here rather than there, now rather than then. . . . The eternal silence of these infinite spaces terrifies me.[14]

The character of Calvin, a small, precocious child in the comic strip *Calvin and Hobbes*, often expressed much the same mood in contemporary and popular terms. Standing alone under the great dome of a starry sky or in the face of the awesome power of nature, Calvin insists that he is significant. Nevertheless, in spite of his protestations, he quietly comes to the conclusion that he is hardly more than a dust speck.

Existential philosophers, theologians and psychologists have suggested that existential anxieties about death and meaninglessness represent threats to our sense of significance. According to Paul Tillich, these anxieties are "existential" in the sense that they are inherently part of the human experience and must be borne.[15] While drugs may deaden our sense of these anxieties, and sexual ecstasy and shopping may distract us momentarily, neither psychotherapy nor religion can remove these anxieties. They must be borne through the "courage to be." Indeed, one of the major functions of religious belief is that of supplying a "sacred canopy" under which the believer lives and which provides a basis for such courage.[16] But the sacred canopy does not remove these anxieties; at best, it helps to undergird the courage needed to bear them.

Anxiety about death may be primary. Ernest Becker argued,

> . . .the idea of death, the fear of it, haunts the human animal like nothing else; it is a mainspring of human activity—activity designed largely to avoid the fatality of death, to overcome it by denying in some way that it is the final destiny for man.[17]

Plato observed, ". . . the true votary of philosophy is likely to be misunderstood by other men; they do not perceive that he is always pursuing death and dying."[18] According to Buddhist traditions, the one who became the Buddha was compelled to pursue his quest for enlightenment because of the "four passing sights" which included disease, old age, and death.[19] And St. Paul, writing to the Corinthians, refers to death as "the last enemy to be destroyed."[20] More recently, Sigmund Freud reflects on "the painful riddle of death" and "the great necessities of fate, against which there is no remedy."[21]

While all mammals die, it appears that human beings are unique in that they come to know that they *must* die. Thus, for human beings, death brings with it certain conceptual problems that other creatures need not face for we must somehow integrate this consciousness of our mortality into the cluster of beliefs which make up our worldview. The idea of death is, when examined, quite complex. Children come to the "adult" view of death in three identifiable stages: 1) that the body ceases to function, 2) the person who died will not return, and 3) *all* persons will some day die. The third level of understanding is usually in place when the child is around ten years of age. Small wonder, then, that religious traditions begin to bring in intellectual defenses against the threat of death in the early years of the second decade.

A major human strategy used in defense of personal mortality is to construct some view which helps the person deny that death has the last word. These views can be identified into various schemes of immortality. Some philosophical positions, such as Plato's, put forward the claim that the human soul is immortal and survives the death of the body which, in life, is the "prison house of the soul." The Biblical traditions (Judaism, Christianity, Islam) speak not so much of an immortal soul as they do of the "resurrection of the body," thus giving the body an affirmation which Plato refused to do. The religious traditions of India have generally muted the sting of death by postulating the theory of reincarnation or transmigration of the soul. But in that tradition, the very thought of the continuous reincarnation was rejected as unbearable; hence, the ultimate goal was that of absorption into the Divine sea of reality—union with Brahman.

Naturalistic thinkers who reject the idea of personal immortality or the resurrection of the body have come to terms with their mortality in a variety of ways. Epicurus, the ancient atomist and hedonist held that death can be explained as the coming apart of the "atoms" which make up all existing things. Since a person is nothing more than a functioning collection of material atoms, at death the person essentially ceases to be. But such an understanding of death has its comforts since it informs us that after death there is no suffering to be anticipated, and the gods cannot punish us in an afterlife since we are no more. During our living years, then, Epicurus taught that we should live a life a pleasure for the self with "pleasure" defined as "absence of pain in body or mind." Our concern for others, he taught, was to be limited to those actions which redound to our own benefit.[22]

Other naturalistic philosophers have suggested various forms of symbolic immortality which function as ways of stripping death of its capacity to annihilate the individual. While these thinkers grant that their own existence as a conscious entity is no longer possible after death, they take some consolation in knowing that their existence will have an influence on future events and future beings in various ways. Thus, the *biological* mode of symbolic immortality is that of living on through one's children, while in the *socio-biological* mode one lives on in the tribe or clan or nation with which one identifies. Another position suggests that a creative person can live on, symbolically, by way of great works of art or heroic deeds. For example, one could say that Shakespeare, Tolstoy, Rembrandt, Newton, and Einstein "live on" through their works. Persons with a deep sense of identity with nature and its vitalities can find a form of symbolic immortality in the understanding that their bodies return to the earth and join in the great creative processes of nature.

Psychiatrist Robert Lifton suggests there are those who find no effective shield from their finitude in either the actual or symbolic forms of immortality. These persons, Lifton observes, may express what he calls "experiential transcendence" as a means of blunting their sense of transience. This transcendence may be found in intense feeling states which cover anxieties and represent forms of denial. Thus, in various forms of ecstasy and rapture one seeks to live only in the intense experience of the moment, or else seeks a state of numbness or insensitivity with the help of various chemicals. The sexuality and drug scenes are alternative routes, while shopping may serve for others. Lifton's "experiential transcendence" is a more modern formulation of Kierkegaard's aesthetic stage of existence.[23]

All these efforts to cope with the threat of mortality are linked to a person's convictions about life's possible fulfillment. Clearly, "God" makes a difference. Traditionally, the concept of God (or Brahman) has provided perhaps the most potent conceptual weapon in the defense against death. Worldviews devoid of God (or Brahman or other spiritual powers) posit the annihilation of the individual at death, except in the symbolic forms outlined above. India's Jainism is a possible exception since the Jains hold that each individual human soul is immortal though no God exists. On the other hand, many naturalistic thinkers reject any form of personal immortality and find refuge in the symbolic forms or in the acceptance of the peace of oblivion.

While anxiety about death may be the most basic of existential anxieties, meaninglessness can also undercut attempts to find a fulfilled life. A common epitaph on grave markers in the ancient world expressed this sense of meaninglessness: *Non fui. Fui. Non sum. Non Curo.* "I was not. I was. I am not. I do not care." Poets have voiced this anxiety with great clarity, as Lucretius in his "On the Nature of Thing," to Shelley's "Ozymandias," and Matthew Arnold's "Dover Beach." While such anxiety has often been reflected in cultures, it is usually muffled by cultural meaning systems, often religious in nature. When these systems of meaning are secure, the question of meaninglessness rarely comes to the conscious level. Successful cultures tend to provide meaning systems which give support to the vast majority of citizens, even at the lower social and economic levels, through explanations of "why things are the way they are." The Brahmin in traditional India felt secure in his high ranking caste, while the person in the lowest caste accepted her situation as the appropriate working out of the cosmic Law of Karma. Plato, in his ancient Greek setting, opined that every culture needs some kind of story or myth to the effect that some persons are made of gold, while others are made of silver, bronze, iron, or clay. Only then will persons in the lower ranks find their positions acceptable. When these established systems of cultural meaning begin to dissolve, transformations take place and the problem of meaninglessness begins to surface.[24]

Human ingenuity may be most strikingly demonstrated by the modes in which persons seek to invent or establish personal significance in the teeth of death and possible meaninglessness. While religious traditions often underline our frailty and brokenness—"Thou art dust, and to dust thou shalt return"—they ultimately seek to provide a grounding of our significance in some eternal dimension. If a religion cannot deal successfully with the basic anxiety of personal insignificance, that religion will never develop or sustain a following. Christianity holds the most pessimistic view of human nature and the human condition since original sin places all people in a state of alienation from God even at birth. But while deepening the human problem, Christianity exalts the gracious nature of God. A crucified Messiah presents a radical solution to a radical problem. Ultimately, the freely given grace of God overcomes the alienation and brings the individual back into eternal relationship with the Divine. Significance is found in being loved and redeemed by God's own self-giving.

Hinduism provides the most expansive basis for significance by identifying our true self with Brahman, the Ultimate Reality. *Tat twan asi.* "That art thou."[25] My individual selfhood is an illusion; my true self is identical with the Divine Reality. Other religious traditions assure their followers that they are among the chosen or the elect, or that every individual soul is created, sustained, and loved by the Infinite. Buddhism's approach to individual significance is, at first blush, paradoxical.[26] The Buddha taught the "no self" doctrine as part of the answer to the suffering that human life confronts. We are not abiding selves, souls, or spirits, the Buddha taught; rather, we are a process which moves from moment to moment with no abiding self "behind the scene" having the experiences. We *are* the experiences. But with the realization of this no-self, we can find the detachment from the world where "ignorant craving" brings suffering.

Historically, religions have tended to provide the worldviews that inform most cultures. But with the erosion of religious worldviews, cultures have become replete with many secular symbols of significance: wealth, power, community status, beauty or strength, intelligence, popularity, creativity. Contemporary advertisements suggest that we gain significance insofar as we wear the right clothes, drive the right car, live in the right part of town in the right kind of house with the right kind of furnishings, engage in the right kind of activities, and belong to the right class or group of people. The psychologists designing such advertising assume to know where our personal significance buttons are located and how they can be pushed.

But a secular point of view can also yield a sense of significance by way of creative contribution to the human community through art, science, industrial production, invention and perhaps even philosophy. Humanists find significance in their commitment to the well-being of the human community and the creative labors which sustain and enrich a culture. Some secularists can also find significance by identifying with nature and preserving the environmental processes which nourish the rich variety of life forms.

Human beings appear to have a deep need to count in some kind of way, a need driven, perhaps, by the shadow of insignificance which haunts our consciousness of mortality. Whether or not the religious answers to the question of significance are more true or more noble remains an open question; but the religious answers are often more egalitarian in the ultimate scheme of things since the concept of God or Brahman suggest that even the most humble of human beings can be affirmed by the Ultimate if the correct pathway is followed. On the other hand, Bertrand Russell's alternative vision of "unconscious matter rolling on its relentless way" requires a different vision of significance and various non-religious strategies can be applied in the quest. Here the urge toward excellence is often underlined, with Aristotle an early formulator of this aspiration. Nietzsche's *ubermenschen* (over-man, superman) is a more contemporary example of this Greek affirmation of significance through power and creativity. For Nietzsche, the great man is "beyond good and evil," and is certainly not the common man.

The history of humankind can perhaps be most clearly understood as the history of creatures conscious of their own mortality and seeking to wring some mark of significance and meaning from the world. In this sense, every person wants to be a "hero" of some kind, if not at the high level of kings and generals, at least as counting for something in one's own family and community. Ernest Becker observed, "The question that becomes then the most important one that man can put to himself is simply this: how conscious is he of what he is doing to earn his feeling of heroism?"[27]

My claim has been that all major moral philosophies, religious or non-religious, have assumed that the moral pathway, however described, is a pathway that leads to fulfillment. In this chapter I have described some of the ways in which the concept of God would shape, for the believer, a view of what properly constitutes fulfillment. While belief in God shapes one view of fulfillment, worldviews which do not include belief in God will include views of fulfillment which differ, largely, from a religious view. No claim has been made about the superiority of one view over the other. The next chapter will deal with the second major issue in all moral systems: How are others related to my own quest for fulfillment? This will raise a series of traditional moral questions: In my quest for fulfillment, do I have an obligation of some kind to assist others in their quest for fulfillment? If so, which others? Furthermore, must I carry through on such obligations even at some genuine cost to my own life's quest for fulfillment?

CHAPTER SIX

SELF, OTHERS, AND RIGHTS

Then conquer we must, when our cause it is just; and this be our Motto—"In God is our Trust."
                                              Francis Scott Key

If you love those who love you, what reward have you? Do not even the tax collectors do the same?
                                              Matthew 5:46

All complete moral theories, I have maintained, must deal with two basic questions: 1) What constitutes a truly fulfilling life? 2) Do persons seeking their own fulfillment have an obligation to help others do the same? Chapter Four explored the first issue and demonstrated how the idea of God shapes beliefs about what constitutes a fulfilled life. This chapter will examine the concept of obligation and the ways in which the idea of God can shape answers to that question. Three distinct issues will be analyzed: 1) What contributions do other people make, positively or negatively, to my own quest for fulfillment? 2) Do I have an obligation to aid others in their quest for fulfillment as I pursue my own? 3) Do certain human rights exist that imply people have obligations toward others?

Regarding the first issue, it is clear that we are linked to others in a variety of ways as we seek fulfillment. Some links are not important because the persons involved touch our lives only marginally. The man teaching school in a distant city or the woman heading a law firm in another nation has no apparent influence on my quest for fulfillment. On the other hand, relationships with some people are so intimate and rich that our own flourishing is inescapably tied to them. Family and loved ones almost always constitute a crucial aspect of any life quest. To the degree that my spouse and children flourish, I also tend to flourish. In my child's death, part of my own life dies. Hence, the quest for personal fulfillment is rarely a totally *selfish* pursuit, though our own *self-interests* are involved. Properly defined, "selfish" actions are those pursued solely for one's own self-interest *without any concern for the interests of others*. Thus, on the one hand, the aid I give to my child in nursing her through a serious illness would not be selfish since I have positive interest in my child's survival. On the other hand, my interest in my child's good fortune is certainly *self-referential* because my child's flourishing will often contribute to my own.

As our life connections to others become distant and less intimate, our active interest in their well-being tends also to recede. The illness of the child next door—or on another continent—does not concern us as much as does the illness of our own child. The influential nineteenth century British philosopher, Henry Sidgwick, once put the matter in the following way:

> We should all agree that each of us is bound to show kindness to his parents and spouse and children, and to other kinsmen in a less degree; and to those who have rendered services to him, and any other whom he may have admitted to his intimacy and called friends; and to neighbors and to fellow countrymen more than others; and perhaps we may say to those of our own race more than to black or yellow men, and generally to human beings in proportion to their affinity to ourselves.[1]

In this analysis, Sidgwick echoes David Hume's observation that the most we can hope for in human relationships is a "confined generosity." A number of contemporary philosophers also reflect Sidgwick's point by suggesting that human beings work out their life commitments in ever-widening circles of identification.[2] The implication here is that the human scene is deeply marked by "tribal" relationships of various kinds.

Two fundamental issues are underlined by Sidgwick's observation. First, it is clear that our own flourishing is linked closely to persons with whom we have affinity. These circles of affinity or identification usually begin with family, but may expand to clan, club, gang, community, ethnic identity, social rank, nation, or religious community. All of these factors reflect how we identify those who are "our own" or "our kind of people." And, in making those distinctions, we also identify those who are "not our own" or "not our kind of people." In just this way we tend to divide the world into "us" and "them," and classify not only those who contribute to our flourishing but also those who stand in our way. As we pursue our self-interests as well as self-referential interests, those distinctions inevitably become part of our life commitments and plans. This line of thought will be developed later in this chapter when the various ways in which persons structure their "us-them" dichotomy will be explored.

The second issue underlined by Sidgwick's observation is how these natural circles of affinity are related to the concept of moral responsibility. The question, here, is that of the appropriate and rational goal for human actions. Is it rational for an individual to pursue only his or her own self-interests, including self-referential ones? Or is it rational, at least at times, to pursue the interests of others at some cost to one's own? Sidgwick, in wrestling with these questions, did not find a satisfactory way to adjudicate between rational egoism and utilitarianism, two highly influential but conflicting moral theories. He called this conflict the "Dualism of Practical Reason." Echoing the ancient Greeks, Sidgwick argued that rational egoism—the fundamental and rational aim of every person is that of his or her own interests—was a self-evident first principle. However, he also concluded that utilitarianism—the greatest good for the greatest number—is also a self-evident first principle. Sidgwick found no way to reconcile this apparent conflict between self-interest and moral duty that has long existed as a basic issue in moral philosophy. Indeed, it is just this conflict that creates much philosophical reflection.

In contrast to Sidgwick, I take the position that the primary self-evident principle is that of egoism and that the utilitarian position, as formulated by Bentham and Mill, falls back on a form of egoism for its justification. This is consistent with my assertion that all classic moral theories always promise fulfillment for the person walking the moral pathway as defined by a particular theory. Morality, finally, is *for us*. My defense of this approach will be more fully developed in Chapter Eight where the question "Why be moral?" will be addressed. To blunt initial criticisms of egoism as a first principle, I note that egoism is not to be identified with selfishness. This seems true since our own interests are often positively linked to the self-interests of others, as noted above. Furthermore, the founder of utilitarianism, Jeremy Bentham, embraced *psychological egoism*, the descriptive theory that people always and necessarily act to satisfy what they perceive to be their best interests.

> Nature has placed mankind under the governance of two sovereign masters, pain and pleasure. It is for them alone to point out what we ought to do, as well as to determine what we shall do.[3]

While modifying certain aspects of Bentham's position, J. S. Mill retained this basic psychological egoism. Indeed, both claimed that various sanctions teach us that our own quest for happiness requires us to become good utilitarians. Both argued that egoism, rationally pursued, leads to utilitarianism. Such an argument implies that rational egoism is the primary principle and that utilitarianism is derivative. The point that both Bentham and Mill seek to make is that our own happiness, which we *necessarily* seek as rational creatures, is inescapably linked to the happiness of others. At one level, such a claim appears to be intuitively or even empirically true; but on another level it raises the question of whether or not our own happiness is tied to the happiness of *all* others, or just those with whom we have the strongest affinity or identification. The question of whether or not our natural tribalism can be overcome is still with us; consequently, we must explore how the idea of God relates to this tribalism. Can belief in

God overcome the conflicts of tribal interests, or does such a belief only construct additional rigid and tragic boundaries?

In order to analyze how the idea of God shapes our sense of affinity with other persons, we must first outline some of the factors that create such connections. In a broad sense, affinity to others is linked to traditions in which we are often rooted. As sociologist Robert Bellah put it:

> Our lives make sense in a thousand ways, most of which we are unaware of, because of traditions that are centuries, if not millennia old. It is these traditions that help us to know that it does make a difference who we are and how we treat one another.[4]

Philosopher Alasdair MacIntyre makes a similar point by showing that our stories are basic in establishing our connections with others.

> . . . man is in his actions and practice, as well as in his fictions, essentially a story-telling animal. . . . I can only answer the question "What am I to do?" if I can answer the prior question "Of what story or stories do I find myself a part. . . .Deprive children of stories and you leave them unscripted, anxious stutterers in their actions as in their words. Hence there is no way to give us an understanding of any society, including our own, except through the stock of stories which constitute its initial dramatic resources.[5]

Another way of underlining the significance of traditions and "stories" is to see them as the background for ideologies, those systems of ideas and beliefs that underlie and inform our social and political actions. Indeed, these ideologies can be seen as systems of ideas we use to justify political and social structures and to distinguish those who "belong to us" from those who are not "our kind of people." Ideologies structure tribalism; they show us to which group we belong.

But what constitutes belonging to a group? How is it that we get into position to make a distinction between *us* and *them*?

Or, as Ninian Smart phrased it: What constitutes "ushood"?[6] One of the most powerful boundaries that shape ushood is that of national identity. A nation is, itself, an entity, a whole in which citizens are a part.

> Its citizens are woven together by the strong threads of rituals—the very speaking of the same language, . . . the shape of values imparted through education, the more explicit rites of the nation through its anthem and flag, the sense of belonging and pride celebrated through football matches and Olympiads, the solemn demands of war, the remembrance of the sufferings of the past and their sad but glory-giving celebration, the feel for the ancestors, the general willingness to join one's country's armed forces, the expectation that to die for one's nation is a great and glories thing. Such consciousness is acknowledgement of a particular and solemn ushood, in which we individuals merge together in solidarity, and are conscious of the nation both as something which is out there and as something in which each one of us participates.[7]

In much of the modern world, as Smart notes, the nation is the ultimate group which generates not only solidarity but also the duties of self-sacrifice. National identity is, in the modern world, the most common and powerful form of tribalism that is expressed in the command to kill as a basic duty. Smart placed special emphasis on the matter of killing.

> . . . because warfare itself is one of the great sacraments of mankind. Warfare is much more than killing or being killed: it transforms men, baptizes them with fire, leads them to the highest sacrifice, gives the nation a sense of its own destiny. It ams at victory, and the aggrandizement of national substance. . . But, above all, in causing and suffering death, warfare feeds the national glory.[8]

A nation, itself, is constituted by many factors where *territory* is basic. A people without land of their own cannot become a nation since it fails to have a territory that grants not only a symbolic significance but also something like sacred space. The Zionist movement is an example of the significance of a land for a people. In its early days, the Zionist movement was driven more by the need to return to a land rather than by deep religious convictions. But ultimately it created a tragic and lengthy struggle with the Palestinians who rallied to defend what they claimed as their territory, a territory that had been taken over by others. This struggle by the Palestinians is not only an expression of the humiliation stemming from the sense of being invaded and displaced, but also an application of Muslim ethics that calls on the faithful to defend their faith as well as their land. In its most radical form, the struggle between the Palestinians and the Zionists involves the combination of territory and religious belief.

The tragedy of the Middle East reflects other factors that often define a nation: language, religion, and biological descent. For many nations, those three factors are shared by the vast majority of the population, as in Italy where the national language is Italian and where Roman Catholicism is the religious identity—perhaps even for those who profess no faith of their own. While in the Far East, the Japanese, for centuries, had found their national identity linked to their language, their biological heritage, Shinto religion, and to their islands--the origins of which are recounted in the Shinto myths. Given their great capacity for adaptation and borrowing, the Japanese were generally open to Buddhism, which entered Japan from Korea in 552 CE. With the restoration of the emperor in Japan in the 1860's, there was some attempt to repress Buddhism and elevate Shinto as the national faith, but the common people found no difficulty in practicing both Buddhism and Shinto. Buddhism, therefore, was eventually granted autonomy. Some religions can learn to live together or even blend without rancor. Tensions between Buddhism and Shinto appear to be more easily resolved than tensions that occur between competing monotheisms. While someone may, without contradiction, practice both Shinto and Buddhism, it is not possible to practice two (or more) of the three major monotheisms: Judaism, Christianity and Islam. There are, of course, attempts to merge these faiths by way of a new religious movement, such as Baha'i, but such syncretisms have essentially left the fold of the faiths so blended.

The challenge the United States faced—and still faces—is that of building a sense of national identity among immigrants that represent a variety of languages, religions, and biological descent. No doubt the dominant Christian background, the English language, European heritage, the developing territories and states, and the rituals of flag and nation all contributed to the early sense of being an "American." The constitutional separation of church and state was, perhaps, never solved theologically; but this principle established a practical sense of tolerance and enabled citizens to feel like loyal Americans even if their religious beliefs were different or absent altogether. The church-state separation also largely eliminated the need to choose between loyalty to one's religious faith or to the nation. At times, of course, specific religious beliefs were over-ruled by the courts if, for instance, they appeared to endanger the life or welfare of a child. Yet, the believers were not forced to choose between faith and nation since they remained citizens even though their practices ran afoul of the law. It is evidently possible to "give unto Caesar that which is Caesar's and unto God that which is God's." Seldom, in the modern world, is there a forced choice between religious belief and national loyalty; therefore, it is difficult to ascertain which of the two might make the ultimate claim for a believer's loyalty.

It appears, then, that our tribalism is defined in a variety of ways. The dichotomy between "us" and "them" can be traced in terms of national identify, biological and racial connections, ideologies, language, territory, social status, and religious beliefs. All these create in-groups and out-groups. This dichotomy, as history generally demonstrates, also prescribes just whom we will care about first and foremost. It appears "natural" for us to support the quest for fulfillment of those with whom we find some affinity. Indeed, evolutionary processes may well have wired our genes for just this sort of "natural" affinity. On the other hand, it also seems "natural" for us to ignore or undercut the attempts of others who seek fulfillment if their quest conflicts with our self-interests or the interests of those we care for. We may claim to love our neighbor, but we still ask, "Who is my neighbor?" As Emerson once said, ". . . do not tell me, as a good man did today, of my obligation to put all poor men in good situations. Are they *my* poor?"[9]

How then, might belief in God shape in-group and out-group boundaries in significant ways? Any attempt to answer this question decisively is riddled with complications. Many current books explore the role religion plays in violent eruptions around the earth and lead to the clear conclusion that religion, as powerful human belief systems, can be used by evil people for evil purposes.[10] Modern technology suffers the same fate. On the other hand, there are examples of movements for justice and fairness that are grounded in religious convictions. The issue is also complicated by the question of causal relationships between the belief espoused and the good or evil actions that appear to be linked to those beliefs. Do religious beliefs *cause* persons to do evil deeds? Or is it that those who already possess evil intentions choose to use religious justifications for their actions? Conversely, do religious beliefs *cause* persons to do good deeds? Or is it that persons disposed to be good use religious beliefs to support their good deeds? The difficult question is whether or not religious belief, by its nature, is basically a force for the general good of humanity or whether it is largely an expression of tribalism that generates divisions and conflict. Empirical data, as such, will not provide conclusive evidence for a definitive answer although specious arguments on both sides abound.

That believers can be powerfully bonded together by shared religious convictions seems beyond doubt and is reflected in scriptures and traditions. The *shema* (hear) in Deuteronomy 6:4-9, declares the unity and commitments of the people of Israel that follows from their status as a people chosen by Yahweh. Influential in shaping the Christian tradition, St. Paul wrote, "There is neither Jew nor Greek, there is neither slave nor free, there is neither male nor female; for you are all one in Christ

Jesus."[11] For Muslims, Muhammad's declaration in one of his last sermons is instructive: "Oh Muslims, know that every other Muslim is your brother." The vow of Buddhist monks reflects the same sense of affinity: "I take refuge in the Buddha, in the Dharma (foundation doctrines), and in the Sangha (the monastic order)." Traditional Shinto religion in Japan reflected, perhaps, the most potent expression of the unity of a people through the Shinto myths. These myths tell not only that the islands of Japan have divine origin, but also that the Japanese peoples themselves are descendants of the kami (spirits, deities, gods). All these declarations and symbols of affinity clearly designate in-group status in these various traditions. The question remains as to whether or not religious traditions have ways of overcoming parochial identities and relate in supportive ways to peoples of other traditions.

Before elaborating on the negative effect of religious belief, a more positive analysis can be suggested by comparing Quakers with primitive head-hunters. At one level, classical Quakers and head-hunters share a basic moral rule: One ought never take the head of someone from your own tribe. The significant difference between these two groups is found in their definition of "tribe." Tribal boundaries are reasonably clear for the head-hunters. If you want a head, you go outside of your tribe to harvest it from dead enemies. The Quaker, on the other hand, has an expanded view of "tribe," since they believe that their tribe encompasses all humanity. Hence, you cannot harvest a head from anyone, for no one is "outside" of your tribe. The implication of classical Quaker pacifism is that all human beings belong to the in-group. There is no out-group. Historically, this conviction of inclusiveness is rooted in the Christian tradition that nurtured George Fox, founder of Society of Friends, and his early followers.[12] As part of the left wing of the Protestant Reformation, Fox put forward the doctrine of the "inner light" drawn from the Gospel of John 1:9. Arguing that the "light of Christ" is available to all, even those who have not heard the preaching of the gospel, Fox held that this light is present as a seed in all persons and can be nurtured so that the Spirit of Christ dwells fully within the heart. Out of this foundation, the Quakers have long demonstrated social concerns reflected in people like Robert Owen, John Woolman and William Penn. They were, for instance, early and powerful opponents of slavery. The Quakers are best known for their consistent pacifism that is rooted in the doctrine of the "inner light."

> It is not lawful for Christians to resist evil or to fight in any cause. . .(war is) as opposite to the Spirit and doctrine of Christ as light to darkness. . . Strange that men made after the image of God should bear the image of roaring lions; tearing tigers, devouring wolves, raging boars. . .[13]

The Quaker position is summarized here as one *example* of how religious belief can provide a foundation for a socially conscious and care-oriented attitude toward *all* persons. It appears, therefore, that some religious beliefs are able supply a strong sense of affinity with all human beings and can help overcome barriers that traditionally create out-groups. But the example of the Quakers is not to be construed as an argument designed to show that the Quaker position represents "genuine" Christianity, or that the Quaker position is either rational or justified in some other way. These questions are left open in this discussion.

Some religions of the Far East have ameliorated tensions between groups and established a more universal sense of identity through the principle of non-injury (ahimsa). In its most fully developed form in Jainism, ahimsa requires the deeply spiritual ascetics to avoid injuring any living entity. Consistent with the claims I am making in this book, the Jains practice non-injury as a means of achieving their own fulfillment since injuring a living creature is believed to be an act which creates bad karma and impedes liberation from the cycle of rebirths. In Hinduism and Buddhism the principle is honored but not as strictly observed. The principle of non-injury was adapted to the nonviolent social and political movements of Mohandas Gandhi and Dr. Martin Luther King, Jr. Gandhi's nonviolent approach toward the British grew out of Jain and Hindu teachings as well the influence of Christian Quakers he had met in South Africa. In order to square his non-violence principle with the *Bhagavad-Gita*, a Hindu spiritual classic, Gandhi chose to interpret the violent passages in that work as allegorical. Dr. Martin Luther King was influenced by Gandhi as well as by his own Christian tradition as he shaped the civil rights movement. Both Gandhi and King represent leaders whose religious beliefs enabled them to escape narrow tribalism and move toward an inclusive view of justice and social policy.

The historical examples above demonstrate that religious beliefs not only bond a community of believers together but can also, at times, develop an inclusive identity with all human beings. On the other hand, history is also replete with examples that demonstrate the divisive and tragic results of religious belief. While other factors were often involved, the list of historical conflicts that included powerful religious dimensions would include the crusades of the Middle Ages with the Christian battle cry of *Deus vol* (God wills it), the spread of Muslim armies across North Africa into Spain and France, and the variety of conflicts resulting from the Reformation. More recently, the Israeli-Palestinians struggle and the Protestant-Catholic bloodletting in Northern Ireland include religious dimensions.

Representatives of radical religious groups that have supported terrorism include: Reverend Paul Hill, the Christian pastor and convicted anti-abortion killer; Dr. Baruch Goldstein, the Jewish physician who gunned down more than thirty Muslims during their morning prayers; Osama bin Laden, the Muslim alleged to have bankrolled terrorist acts including the 9-11 destruction of the Twin Towers in New York City; and Simranjit Singh Mann, a Sikh political leader suspected of masterminding the assassination of Indira Gandhi.[14] The history of the Mormons provide an example of how a charismatic leader and a claim to revealed and absolute truth can lead true believers to acts of horrific violence.[15]

In spite of certain evidence that belief in God has helped create peace and justice among peoples, can religion in general be defended in the light of the bloody history involving various

SELF, OTHERS, AND RIGHTS 137

faiths? Defenders of religion could suggest that the Nazi and Communist movements, both enemies of religion, produced tragedies of immense proportions. But those examples show only that evil can be perpetrated from a variety of ideologies; they do not excuse the evil done in the name of God. The jury is still out on this issue and a variety of voices hold court. A closing note on this issue comes from a scholar who has studied religiously motivated violence and nevertheless holds a hopeful view regarding religion's role in the human enterprise.

> Religion gives spirit to public life and provides a beacon for moral order. At the same time it needs the temper of rationality and fair play that Enlightenment values give to civil society. Thus religious violence cannot end until some accommodation can be forged between the two—some assertion of moderation in religion's passion, and some acknowledgment of religion in elevating the spiritual and moral values of public life. In a curious way, then, the cure for religious violence may ultimately lie in a renewed appreciation of religion itself.[16]

Having explored the first two issues raised in this chapter, the question of human rights must now be examined. In claiming that a person has a right of some kind, two assertions are being made. First, a person is entitled to behave in a certain way under certain circumstances. If free speech is a right, then a person has a right to express his or her views or opinions—under certain circumstances. Second, a person should have certain expectations about the behavior of other persons in their relations with the person who has a particular right. Thus, if a person has the right to life, this right would restrict any attempt by another to take the life of the person with that right. These two assertions suggest that claims about rights have to do with what a person may be allowed to do and what constraints may be placed upon the actions directed at another person. Rights, in this way, reflect both freedoms and restraints.

Among the many and complex issues raised by the question of human rights are the following: 1) Are there such things as human rights; and, if there are, what are they? 2) Are human rights "discovered" as part of what might be called the nature of things; or are human rights "invented" as a means of dealing with moral and political issues? 3) How is a claim about human rights to be justified? 4) If human rights exist, do these rights imply obligations on the part of others? 5) What types of sanctions are appropriate if someone (or some group) fails to honor certain obligations imposed on that person (or group) by the existence of certain rights? 6) How does the idea of God (or some correlate) inform certain claims about human rights, and can such claims be sustained in the absence of belief in God? While a detailed examination of the concepts of rights, liberties, and duties cannot be accomplished in this work, some distinctions regarding language about rights would be helpful at this point. After these distinctions are made, the question of the existence of human rights and their possible justifications will be pursued.

Legal rights exist and have an adequate grounding in the actions of an appropriate governing body. The first ten amendments to the Constitution of the United States, commonly known as the Bill of Rights, are examples of legal rights. While such legal rights are generated by the action of some governing authority, some persons believe that such rights are, themselves, grounded in objective and universal moral principles. On the other hand, some believe that legal rights exist just because a governing authority has declared such rights. Further grounding or justification is neither needed nor available. *Civil rights* are a special case of legal rights that deal largely with matters of justice and fairness. *Natural rights*—if they exist—are independent of the actions of any specific governing body or legal entity, but are, instead, human rights which exist in the very nature of things. They are often thought of as being rooted in some metaphysical or religious reality. Thomas Jefferson (1743-1826) included "life, liberty and the pursuit of happiness" as examples of such natural rights. The task of a government, for Jefferson, was not to invent or formulate such rights, but to "secure them" by forming legal structures which protect such rights.

A differing view of natural rights is found in the works of Thomas Hobbes (1588-1679), who held that in the "state of nature," where no civil authority or governing body exists, all people would have a "right of nature" to "do what he would, and against whom he thought fit, and to possess, use and enjoy all that he would, or could get."[17] For Hobbes, to "have a right" in that setting is equivalent to "having the power." In this sense, the lion has the "right of nature" to kill and eat what he or she can. For Hobbes, this right of nature has no moral implications whatsoever.

Human rights—if these exist—are important rights generally considered to be universal in that they apply to all human beings. As "inalienable," such rights cannot be given away by a person holding them, nor can they be taken away by others. The assertion of human rights has appeared conspicuously at two points in history, one being in the Declaration of Independence made by the Second Continental Congress on July 4, 1776. The language of that declaration contains clear religious affirmations in appealing to the "Laws of Nature and of Nature's God." And, of course, the famous lines: "We hold these Truths to be self-evident, that all Men are created equal, that they are endowed by their creator with certain unalienable Rights, that among these are Life, Liberty, and the Pursuit of Happiness." Another significant claim about human rights appeared in 1948 with the Universal Declaration of Human Rights formulated by the United Nations. This document differs in a significant way from the Declaration of Independence in that it avoids specific religious grounding for such rights. Instead, in Article 1, it makes a number of assertions which stand without any attempt at justification: "All human beings are born free and equal in dignity and rights. They are endowed with reason and conscience and should act toward one another in a spirit of brotherhood."[18] The authors of this Universal Declaration of Human Rights either believed that such claims are sufficiently self-evident, or they deliberately chose to avoid any philosophical or religious defense of such assertions. Agreement on the claims themselves was easier to achieve than an agreement on the justification for such claims. The aim of this 1948 Declaration is expressed in the words of the Preamble as "a common standard of achievement for all peoples." These rights serve as goals to be pursued as well as a basis for protest and for policy reform. Not all philosophers would accept such rights as self-evident and would call for some type of justification of these claims; nevertheless, this Universal Declaration has been widely honored in word if not in deed.

The shift from the use of religious language to justify claims about human rights in the Declaration of 1776 to the absence of any justification at all in the 1948 Universal Declaration illustrates the question at hand. This question can be formulated in two ways: 1) How can we *know* that human rights exist? 2) How can claims about human rights be *justified*? In keeping with the general intent of this work, no attempt will be made to provide any justification of human rights claims. Instead, some of the major options that have been proposed by philosophers will be explored. The following list should not be considered exhaustive; rather, these examples suggest certain ways of responding to the question.

The idea of human rights comes on the scene comparatively late in our history. Indeed, it appears that Thomas Paine was the first to use the specific expression "human rights" in his *Rights of Man*, published in 1791.[19] Long before rights language was formulated, the focus had been on the concept of duty. Duty, in turn, was related to the idea of some type of universal laws (God or nature) which set forth the duties required of persons. As Gandhi observed in the twentieth century, "The true source of rights is duty."[20]

One attempt, then, to justify the claim that human rights exist is to ground the claim in some religious belief. This approach, of course, could be judged as successful only if the religious claims themselves can be justified—an issue I leave as an open question. In this justification of human rights, the religious belief would include the concept of duty linked to laws understood as given by God. Later, the concept of rights would be developed as a logical concomitant of those duties. One argument would go something like this: If God commands that I ought not kill my neighbor Y, then I have a duty not to kill Y. But if I have a duty not to kill Y, then it follows that Y has a right to his life that I must honor.

Another approach to justifying the claim that human rights exist involves an appeal to natural law. Historically, this appeal was almost always linked to some idea of God or a divine reality that brought such laws into being or sustained and enforced them. Hence, the appeal to natural law is another way of grounding rights in a religious belief system. The first century BCE Stoics were the first to speak of natural law as a set of essential, eternal laws required for the happiness of individuals and for social harmony. For these Stoics, the entire universe was governed by the laws of a rational God. Physical laws governed the movements of objects, while moral laws expressed the right actions to be undertaken by human beings. These laws can be discovered because individuals have within them a divine spark or rational seed. Furthermore, these laws were understood to be universal and objective, applying appropriately to all human beings at every time or place.

Thomas Aquinas (1225-1274) adapted both Stoic thought and that of Aristotle in formulating his own view of natural law. Key elements in his natural law theory included several claims. 1) God created human beings with a rational nature that enables them to discover those laws that help them to live and flourish in ways appropriate to human nature. 2) These laws can be known by reason, without revelation or knowledge of God. 3) Since these laws are unchangeable and universal, they should be used by all human communities to evaluate the laws of their societies. 4) Civil laws which are not in line with natural laws lose their status as *true* laws. Applying this natural law approach, for instance, Aquinas held that it is natural for persons to desire to sustain and continue their lives; therefore, one is obligated to protect life and health, and to avoid suicide and carelessness.

John Locke (1632-1704) reflected the natural law tradition in his conviction that by the use of reason human beings could discover the moral rules that conform to God's laws. Furthermore, this divine law was to be seen as "the only true touchstone of moral rectitude." Locke extended the concept of natural law by claiming that there are natural *rights* that represent the other side of the duties entailed by natural law. If there is, for instance, a natural law and a duty to preserve life, then a human being has a "right to life." This type of argument led Locke to affirm that three fundamental rights exist—the right to life, liberty and property. A century later, Thomas Jefferson drew upon John Locke's views when he penned the Declaration of Independence with its claim that "all men are endowed by their creator with certain unalienable Rights." For the third right, Jefferson substituted "the pursuit of happiness" for Locke's "property."

Another attempt to justify the claim to human rights grows out of the conviction that each human being has some special status as a person who must be honored. This view is often linked to a religious justification of rights through the claim that the creative act of God endows each person with a basic sacredness. Some argue that the claim of the "sacredness of personality" or the "infinite worth" or the "dignity" of a human being requires a link to a religious claim of some kind.[21] On the other hand, however, some maintain that the claim of a special status for persons need not be rooted in a religious claim as such. For instance, some in the human rights field hold that the concept of human dignity itself is the ultimate justification for human rights.[22] So when the question is raised about why one should respect human rights, the response would be that human dignity is violated if such rights are not respected. While this argument—or claim—has a certain persuasive power because of its rhetorical force, it betrays a certain circularity. What, after all, is the basis for human dignity? And just why should such presumed dignity be honored?

John Stuart Mill (1806-1878), the utilitarian, suggested another approach to the justification of human rights claims by grounding such claims in terms of general utility. Mill argues,

> To have a right, then, is, I conceive, to have some thing which society ought to defend me in the possession of. If the objector goes on to ask why it ought, I can give him no other reason than general utility.[23]

Rights, for Mill, are not a matter of abstract principles or of God's rules or natural law; rather, they are ways of thinking about freedoms and actions which tend to bring about the greatest good for the greatest number. But a personal right may be qualified. I may have the right to possess a certain property; but if the generally happiness of the community would be enhanced by building a highway through my property, then my right to hold the property is trumped by the needs of the community. Whether this approach to human rights is successful will depend on whether or not utilitarianism can be defended.

Richard Rorty, a contemporary philosopher, questions whether we need to justify claims to human rights or any other moral claims.[24] Rorty supports human rights efforts as a way of developing a humane, secure, and prosperous human community. But he believes that this end is best achieved through what he calls a sentimental education rather than through argument and reasoning. The debates over just how to justify human rights in some theoretical way, he believes, have been endless and generally fruitless. Such debate, though reflecting careful analysis and reasoning, will do very little to change the heart or mind of those who violate human rights. What is needed, instead, is some way that helps us arrive at an emotional and personal identification with others. Respect for human beings and rights is best obtained, Rorty believes, through the main cultural instruments of literature, film, television and journalism. Many thinkers, however, believe that Rorty has abandoned the philosophical ship and is cast adrift in some kind of unfounded confidence that human emotions can lead to a better community.

In his *Social Philosophy*, Joel Feinberg searches for a justification of claims for human rights, but concludes that such rights claims are expressions of "attitudes." In contrast to Jefferson's language in the Declaration of Independence, Feinberg avoids grounding claims about human rights in religious assertions. Instead, he suggests that the idea of human worth expresses not so much some *fact* about human beings but rather an "attitude of respect—toward the humanity in each man's person." He then concludes,

> That attitude follows naturally from regarding everyone from the 'human point of view,' but it is not

grounded on anything more ultimate than itself, and it is not demonstrably justifiable.[25]

The human rights skeptic might well ask Feinberg just what is the basis for holding this attitude of respect in a world where far too many persons seem to merit precious little respect in terms of their actions and attitudes

In the two centuries between Jefferson and Feinberg, it appears that human rights have lost their status as truths rooted in the creative act of God and have become attitudes without any "demonstrable justification." Nevertheless, we can be assured that the dialogue will continue. The very idea of human rights is both too deep and too precious to be relegated solely to the realms of attitude and emotions.

CHAPTER SEVEN

THE CHALLENGE OF ETHICAL RELATIVISM

If your heart does not want a world of moral reality, your head will assuredly never make you believe in one.
William James[1]

    In the fifth century BCE, Protagoras put forward an early form of ethical relativism, the view that no moral code exists which properly applies to all persons in all places at all times. He came to this position, at least in part, because of the great variety of moral views he encountered in the ancient world. The review of a number of significant moral theories in Chapter Three raises the same issue Protagoras faced. Given the history of conflicting moral codes and theories described in that chapter, is it not presumptuous for any of them to claim that *their* view is the objectively proper view for all persons at all times? Could ethical relativism be a solution to that history of conflict and diversity?

    Ethical relativism is a theory that provokes lively discussions at the popular level and arises as an issue in almost all introductory courses in ethics. It is also an example of a typical philosophical issue in three ways. First, it is clearly *not* a scientific problem since it cannot be solved on the basis of purely empirical evidence. Secondly, it is an issue where some progress in the debate can often be made by way of analysis and argument. Compelling arguments can be constructed even though such arguments are not rooted in the hard facts of scientific observation. Finally, this issue is philosophical in that much of the debate involves both a careful clarification of terms and an analysis of the logical implications of certain beliefs. To call it philosophical, of course, neither glorifies nor demeans the issue; it merely identifies the nature of the theory and the processes needed to arrive at a rational solution.

Some preliminary semantic housecleaning is required since much disagreement is often merely verbal confusion. The debate often ensues only because the parties involved hold different understandings of the terms and theories under discussion. Clear definitions can lead to constructive arguments. One approach to clarifying the theory of ethical relativism is to first define the theory it contradicts—ethical absolutism. According to ethical absolutism, there is at least one moral rule or principle that properly and objectively applies to any person at any place and at any time. Ethical absolutism does not imply that all persons *know* of any such moral rule or principle that so applies. Absolute moral laws may exist, just as laws of science exist, without all persons (or any person) knowing of their existence. Neither do ethical absolutists necessarily claim that they know for certain just what those moral rules might be. To be sure, many absolutists often make such claims to knowledge, but one can believe ethical absolutism to be true without claiming to know what the precise moral rules are. No doubt that the philosophers who seek to defend some moral absolute already believe that one exists.

Ethical relativism, then, contradicts the claim of ethical absolutism by asserting there are *no* moral rules or principles that properly and objectively apply to all persons in all places and at all times. The ethical relativist will grant that there are moral rules of some kind since every culture reflects ethical guidelines. But the relativist claims that none of these existing rules are absolute in the sense that they apply properly and objectively to all persons at all times in any culture. Most ethical relativists will also grant that there are certain moral rules that can be called the right moral rules. Usually these relativists maintain that the right rules for any culture are those that are generally accepted by the people of that culture. But these relativists also claim that the moral rules accepted by one culture have no proper authority over another. Culture A's rules may differ from those of culture B, but A's moral rules are right for A and B's rules are right for B. Furthermore, for the ethical relativists, these are the only kind of moral rules that exist, since there are no objective and universal moral rules that can be used to evaluate the moral rules of specific cultures.

Another theory, *cultural relativism*, needs to be identified to avoid confusion. Sometimes called "descriptive relativism," cultural relativism is the theory that moral values or rules do, in fact, vary from culture to culture. For example, some cultures allow plural marriage, others do not. Some cultures allow for the holding of slaves, others do not. Cultural relativism, as defined, is not a philosophical issue; instead, it is a purely descriptive claim that can be empirically tested by examining various cultures to see if differences in moral beliefs do exist. Social scientists generally agree that cultural relativism is true. However, even if one believes that cultural relativism is true, that does not commit one to the belief that ethical relativism is true since the two theories are quite distinct. This point will be more fully examined in the context of an argument given in support of ethical relativism; but, it is important to understand the distinction between the theory of cultural relativism and any form of ethical relativism, since confusion about this distinction causes fruitless debate.

Another distinction must now be made between "principle ethical absolutism" and "rule ethical absolutism." The latter holds that there are specific moral *rules* that all persons should honor. Familiar examples of rule absolutism are found in religious traditions. "Thou shalt not steal" is an example, since it states a *specific* rule. An absolutist who accepts this rule believes it appropriately applies to all persons at any place and any time. This absolutist may grant that some persons do not know about the rule while others may not accept it. Nevertheless, this absolutist believes it is a moral rule that everyone *should* learn and follow.

Principle ethical absolutism, on the other hand, holds that there is one general moral *principle* that everyone should follow even though there may be no specific *rules* that are always applicable.

Examples of principle ethical absolutism can be found in both religious and philosophical traditions. "Love your neighbor as yourself" could function as a principle absolute in that it does not identify a *specific* kind of act to avoid or carry out. Instead, it provides a *general principle* to be applied to all morally significant actions. The utilitarian principle, "Always pursue those actions which produce the greatest amount of happiness for the greatest number of persons" is also a principle absolute. Even the advice of Epicurus, "Always do that which maximizes your own experience of pleasure" is a principle absolute. It is clear that rule absolutists have not always agreed on *which* rules are the correct ones; and neither have principle absolutists agreed on the *principles* to be followed. Yet those who offered the principles listed above all believed that the principle they defended was one that properly applies to all human beings at any place and at any time. The utilitarians and Epicureans are ethical absolutists as much as religious moralists tend to be.

The question of truth-telling demonstrates the distinction between rule and principle absolutists. A rule absolutist who holds that lying is wrong believes that lying is *always* wrong. The principle absolutist believes it is not that simple since there may be times when lying is morally acceptable. An absolutist committed to the principle of "love your neighbor" may claim that truth-telling is almost always the loving thing to do, but there may be times when lying is required in order to honor the principle of love. For example, one would be morally justified to lie to the Nazi secret police if they knocked on your door and asked where your Jewish friends were hiding. The principle of love almost certainly would *require* lying in that situation. On the other hand, if lying is always wrong, as some rule absolutists hold, then lying to the Nazis would be immoral.

This distinction between rule absolutism and principle absolutism leads some to believe that so-called "situation ethics" is a form of ethical relativism. Situation ethics holds that ethical decisions can be made only within a particular situation since no standard specific rule, such as "Do not lie," can be appropriately applied to all situations. Each situation must be evaluated to see if lying is or is not morally acceptable in that context. Both utilitarian ethics and the religious principle of "love your neighbor" function as situation ethics. But neither of these principles lead to relativism since both theories maintain that the principle is universally binding. Nevertheless one needs to discern the best way of honoring that principle in each situation. While the principle is absolute, some rules are not. In some situations, truth-telling may be the most appropriate way of honoring the principle of love. But in other settings, as with the Nazi scenario, that principle may require lying. While the application of the principle may vary, the principle itself is always absolute, never relative.

There are also two forms of ethical relativism: 1) cultural ethical relativism and 2) individual ethical relativism. Both are forms of ethical relativism since both deny there are any absolute rules or principles. The cultural ethical relativist holds that the right moral rules for a culture are the rules generally accepted by all. If these people generally believe that plural marriage is morally acceptable, then, indeed, plural marriage *is* morally correct in that culture. But if an individual in that culture believes that plural marriage is immoral, then that individual would be morally mistaken, according to cultural ethical relativism, since that person disagrees with the generally accepted view.

On the other hand, the *individual* ethical relativist asserts that the individual is the proper judge of moral actions. This relativist holds that the right moral rule for any person is the rule believed to be right by that person, not the rule that the people of the culture generally believe to be correct. Within a specific culture, according to individual ethical relativism, individual P may disagree with individual Q, but P cannot objectively maintain that Q is mistaken in her beliefs, nor can Q maintain that about P. What P believes to be morally correct is morally correct for P, and what Q believes to be morally correct is morally correct for Q. Furthermore, according to this form of relativism, what P believes to be morally correct is, in fact, morally correct even though the majority of persons in that culture disagree with P's beliefs.

The first argument to be considered in support of cultural

ethical relativism has ancient roots. Offered by Protagoras in the fifth century BC, this could be called the *argument from practical benefit*. This argument claims that the moral rules generally accepted by a culture are the right ones because they help the people of that culture to survive or flourish The argument takes the following form: Premise 1) Moral rules R are rules believed to be right by culture Q. Premise 2) The moral rules believed to be right by culture Q are the moral rules that help culture Q to flourish. Hence, subconclusion 3) Moral rules R help culture Q to flourish. Premise 4) The moral rules which help culture Q to flourish are the right moral rules for that culture since flourishing is assumed to be an objectively appropriate goal. Subconclusion 3) and premise 4) yield the conclusion 5) Moral rules R are the right moral rules for culture Q. This argument is valid in form. If its premises are true, its conclusion must also be true since it follows logically from the premises.

An examination, however, reveals a number of problems with this argument. While premise 1) could be shown to be true through the use of polling, premise 2) is doubtful because it seems probable that some cultures would be better off if they revised certain of their moral rules—e.g. a culture which permits slavery. Furthermore, premise 2) is not self-evidently true, and would be difficult if not impossible to test. But the failure of the argument lies in premise 4) since it actually asserts a form of ethical absolutism. For, in claiming there are some "right moral rules" one surely means there are rules that a culture *ought* to follow. Thus, in claiming that the moral rules that help a culture flourish are the right ones for that culture, the relativist would be claiming that 6) A culture ought to follow those moral rules that help it to survive. In claiming 6), the relativist would be making a principle absolutist claim, namely: "Any culture at any place and at any time ought to follow those moral rules that help it to flourish." A relativist who endorses such a claim does so at the cost of abandoning relativism.

Furthermore, the claim that "any culture at any place and at any time ought to follow those moral rules that help it flourish" appears to be false. There may, after all, be some rule that would help a culture to flourish, such as "steal from neighboring cultures whenever you can do so without being punished in some way." Yet such a rule does not appear to be an acceptable moral rule. Some might suggest that this claim has the support of Darwinian evolutionary theory, since the "survival of the fittest" could apply to species, and cultures. According to this use of Darwinian theory, cultures ought to pursue that which helps them to flourish in spite of what this might to do other cultures. But this type of argument misrepresents the claims of evolutionary science, for the theory of evolution holds only that those species that adapt best to their environments are those that survive. This is a purely descriptive claim and in no way implies that species or cultures *ought* to so adapt; nor does it claim that surviving species are somehow more "worthy." Furthermore, as others have noted, the "survival of the fittest" is a curious phrase since "the fittest" is *defined* in terms of survival. The fittest *are* simply those who survive. Thus the "survival of the fittest" can be reformulated as "the survival of those who survive." This may be true, but it is only a verbal truth empty of factual content. The question of whether or not evolutionary theory yields any moral truth will be examined in Chapter Nine.

A second argument sometimes given in support of ethical relativism is the *argument from tolerance*. Premise 1) Ethical relativists are more tolerant than ethical absolutists. Premise 2) Tolerance is a moral good. (One *ought* to be tolerant.) Conclusion: Ethical relativism is morally preferable to ethical absolutism, hence it must be true. On the face of it, premise 1) appears to be true since some expressions of absolutism, especially in religious forms, seem intolerant, narrow and inflexible. Yet not all forms of ethical absolutism reflect this attitude; for many utilitarians are tolerant, and persons committed to the Biblical principle of loving your neighbor are also. Of course if one means by "intolerant," any view that maintains that moral views conflicting with their own are wrong, then the absolutist is intolerant by definition. Most absolutists, for instance, believe that the holding of slaves is wrong, and would also disapprove of muggers, rapists, and promoters of genocide. But surely such intolerance cannot be morally faulted. Therefore, premise 1) cannot be true as a general claim. Finally, this argument from tolerance fails to support ethical relativism since one of its premises involves an absolutist claim. In asserting that tolerance is a moral good, premise 2) claims that tolerance is a universally appropriate moral principle that everyone should accept and practice. In making that absolutist claim the ethical relativist has abandoned his theory.

A third argument commonly used in support of ethical relativism is the *argument from cultural relativism*. Its common formulation is as follows: Since varying cultures hold varying moral beliefs (cultural relativism), ethical relativism must be true. But even a casual analysis of that argument reveals that it is incomplete for there is a logical gap between the premise and the conclusion. It is clear that the premise does not, by itself, entail the conclusion since, as noted earlier, cultural relativism differs substantially from ethical relativism. To complete this argument the hidden premise(s) must be added. Premise 1) Varying cultures hold varying moral beliefs (cultural relativism). Premise 2) If cultures hold varying moral beliefs, then ethical absolutism cannot be true. Sub-conclusion 3) Therefore, ethical absolutism cannot be true. Premise 4) Either ethical relativism is true or ethical absolutism is true. Conclusion 5) Therefore, ethical relativism is true.

Since this argument is valid in its form, the conclusion must be true if the premises are true. But some of the premises are problematic. Most social scientists would agree that premise 1) is true; indeed, most ethical absolutists would also agree with it. Premise 4) is a logical truth since its truth depends entirely on the meaning of the words, not on any factual data about the world. Ethical relativism and ethical absolutism, as defined, exhaust the alternatives; hence, one of these theories must be true. And since one contradicts the other, they cannot both be true. The argument hinges, then, on premise 2), since if 2) is true, we have successfully shown that ethical relativism is true. However, premise 2) is clearly false. Ethical absolutism can be true even if varying cultures do hold varying moral beliefs. Every ethical absolutist grants that cultures do vary in that way. Some cultures hold slaves while some do not. Some cultures allow plural marriage while others do not. The absolutist does not claim that all cultures believe the same moral rules; rather, the absolutist claims that there are some moral rules that every culture *ought* to believe and follow. Some cultures, according to the absolutist, are simply wrong in their beliefs. Furthermore, the absolutist would add, the fact that cultures disagree about moral rules does not mean that there are no objectively right moral rules. Many have disagreed about the shape of the universe (heliocentric or geocentric); but, that disagreement does not, in itself, imply that there is no objectively correct theory about the shape of the universe. Since premise 2) appears to be false, the argument from cultural relativism fails.

A purely logical point must now be made. Even though the arguments in support of ethical relativism appear to have failed, the theory could still be true. A failed argument fails only to *prove* that the conclusion is true, but the conclusion of the argument may still be true. In fact, the conclusion of an argument could be true even if the argument is invalid in form and its premises are all false. Some beliefs may be true even though we cannot supply arguments or evidence for proving them. Certain religious beliefs rely on that logical point. Nevertheless, many persons prefer to have *knowledge* supported by evidence and sound arguments, not just *beliefs*.

A fourth argument given to support ethical relativism can be called the *argument from lack of proof*. In popular and incomplete form, this argument claims that since no one has successfully shown that ethical absolutism is true, then ethical relativism must be true. Putting the argument formally can expose the hidden premise. Premise 1) No one has proven that ethical absolutism is true. Premise 2) If a theory has not been proven to be true, it must be false. Sub-conclusion 3) Therefore ethical absolutism must be false. Premise 4) Either ethical absolutism or ethical relativism is true. Conclusion: 5) Ethical relativism is true. The form of the argument posed is valid; therefore, if the premises are true, the conclusion must be true. Premise 4) is true on the basis of the analysis given above; but premise 1) is problematic since a number of philosophers have defended forms of ethical absolutism and have convinced many others of the truth of their position. On the other hand, no one has succeeded in convincing all other serious thinkers of the truth of a particular form of ethical absolutism. That being so, we could grant that premise 1) is true. Premise 2), however, is blatantly false. The mere fact that a theory has not been proven true does not entail that the theory is false. No one, for instance, had proven the truth of the heliocentric view of our solar system by the twelfth century; yet that lack of proof did not show that the theory was false. It was presumably true at that time, though no one apparently *knew* that it was true. Thus, the argument from lack of evidence fails since a crucial premise is false. Nevertheless, the lack of a generally persuasive argument in favor of some form of ethical absolutism tends to call into question the adequacy of the theory. And, of course, ethical relativism may be true even if arguments fail to demonstrate its truth.

If arguments supporting ethical relativism are not compelling, are there any cogent arguments which demonstrate that ethical absolutism is true, or, conversely, that ethical relativism is false? One conclusive approach would be to prove that a particular form of ethical absolutism is true. As Chapter Three illustrated, many thinkers from Plato to contemporaries have attempted to do just that, but any such attempt would run beyond the intentions of this chapter and this book. Hence, arguments here will be limited to those that attempt to show that ethical relativism is false. If this attempt is successful, then some form of ethical absolutism must be true—leaving open the question of just which form that might be. Three lines of argument will be pursued. The first will seek to show that ethical relativism is incoherent upon analysis. The second will offer a number of *reductio ad absurdum* arguments against ethical relativism. Finally, the suggestion that ethical relativists are really hidden egoists will be examined.

The charge that ethical relativism is incoherent stems from an attempt to clarify what precisely is being asserted in claiming, as some relativists do, that the *right* moral rules for a culture are the

THE CHALLENGE OF ETHICAL RELATIVISM

rules generally *believed* to be right by the people of that culture. But what coherent connection can be made between the apparent fact that a culture believes some rules to be right and the claim that such rules are, then, the right moral rules for that culture? This question leads to an attempt to impale the ethical relativist on the "horns of a dilemma." It seems that the relativist must hold either (first horn) that there are good reasons for the persons of that culture to hold the moral beliefs that they do, or (second horn) there are no such good reasons. Now if the relativist asserts the first horn and claims there are good reasons to support the moral beliefs of a culture, then he or she is committed to some form of absolutism. For if the relativist grants that "good reasons" can be given, then these reasons would surely justify the same kind of moral rules for any culture. Compare: If good reasons for holding your beliefs can be given, then I should be led to hold the same beliefs. If "good reasons" justify your actions, then the same reasons would justify the same actions for me. But if such "good reasons" exist for some moral beliefs, then these reasons establish objective justification for such moral beliefs. In short, some form of absolutism has been established.

Consider the second horn of the dilemma. Perhaps there are no "good reasons" for a culture to hold the moral views that they do. But if the relativist is not claiming that the moral rules in question can be right for the culture on the basis of good reasons, then on what grounds is the relativist claiming that such rules are "right"? It appears that we are left with the claim that such rules are right merely because the persons in that culture have come to believe such rules are right even if they have no "good reasons" for believing as they do. Yet it would seem absurd to claim that certain moral rules are the right moral rules merely because a culture happened, without good reason, to belief what they believe. Surely such a position would be a desperate view of the human quest for morality.

There is, of course, the position of the moral nihilist who claims there are no such things as moral facts or moral rules. However, even the nihilist is forced to make life decisions regarding the two issues I have traced in this book: 1) What is the most fulfilling human life that a rational person could pursue? 2) As a person seeks his or her own fulfillment, does that person have any obligation to aid others in their quest for fulfillment? The nihilist must answer those questions as he or she lives out her life—whether or not that nihilist identifies them as moral in nature.

Various *reductio ad absurdum* arguments are often used to defeat ethical relativism. These arguments attempt to show that since ethical relativism leads to absurd implications, the theory itself must be absurd. This approach takes the following form: Theory P implies Q; but Q is absurd; therefore, P must be absurd. A series of such arguments follows.

Reductio 1): A) If individual ethical relativism is true, then an individual can never be mistaken in her considered moral judgments. B) But it is absurd to hold that an individual can never be mistaken in her moral judgments. C) Hence, individual ethical relativism must be absurd. The hypothetical premise A) is true because of the meaning of individual ethical relativism, since that theory holds that the right moral rule for an individual is the rule that individual believes to be right. Hence, if Jill *believes* moral rule M is the right moral rule, then M *is* the right moral rule for Jill to follow. No one can, in principle, claim that Jill is mistaken. But surely it would be absurd to hold (B) that no one has ever been mistaken in their moral judgments. For instance, Adolph Hitler would be a common example of an evil person. But, according to individual ethical relativism, he was not mistaken in his moral judgments. In fact, according to this form of relativism, Hitler would be considered a moral equal, objectively, of St. Francis of Assisi or any other paradigm of goodness. Surely such a judgment would be absurd.

Furthermore, individual ethical relativism involves a curious implication. What if, for instance, Jill changes from believing moral rule P to believing moral rule Q? According to individual ethical relativism, while Jill *believed* P, then P would be the right moral rule for her and rule Q would have been wrong. But when she no longer believed moral rule P and came to believe moral rule Q, then rule Q would be right for her and P would be wrong. Nor could Jill claim that she was mistaken when she believed moral rule P, since individual ethical relativism does not recognize a basis for any such "mistake." What Jill believed was what she believed and, hence, was the right moral rule for her. All this leads to the odd conclusion that P, which was once the right moral rule for Jill, is no longer truly the right moral rule for her; nevertheless, Jill was not mistaken when she believed that moral rule P was right for her. The point, of course, is that any theory that generates such curious and paradoxical implications must surely be false.

Reductio 2): A) If cultural ethical relativism is true, no culture can never be mistaken in its moral judgments. B) But it is absurd to hold that no culture has ever been mistaken in its moral judgments. C) Hence, cultural ethical relativism must be absurd. This argument can be fleshed out in terms analogous to *reductio* 1) above by substituting a certain culture or society that is generally held to be evil. Examples include cultures that practiced slavery and traded in slaves, or a culture that practiced ethnic cleansing. Surely it would be absurd to claim that the moral patterns of such cultures were right just because they were generally accepted in those cultures.

Reductio 3): A) If cultural ethical relativism is true, then the moral beliefs of a culture can never improve or decline. B) But it is absurd to hold that the moral beliefs of a culture can never improve or decline. C) Hence, cultural ethical relativism must be absurd. This argument holds because of the meaning of "improve" and "decline." If a culture is to improve in its moral beliefs, then it must reflect a movement toward some morally correct position. But according to cultural ethical relativism, there cannot be any such correct moral position for a culture aside from the one held by that culture. Therefore, nothing like improvement or decline is possible. To be sure, *changes* in belief would be possible; but no change could represent improvement or decline. Therefore, a culture that moves from slavery to non-slavery has not improved even though beliefs have changed. Nor would a culture improve if it moved toward giving women rights equal to men. Such implications appear to be absurd; thus, cultural ethical relativism must be absurd. A parallel argument could be made against individual ethical relativism.

Reductio 4): A) If cultural relativism were the case, then all moral reformers are mistaken when they initiate moral reform within a culture. B) But it is absurd to claim that moral reformers are mistaken when they undertake reforms. C) Hence cultural ethical relativism must be absurd. Premise A) is true since a moral reformer is, by definition, one who seeks to change the moral patterns of a culture; but according to cultural ethical relativism, the correct moral beliefs for any culture are those that are generally accepted. Hence, anyone who disagrees with those generally held beliefs must be mistaken. In that case, anyone promoting emancipation in a culture that generally accepts slavery is mistaken in her moral judgment; and any person seeking equal rights for women in a traditionally male dominated culture is morally mistaken. Paradoxically, if the reformer succeeds in changing the moral beliefs to her reformed position, then she is no longer mistaken but now holds the correct moral beliefs since they now correspond with those of the culture. Such are the absurd implications of cultural ethical relativism.

There is, however, a straightforward response that a relativist could make to the attempted *reductio* arguments given above. The relativist need only claim that while those various consequences are entailed by ethical relativism, they are not absurd. The relativist just asserts that: 1) no individual (or culture) can be mistaken in his or her (their) moral beliefs; 2) no culture can make moral progress in its beliefs; 3) moral reformers are always mistaken when they attempt moral reform; 4) Hitler was the moral equal to any saint figure one would care to suggest. While all of these assertions may be the true, they are largely counter-intuitive. Perhaps the argument reduces to what could be called the moral intuitions of the relativist and his or her opponent.

A final line of argument against ethical relativism is the suggestion that the relativist, when unmasked, is found to be an ethical egoist. For instance, persons may be initially attracted to the relativist view since it appears to be a way of escaping from the hook of moral responsibility.[2] The purported individual ethical relativist claims, "What I believe to be right is right for me; and what you believe to be right is right for you. Such is the good old American individualistic tradition." But if the arguments given above are at all cogent, such a claim seems to be incoherent to the extreme. Thus, what the relativist probably intends to assert is, "After all, I want to do what I think is best for myself, and others can do what they think is best for themselves." That would be a coherent position, but it would be correctly identified as ethical egoism that holds to the following moral principle: "The morally correct action is that action which results in advantage to oneself." Epicurus defended that view centuries ago and it has contemporary advocates. It is, however, a form of ethical absolutism, not ethical relativism.

The arguments given and critiqued above were generally designed to support some form of ethical absolutism. However, that attempt may appear to run counter to the general thesis of this book; namely, that belief in the existence of God entails a moral perspective that differs widely from a variety of moral beliefs rooted in a non-religious worldview. While this general thesis commits me to descriptive or cultural relativism, it does not commit me to ethical relativism. In Chapter Three, I described a number of ethical theories held by various philosophers, each within the context of that particular philosopher's worldview. A number of them represented a form of ethical absolutism. In that chapter, I made no claim that any of the theories were true or more adequate than the others. Nor did I argue that any of them were clearly false. However, it is possible that one of them could be true. If that were the case, then some form of ethical absolutism would be true and relativism would be false. Hence, my general thesis does not commit me to ethical relativism. I have claimed only that belief in God shapes the nature of the resulting moral perspective—without asserting that belief in God yields an objectively true or more adequate moral pathway.

CHAPTER EIGHT

WHY BE MORAL?

If moral persons were not to eventually gain happiness, then morality, in the many cases where it brings no recompense on earth, would be just stupidity.
C. J. Ducasse[1]

...one of the things we ought to have learned from the history of moral philosophy is that the introduction of the word "intuition" by a moral philosopher is always a sign that something has gone badly wrong with the argument.
Alasdair MacIntyre[2]

The question, "Why should I be moral?" has a variety of possible interpretations. The question would be pointless if it asks for moral reasons for being moral. The real question is whether or not there are good reasons for being moral when such actions would entail some genuine cost to the individual choosing to act morally. In short, is there an inescapable conflict, at times, between rational self-interest (prudence) and the demands of morality. For the purposes of this chapter, I will address the issue by way of two related questions: 1) Why should societies develop some system of morality? and, 2) Why should any individual act morally?[3] My answer to question 1) was given earlier in this work where I asserted that some type of system must *of necessity* be worked out in any society because of the conflicting wants, needs, and desires (WNDs) of people in that society. Societies must formulate some type of moral patterns. I stipulated that *any* such system could properly be called a system of morality since the very point of morality is that of arbitrating such conflicts. Every society addresses those conflicts formally or informally, usually drawing on long religious traditions for justification. Some such systems may, of course, be profoundly mistaken, yet the point of any such system is that of arbitrating conflicts of interests. Interestingly, in the animal kingdom such conflicts of interests are usually settled on the basis of power or other skills while human societies have used a variety of strategies—including the use of power. While I argued that *any* system which seeks to appropriately arbitrate among the conflicting WNDs should be designated as *a* system of morality, I left open the question of whether or not any of these systems can be rationally justified.

In addressing the question, "Why should any individual act morally?" the following lines of argument will be pursued. First, I will claim, in contrast to a number of philosophers, that rational egoism—the pursuit of long-range self-interest—is the primary moral principle and trumps the apparent demands of moral rationality—the call of duty. The specific details of rational egoism in practice will depend on the belief system (worldview) held by the individual. Thus rational egoism in a religious context (e.g. St. Augustine) would provide moral guidelines that would vary from rational egoism in a non-religious context (e.g. Epicurus). For Saint Augustine, long-range self interest would involve the quest for Heaven and the Beatific vision of God. For Epicurus, since, death ended the individual, self-interest involved only the quest for pleasure during embodied life. Next, I will argue that "*the* moral point of view," as defended by several philosophers, is a dubious concept since it relies on intuitions rooted in a long cultural heritage. This cultural heritage that has shaped our intuitions may well have provided what could be called a "received tradition" in morality; but this tradition cannot be identified as *the* moral point of view. Other traditions that have shaped other sets of intuitions also exist. Finally, an analysis of the role of sanctions—punishment and reward—in moral systems will be pursued.

The distinction between rational egoism and moral rationality can be expressed in the following way: rational egoism holds that pursuing one's own long-term self-interest is a completely rational motive for *any* action, while moral rationality claims that there are times when reason shows us that moral duty can, at least for some actions, override one's self-interest. This distinction exhibits the tension or contradiction between the two and represents the principle issue in practically all systems of morality that have been proposed. Contemporary philosopher Ronald Green, for instance, reflects this problem in his *Religious Reason* where he argues that it is rational for any society to construct principles and methods for settling conflicts and achieving cooperation (moral rules).[4] Nevertheless, he suggests that it is not necessarily rational for an individual member of such a society to sacrifice his or her own fulfillment in order to benefit the society as a whole. Green maintains that this tension between what is rational for a society and what is rational for an individual "plagues moral reasoning from beginning to end." His solution to this problem will be examined later in this chapter.

The apparent tension between rational self-interest and the call of moral duty is what underlines the significance of the question "Why should I be moral?" This question asks for a justification for being moral and implies that there may also be reasons for *not* being moral. The prudential justification of morality would claim that being moral is an important aspect of the quest for a fulfilling life; in short, it pays to be moral. A variety of non-prudential answers have been suggested such as "Because it is right," or "Because it is one's duty," or "Because one is obligated to be moral." These responses fail to give a complete answer since one can respond, "Why should I do what is right?" "Why should I do my duty—if I have one?" or, "Why should I do what I am obligated to do—if I am so obligated? An answer that puts an end to this sequence of "whys" appears to be required.

The question "Why should I be moral?" could, for instance, be answered from a traditional religious position by claiming that God wills that we should be moral. However, one could ask

"But why should I do what God wills?" (Just as one might ask, "But why should I do what Judy wills?") The response in this context surely would be something like: "You should do what God wills because such obedience promises to be the path to the highest possible fulfillment and failing to do what God commands will lead to dire consequences." If one believes this response to be true, then the series of questions "But why should I . . .?" appears to come to a halt since it would seem odd to ask "But why should I pursue my highest possible fulfillment or seek to avoid dire consequences?" In general, the pursuit of happiness or the "good life" (in the non-moral sense) seems not to need a rational justification. Though there are differing views about what constitutes happiness or fulfillment, such pursuit is rational by its very nature Some might object that this prudential justification of religious morality is not in keeping with traditions that urge self-sacrifice and self-forgetting. A response by W. D. Hudson calls such an objection into question.

> Is it not significant that those who advocate self-sacrifice usually present it as a path to self-realization? 'He who loseth his life shall find it.' However difficult it may be to make sense of this, and I do not personally find it difficult, the fact remains that to those who advocate it, and to those who heed them, self-sacrifice appears to be a duty *because* it is the way to some kind of self-realization.[5]

The review of a number of philosophical and religious systems of ethics in Chapter Three revealed that they all reflect an answer to "Why should I be moral?" that is parallel to the religious answer expressed above. Each thinker reviewed in Chapter Three who supported a moral code or principle argued that the path to human fulfillment was also the moral pathway—as the individual thinker envisioned fulfillment and the moral pathway. In none of them was there, finally, a tension between doing what is moral and doing what is in the long-term best interest of the self. All of them, of course, would have granted that there may be times when an action that might serve *immediate* self-interest should be avoided since that action would undercut long-term self-interest. Thieving my neighbor's Twinkie or Porsche may meet my immediate self-interests, but the long-range results may well be costly to me. Reason can serve the aims of long-range self-interest by helping us to see the consequences of certain actions. In Hume's terms, reason can help show us the way to get what we truly desire.

Given that the long history of moral philosophy has consistently maintained that there is no fundamental conflict between moral duty and the quest for fulfillment, one is led to wonder just why some contemporary thinkers have proposed just such a conflict. William Frankena, for instance, wrote ". . . it must be admitted in all honesty that one who takes the moral road may be called upon to make a sacrifice and, hence, may not have as good a life in the nonmoral sense as he would otherwise have had."[6] Frankena's position will be analyzed later in this chapter. At this point, following the pattern of the important historical moral theorists, I maintain not only that it is always reasonable to pursue one's own interests, but also that so-called moral reason never trumps rational self-interest but is compatible with it. Put more directly, I claim that rational egoism as the long-term pursuit of self-interest is never in conflict with moral duty.

Rational egoism, however, is not to be identified with selfishness. To clarify this point, distinctions need to be made among self-interested, selfish, self-referential, and altruistic acts. A *self-interested* act is one pursued for one's own interest but may or may not include concern for the interests of others. A *selfish* act is one pursued *only* for the interests of the self without any regard for the interests of others. A *self-referential* act is one pursued for the interests of another while it also has a self-interested component. For example, a parent who spends a sleepless night nursing a sick child through a crisis is positively interested in the child's welfare, but is also clearly pursuing a *self-interested* activity though not a selfish one. The child's flourishing is a significant aspect of the parent's own flourishing. A deed which contributes to the welfare of another in this way is certainly not a *selfish* deed, but it can be *self-referential* if it also contributes to the welfare of the one performing the deed. Hence, there can be unselfish acts that are also self-referential. For the sake of clarity, such self-referential acts should be distinguished from *purely altruistic* ones in that a *purely altruistic* act demonstrates concern for the welfare of others *without any regard* for one's own welfare or interests. Hence a *purely altruistic* action would have no self-referential dimensions whatsoever. (The phrase "purely altruistic" is used here since "altruism" is often defined as "unselfish concern for the welfare of others." But such a definition does not clearly distinguish between a concern for others that has a self-referential component and one without such a component.) With these definitions in place my thesis of rational egoism would maintain that unselfish but self-referential actions *can* be rationally grounded, but purely altruistic actions are *never* rationally grounded. In short, it is never rational to act in such a way as to increase the welfare of another at a net cost to one's own self-interest—which would include one's interests in the welfare of those about whom we care. Recall that parental investment in a child's welfare, for instance, is also in the self-interest of the parent.

One assertion supporting rational egoism is central to this book: morality is "for us" in that the moral pathway always promises fulfillment and is, therefore, fully compatible with rational egoism. To defend this assertion, I first make a bald appeal to the authority of a number of thinkers. Chapter Three demonstrated that major theories of ethics, religious or non-religious, always claimed that the moral pathway is, in fact, the fulfilling pathway. The nature of the "fulfillment" envisioned differed considerably, however, among these theories. Plato, for instance, argued that the wise person is the good person since the wise person is just and the just soul is the most fulfilled soul. Aristotle argued that every action is thought to aim at some good and that what people aim at intrinsically is the good of a human being as human being. His theory of ethics is an elaboration on the quest for personal fulfillment by way of human excellence. Epicurus advised that the proper goal of the individual is that of pleasure for the self within the limits of our mortal life span. Augustine and Aquinas, who shaped much of Christian theology, held that the moral pathway was always part of the journey toward eternal bliss in God's presence. Jeremy Bentham and J. S. Mill, the founders of utilitarianism, were both psychological egoists in claiming, as Bentham put it, that "Nature has placed mankind under the governance of two sovereign masters, pain and pleasure. It is for them alone to point out what we ought to do, as well as *determine* what we *shall* do." (My emphasis.) Bentham informs us that physical, political, moral, and religious sanctions teach us to be good utilitarians as we *necessarily* seek to maximize our own pleasure. Finally, Immanuel Kant, though arguing that the truly moral deed is one done solely because it was morally binding, maintained that the very idea of morality includes the conviction that the morally good person will be rewarded and the evil person punished. To sustain this claim, Kant needed to posit freedom of the will, the immortality of the soul, and the existence of God.

These diverse thinkers agree that, in the end, the moral person (however the particular view of morality is described) is the person who will become the fulfilled person. Some perceive this fulfillment as something like delayed gratification since such fulfillment is seldom experienced during this lifetime (Augustine, Aquinas, and Kant). Others hold that fulfillment must come in this life since this is the only arena in which we can be fulfilled (Aristotle, Epicurus). While this persistent link between the moral pathway and personal fulfillment does not appear to be some form of logical entailment, it does appear to be a highly rational reading of the human venture. What rational person, for instance, would find any interest in a suggested moral pathway if that pathway promised only that you would suffer and be discarded for no good purpose? No moral philosopher ever held to such a theory—probably well aware that no person would find this position either attractive or rationally compelling. Richard Taylor made this point nicely:

> However one approaches ethics—whether from the ancient standpoint of virtue, or the modern one of duty, or from any other—what one finally asserts has to be something that makes a difference and this,

in the last analysis, must be a difference with respect to human happiness. Otherwise, whatever is said will be simply pointless.[7]

There are, of course, philosophers who would challenge my contention that rational egoism is the primary moral principle. Some argue that the principle of rational egoism is contradictory to the very concept of morality and thus cannot be a *moral* principle. William Frankena, for instance, in his criticism of ethical egoism maintains that "living wholly by the principle of enlightened self-love (my "rational egoism") just is not a kind of *morality*."[8] This assertion is linked to his claim that "The moral point of view is *disinterested*, not 'interested'." Frankena appears to maintain that while self-interest is not necessarily immoral, true morality moves beyond any kind of self-interest, even of self-referential actions that are not selfish. Evidently the parent caring for the sick child is not demonstrating morality since the parent's actions are clearly interested, not disinterested. Frankena would not claim that the parent was being immoral even if the act would evidently not classify as a truly moral one for Frankena. Instead, he would hold that such actions are to be seen as morally neutral or non-moral.

Other philosophers commonly understand the term "moral" in a way that would reject rational egoism as a possible *moral* theory. John Mackie implies this when he writes "Morality has the function of checking what would be the natural result of prudence alone."[9] Mackie's "prudence" would carry much the same meaning as my "rational egoism." David Gauthier makes much the same point:

> Morality is a system of principles such that it is advantageous for everyone if everyone accepts and acts on it, yet acting on the system of principles requires that some perform disadvantageous acts.[10]

In those passages, neither Mackie nor Gauthier commit themselves to the proposition that some must perform acts that are *long-term* disadvantageous. Short-term disadvantage would be acceptable to practically all moral theories if such disadvantage is needed for long-term advantage or fulfillment. I might, for instance, spend time and effort to help a person get her car out of the snow. The immediate disadvantage is clear, though in the long-term I could consider such actions to be part of what I should do to be seen as a virtuous person in my community. I could also hope that my actions may influence others who could, some day, be of help to me in a similar situation. Furthermore, such actions would support my own self-image as a virtuous person and, therefore, help confirm an image of myself as a good human being—an image that might well support my sense of fulfillment. Hence, such actions may have long-term advantages that can outweigh any short-term disadvantages. A more direct illustration would be that of various saints from a variety of religious traditions who obviously forego, through vows of poverty and celibacy, what many of us would consider to be advantageous experiences. Yet those taking such vows *always* understand them to be part of the pathway that leads to ultimate fulfillment. For such saints, long-term advantage requires what some would judge to be short-term "sacrifice."

Another philosopher, Kurt Baier, argues that

> "... being moral is following rules designed to overrule self-interest whenever it is in the interests of everyone alike that everyone should set aside his interest."[11]

Baier appears to argue that morality contributes to advantage in a way that prudence alone cannot. Yet his claim that "it is in the interests of everyone alike" to overrule self-interest has an air of paradox about it for the claim would apply also to the one who is *overruling* his or her self-interest for *the sake of his or her self-interest*. It is, apparently, in my self-interest to over-rule self-interest. But the issue, again, is whether or not Baier is speaking of short-term or long-term interests. Most would agree that it would be rational to sacrifice some dimensions of self-interest on some occasions if that sacrifice would promote one's long-term advantage. If that is Baier's contention, then his position is not in conflict with the rational egoism I am proposing.

I would claim, at this point, that Frankena, Mackie, Gauthier, and Baier all reflect what could be called a "received tradition" in moral thought and, in this way, represent a type of moral intuitionism. In ethical theory, intuitionism holds that the good or the right thing to do can be known directly through some faculty of intuition. None of the four present *arguments* designed to show that morality must be disinterested or must involve an overruling of self-interest. Nor do they stipulate some definition of "morality" that would involve such considerations. Instead, they claim that this is what "moral" or "morality" means or implies; and in doing so they reflect a type of intuitionism that just "sees" morality in that way. Fully developed forms of ethical intuitionism are generally rejected at this point in history. It is rejected, in part, because there seems to be no way of adjudicating between conflicting sets of intuitions—as when the intuitions of X conflict with the intuitions of Y. Furthermore, it is difficult to identify just what this faculty of intuition might be. When a philosopher falls back on claims of intuition to support his or her position, I suggest that his or her arguments have gone wrong—as MacIntyre claims in the epigraph to this chapter.

I would grant that most persons in our modern Western culture world do share what appears to be certain moral intuitions. These intuitions are usually similar to the content of our conscience. But surely such intuitions have been shaped by certain cultural traditions that have made their way into our moral language and consciousness. They are not insights into the fundamental and objective nature of morality. Furthermore, these intuitions run strongly counter to a variety of moral theories that have been presented throughout history. Epicurus, for instance, clearly argued that self-interest is the central principle of morality as he saw it. I would add that his moral philosophy is found in all works that deal seriously with the history of ethics, thereby indicating that the authors of such works consider Epicurus's egoistic hedonism as a moral theory—in spite of Frankena's claim that it is "just not a kind of *morality*." Aristotle's ethical theory would also reject the claim that true morality must of necessity result in some long-term cost to some of those who walk the moral pathway. Finally, Bentham and J. S. Mill, the founders of utilitarianism, both held to psychological egoism—the theory that we *of necessity* always choose those actions that we believe to be in our self-interest. They argued that various sanctions would eventually shape us into good utilitarians as we discover how our true self-interests could best be met. My point, then, is that the history of moral philosophy shows that "moral" just does not have the meanings that Frankena, Mackie, Gauthier, and Baier suggest. They draw on a received tradition that has shaped their intuitions. This tradition will be explored later in this chapter.

Another challenge to my position that reflects another form of intuitionism is found in the concept of "the moral point of view." One such position is explored by William Frankena in his *Ethics* where he develops an analysis of "the moral point of view."[12] In another essay, Frankena puts the point bluntly: "I believe... that morality requires genuine sacrifice, and may even require self-sacrifice."[13] Later Frankena makes an observation fully in keeping with the theory about morality I have been proposing:

> ...it seems clear to me... that a universal coincidence of being moral and achieving the best score can be shown to be false—unless it is posited that there is a hereafter in which God will readjust the balance.[14]

Given his understanding of what constitutes true morality, Frankena's last observation is fully compatible with the theory I am presenting in this work. Kant anticipated Frankena's point and proceeded to posit that the existence of God as necessary if morality, as he understood it, is to be rational.

In examining the question of just what it might mean to take "the moral point of view," Frankena reviews and then rejects a position related to that of Immanuel Kant that holds "one is taking the moral point of view if and only if one is willing to universalize one's maxims." A maxim, here, is some action-guiding rule a person might apply in making a choice among possible actions. To be willing to universalize such a maxim one must be willing to view it as a *law* that everyone ought to obey. If one is unwilling to universalize the maxim selected, then one has failed to take the "moral point of view" as Kant saw it. An example of such a maxim would be "Always tell the truth in a situation where one must choose between lying and truth-telling"—a maxim of which Kant would approve. On the other hand, Kant would reject the maxim "Lie when it is to your advantage." Kant argued that one could not consider such a maxim to be a universal law. His complete argument need not be traced in this context. Frankena rejects this form of "the moral point of view" and supplies a variety of reasons often given for such rejection.

Another characterization of "the moral point of view" was proposed by Kurt Baier. He held that

> ...one is taking *the moral point of view* (my emphasis) if one is not being egoistic, one is doing things on principle, and one is willing to universalize one's principles, and in doing so considers the good of everyone alike.[15]

The relationship to Kant's position is clear. Note that both Frankena and Baier write of *the* moral point of view—not *a* moral point of view—thereby implying that it is possible to formulate something like a universally true, objective, and rationally grounded "moral point of view."

Only Frankena's position will be analyzed at this point since his position reflects the central claims of those who defend something like "the moral point of view." Several features of his "moral point of view" are parallel to aspects of my own position presented earlier in this work. I agree with Frankena on the following: 1) Reasons for moral judgments involves facts about just how an action would affect the lives of sentient beings in terms of the distribution of non-moral good and evil. (In other words, moral judgments involve appropriate arbitration among various competing wants, needs, and desires—WNDs.) 2) When the judgment is about oneself or one's own actions, the facts about just how one's actions or disposition affects the lives of other sentient beings are part of the consideration.

A central factor, however, in Frankena's description of "the moral point of view" is problematic, namely his claim that in making a moral judgment one must be willing to universalize that judgment. In this, Frankena follows the language of Kant, Kurt Baier and many other philosophers. Let us call this the "universalizing principle." The difficulty with this principle involves at least two concerns. First, the "precise nature and definition (of this principle), and the implications it has for moral reasoning, are disputed."[16] Second, the foundation or justification of the principle is not clear. An extended discussion of these concerns is beyond the intentions and range of this work. I will, therefore, outline the major reasons why I call into question the validity of claiming that the universalizing principle and the moral point of view are necessary conditions for a moral judgment.

The central meaning of the universalizing principle is that one cannot make oneself an exception to some moral rule or judgment. According to this principle, if I make the moral judgment that some act X is morally wrong for Mr. Z to do, then I must also judge that I would also be morally culpable if I carried out X. The judgment involved, however, would have to be of a general nature, not of a specific action. For instance, I would judge that it would be morally wrong for Mr. Z to have sexual relations with my wife, but the universalizing principle would not lead me to conclude that it would be morally wrong for me to have sexual relations with my wife. There are factors regarding Mr. Z, my wife, and me, that make significant moral differences. If, however, I judged that it would be morally wrong for Mr. Z to have sexual relations with another man's wife, then the universalizing principle would entail that it would also be wrong for me to have sexual relations with another man's wife. The idea of universalizing is clearly related to the ideas of fairness and impartiality. I must judge my own actions by the same standards that I judge others. Furthermore, I cannot claim special considerations just because of certain factors in my own biography such as race, family lineage, national identity, religious beliefs or lack of, educational status, etc. Another human being has equal moral status with me purely on the grounds that he or she is a human being.

This intuition of fairness and impartiality is so deeply imprinted in our cultural heritage that to question it seems odd if not outright absurd. It is not my intent to question the validity of this fairness intuition. I maintain, however, that the universalizing principle that underlies this sense of fairness is, itself, based on intuitions rooted in thought forms and moral theories that have shaped our culture. Universalizing, therefore, is not some objective principle somehow rooted in the structures of human rationality or language. In other words, the universalizing principle reflects a worldview or metaphysical vision that provides the context within which such universalizing can be seen as rational. Alasdair MacIntyre makes a similar point in his discussion of rival justices and competing rationalities. He notes that a "number of academic philosophers" have argued that rationality will bring us to "a genuinely neutral, impartial, and, in his way, universal point of view, freed from the partisanship and the partiality and one-sidedness that otherwise affect us."[17] This view of the role of rationality, MacIntyre claims, begs some key questions.

> For it can be argued...that this account of rationality ... covertly presupposes one particular partisan type of account of justice, that of liberal individualism, which it is later to be used to justify, so that its apparent neutrality is no more than an appearance,..

In this context I want now to consider a claim made in Chapter One: "The substance of a morality rooted in theistic religious traditions cannot be successfully defended on non-theistic or naturalistic foundations." One approach to a defense of that claim was made in Chapter Six where the ability of theistic traditions to move beyond narrow tribalism to a universal affirmation of all human beings was analyzed. According to theistic traditions, since God is the creator of all, then all persons have equal status before the creator. The concept of God made universalizing possible. (That chapter also recognized that theistic traditions can also be tragically divisive.) Purely naturalistic systems, such as those of Aristotle, Epicurus, and Nietzsche, provide little or no basis for such universalizing. The mere *fact* that all human beings are equally the product of natural forces such as evolution does not logically entail the *moral* proposition that all persons should be equally respected or fairly treated.

A further defense of my claim can be linked to the concept of justice as it developed in Western thought. Alasdair MacIntyre has noted the contrast in the scope of justice from the ancient Greek (fifth or fourth century) view to that reflected in modern liberal thought.[18]

> For a modern liberal the norms of justice are to govern the relationships of human beings as such; . . . For Aristotle, by contrast, justice properly so-called is exercised between free and equal citizens of one and the same *polis* (political community, as a city-state). .

The scope of justice for modern liberalism is universal in that differences in political societies, social status, racial identity or other boundaries are viewed as irrelevant in any given transaction. Persons must be respected as persons. For Aristotle and other Greeks justice is confined to the boundaries of a particular *polis*, and the content of justice varied with social and citizenship boundaries. Doing justice may mean treating others as is their due, but the sticky issue is always that of deciding the content of what is *due*. What was due to those whom Aristotle viewed as natural slaves differed substantially from what was due to the land-owning and aristocratic citizen of Athens. Some Greeks, it seems, found various levels of tribalism to be a natural part of their theory of justice.

In tracing the extension of justice to that of universal application, MacIntyre notes, "When in the ancient world justice was extended beyond the boundaries of the *polis*, it was always as a requirement of theology." Socrates, for instance, appealed to the unwritten laws made by God when acknowledging that the scope of justice could move beyond the boundaries of the *polis*. The Stoics developed a notable extension in theory and practice.

> The Stoics were the first thinkers in the Greco-Roman world to assert systematically that the scope of justice is humanity as such, and they did so because they understood every human being, . . . to be a member of one and the same community under one and the same law.

The Stoic claim that all human beings are under the umbrella of *humanity* is based on their notion that God is in everything as a force and rationality that pervades all. The Stoic conception of God was not that of some being in a single location, but as a rational substance that exists in all things and that controls not only the structure of nature but also the events in the world.

This view of God pervading and directing the universe led to the Stoic attitude of acceptance of things as they are. The Stoic Epictetus reflected this attitude in saying, "Demand not that events should happen as you wish; but wish them to happen as they do happen."[19] The Stoics held that the soul of the human being is also part of God as a divine spark, and human reason is rooted in the divine *logos* or reason. This universal participation in the divine provides the basis for the universal application of justice, which is divine, to all persons. Cicero makes a Stoic point in saying, "this whole world is one city to be conceived of as including gods and human beings."[20] Since divine reason pervades and directs events, then this reason is reflected in the ruling status of Rome and the laws of that community. The duties reflected in these laws and customs varied with relationships. As Cicero explained

> Our highest duties are to parents and fatherland (*patria*), that state in which we have citizenship; next come children and the rest of the immediate family; then remoter kin; and finally those friends who deserve well of us."[21]

Here, again, the old patterns of tribalism appear.

One limitation to this Stoic view of justice and law is found in their identification of the standard Roman Law and practice with this universal divine justice. According to the Stoics, such laws apply to all persons but there existed no means of criticizing these laws. There was no reference point from *outside* that law by which to bring criticism *of* that law. MacIntyre notes

> Any conception of justice which not only had a scope which extended beyond the citizens of those polities to all mankind but also provided a standard for evaluating them independently must come from elsewhere.

This source, MacIntyre claims, is the Abrahamic history and the development of the Torah as divine commands. What the Torah in its developed form brings is not only specific details (as in the Ten Commandments) but also a sense of justice that is not restricted to Israel. Justice is expressed as a law holding for all nations. MacIntyre traces the development of this law conception of morality through St. Paul and the Christian tradition with special focus on the St. Augustine's analysis of the universal law of love. In quoting St. Paul, Augustine presents love as the divine standard for justice, "so as to owe no one anything, but to love one another."

The analysis being pursued, here, is not designed to show that this line of justice traced into Christian history is the *correct* understanding of justice. That question I leave open. What I suggest, however, is that the modern liberal view of justice with its call for the universalizing principle and its emphasis on fairness and impartiality has its roots in this history. For good or ill, this long history of Christian thought has made its way deeply into Western culture and has shaped our intuitions about morality and justice so deeply that these intuitions strike us as either common sense or patently obvious. When Kant, for instance, writes of the "very idea of morality" he clearly reflects the Protestant tradition in which he was nurtured, even though he seeks to ground this morality in human reason as such. Kant seems to confuse his intuitions with what he claims to be the objective structures of reason. His own dependency on this religious tradition becomes transparent when he argues that freedom of the will, eternal life, and God must be posited if morality is to be rational. Given his view of morality, small wonder that those posits were developed. If one begins with a view or morality shaped by a theistic tradition, it would not be surprising to justify it by appealing to a form of theism. Philosopher Ronald Green makes an argument parallel to Kant's by arguing that our given understanding of the nature of morality will finally require reason to posit a religious worldview.[22] It is not surprising that Green, as Kant, ends up insisting that moral reason leads to religious belief since his view of morality draws on intuitions from the theistic traditions of the West. (If one begins with Aristotle's ethics or the moral views of Epicurus, "moral reason" would hardly lead to religious belief.) More contemporary philosophers, when speaking of "the moral point of view" are also drawing on this tradition for content though they may be rejecting the theology which originally developed and sustained it. Their construction of "the moral point of view," I claim, ends up being a form of intuitionism rooted in a long cultural heritage. These philosophers seek to keep the universalizing principle but seek to justify it on some basis other than religious belief. The question remains whether or not this attempt can be successful.

Other philosophers have argued in similar fashion that the content of most of our moral terms has been shaped by Western religious traditions and that these terms have become meaningless or even harmful when the religious beliefs are given up. Philosopher G. E. M. Anscombe argued both that Christianity constructed the law conception of ethics from the Torah and that the long dominance of Christian ethics has deeply embedded this conception in our language and thought.

> (T)he concepts of obligation, and duty... and of what is *morally* right and wrong, and of the *moral* sense of "ought," ought to be jettisoned if this is psychologically possible; because they are survivals, or derivatives from survivals, from an earlier conception of ethics which no longer generally survives, and are only harmful without it.[23]

Richard Taylor puts his case directly:

> ...religion introduced the idea of right and wrong at a higher level than that resulting from human custom and law, namely, one resulting from divine law. Modern philosophy thenceforth *kept* the distinction between moral right and wrong, making it the pivotal idea of moral

philosophy, but *cast aside* the context that gave it meaning, namely God's will."[24]

Since Taylor rejects the idea of God, he argues for a return to the Greek view of ethics as the pursuit of a life of "excellence," rather than an ethic of duty. He brings Aristotle's views back into the modern world.

The question "Why be moral?" leads to a consideration of the role of sanctions, rewards or punishments, in morality. Given my theory about moral theories as developed throughout this work, sanctions represent an inescapable aspect of morality. I have claimed, for instance, that all major moral theories have maintained that the moral pathway is the most fulfilling pathway. That claim would evidently entail the view that failure to walk the moral pathway would in some way undercut or hinder life fulfillment. Such an entailment can be discerned in the moral theories reviewed in Chapter Three. Representative voices can be cited. Plato argued that the unjust soul could not be a contented soul. Failure to follow the ethical pathway, Aristotle maintained, would result in a life that falls below excellence. Even Epicurus, with his egoistic hedonism, would claim that failure to follow his moral advice would lead to more pain and less pleasure. And the major traditions of religious ethics are filled with promises of rewards and/or punishments: Heaven and Hell (traditional Judaism, Christianity and Islam); reincarnation in lower forms of life (Hinduism); failure to find peace (Buddhism).

A variety of thinkers have linked serious morality to the idea of God as the final arbiter of justice in terms of rewards and punishments. Plato held that belief in God was necessary for the maintenance of a stable and just community. A long line of theologians and religious philosophers, including Augustine, Aquinas, Maimonides, and John Calvin maintained a similar position. Even Sigmund Freud—no supporter of religious views—believed that the threat of religiously-based sanctions did, in fact, help restrain some of the nastier elements of human nature. John Locke, the 17th century English philosopher, although not an orthodox religious thinker, believed that one had little basis for trusting an atheist. Jeremy Bentham and J. S. Mill, who shaped utilitarianism, both held—at least in their writings—that sanctions delivered by God helped to make good utilitarians out of self-interested human beings. Even Thomas Jefferson, the enlighten-ment deist of the 18th century, held that "no System of morality however pure it might be" could survive "without the sanction of divine authority stampt upon it."[25] This history of reflection on morality suggests that any system of morality would lose not only its point but its seriousness if sanctions were not part of the moral pathway prescribed. Morality may be "for us," but moral failure would appear to be "against us."

To be sure, many moderns no longer take divine sanctions seriously; but most still take into account that sanctions may still be delivered by other human beings if they detect what they deem as your evil acts and if they have the power to level sanctions against you. However, if one has sufficient power or stealth, the threat of human sanctions can be largely diminished. The theory of divine sanctions, on the other hand, contains a dimension not to be found in sanctions delivered only by other human beings—one can neither escape from the eyes of God nor hope to deceive God. Whether or not the concept of Divine eyes has contributed to a more adequate moral scene I leave as an open question.

CHAPTER NINE

EVOLUTION AND ETHICS

Ultimately our moral sense or conscience becomes a highly complex sentiment—originating in the social instincts, largely guided by the approbation of our fellow-men, ruled by self-reason, and confirmed by instruction and habit.

Charles Darwin[1]

... biologists do not have special abilities to assess what is ethical;.. there are within biology no magic solutions to moral problems.

Richard Alexander[2]

William James' analysis of morality, explored in Chapter Two, concluded that the point of moral philosophy is that of discovering the appropriate way of arbitrating between the conflicting wants, needs, and desires (WNDs) of sentient creatures. According to that analysis, our current moral setting involves some six billion human beings (and multitudes of other sentient creatures), each with wants, needs, and desires. Certainly not all of them can be honored; hence some must go unfulfilled. This current moral setting with its struggle of need against need and creature against creature is parallel to the scene reflected in theories proposed by the Reverend Thomas Malthus (1776-1834), English economist and philosopher. He concluded that the ability of the human species to reproduce its kind would, if not restricted in some way, lead to a growth in population that would far exceed the resources needed to sustain it. There would be, as Malthus put it, a "struggle for existence." The gap between population demands and available resources seemed inevitable unless population increase was somehow limited. This limitation, Malthus observed, would come about by way of premature death through disease, starvation, and war as well as attempts to check the birth rate. Since the latter seemed ineffective, it was left largely for early death to keep population in check.

While Malthus maintained this pessimistic view of the human scene, he worked out a way of fitting his theory into the structure of his own religious faith, which was not strictly orthodox at all points. Even though he suffered some abuse by those more optimistic about the scheme of things, his theories did attract the attention of others. The most significant impact made by Malthus on future thought was through his influence on Charles Darwin (1809-1882), whose theory of evolution through natural selection was prompted, in part, by the Malthusian description of the "struggle for existence."

In *Darwin's Dangerous Idea*, Daniel Dennett confesses that he would give Charles Darwin an award for "the single best idea anyone has ever had." The idea of evolution by natural selection is "not just a wonderful idea. It is a dangerous idea."[3] However Darwin might be rated, there is little doubt that his theory of evolution has had an immense impact on many sciences. It also has the marks of a very successful scientific theory. Great scientific theories are marked, for instance, by their ability to unify many fields of learning. "In a single stroke, the idea of evolution by natural selection unifies the realm of life, meaning, and purpose with the realm of space and time, cause and effect, mechanism and physical law."[4] Great scientific theories also have explanatory power. The aim of any scientific theory, after all, is that of explaining observed phenomena in some way. While Darwin initially aimed primarily at explaining just how various species came into being, his theory now encompasses many other aspects of animal and human life. A variety of questions, including the following, have been explained by evolutionary theory. Why do males in many species develop tusks, fangs, horns and other weapons? Why, in many species, do only a few males do most of the copulating? What accounts for acts of infanticide on the part of males (lions, chimpanzees, human beings)? Why do females, in most bird and mammalian species, tend to make a larger "parental investment" in their offspring than the males by giving more time and energy to raising their children than do the males? Why have human societies moved largely to monogamous marriages—at least in terms of legal patterns?

For several decades, biologists and philosophers have expanded the explanatory range of Darwin's theory by seeking to apply it to morality. Evolutionary theory has been used to explain just why human beings have developed and expressed patterns of behavior that reflect moral issues: violence of all kinds, selfishness, kindness, altruistic behavior, cooperation, cheating, truth telling, lying, mating patterns and rules of sexual conduct, and schemes of justice and fairness? The literature is both fascinating and abundant.[5]

Central issues in the various discussions include: 1) Can morality be reduced, ultimately, to biological facts so that biology can not only *explain* but also *justify* moral patterns? 2) To what extent can cultural patterns and belief systems (as religion) alter behavioral tendencies rooted in biological heritage? 3) If biology cannot fully explain and justify moral patterns, can it provide insight for those who attempt to construct or enforce moral patterns? The old question of "nature vs. nurture" is clearly involved and the answers given by various writers vary within the nature/nurture spectrum. Edward O. Wilson emphasizes the nature component:

> The genes hold culture on a leash. The leash is very long, but inevitably values will be constrained in accordance with their effects on the human gene pool. The brain is a product of evolution. Human behavior—like the deepest capacities for emotional response which drive and guide it—is the circuitous technique by which human genetic material has been and will be kept intact.[6]

While Michael Ruse makes a striking claim:

> In an important sense, ethics as we understand it as an illusion fobbed off on us by our genes to get us to cooperate.... Furthermore the way our biology enforces its ends is by making us think that there is an objective higher code, to which we are all subject.[7]

R. D. Alexander, while deeply impressed by the power of biological heritage, suggests that nurture through culture has a creative role to play in constructing moral values.

> We are thus evolved to be nepotists, even though, because of the role of social learning and the nature of consciousness, purpose, and deliberation, we are not *obliged* to be nepotists.[8]

I will not engage directly in the nature/nurture debate. Instead, I will outline conclusions generally established by biologists and philosophers about how evolution has shaped values and behavior and then explore the relationship of these conclusions to moral theory.

A clarification needs to be made about various terms that will be used in the following pages such as "intention," "designed," "strategy," "selfish," and "atruistic." When these terms are applied to the processes or results of evolution they are meant to be understood metaphorically. Biologists presently hold that no entity as "evolution" exists that can do anything like intend, design, etc. Furthermore, most biologists we will be quoting also generally believe that there is no mind or consciousness within, under, or beyond nature that does the designing or has certain intentions. There is no God behind the scene. Instead, evolution is a name for a process reflected in nature that explains many phenomena of the natural world. Evolution, itself, is taken as a "brute fact" that cannot be explained in terms of some other theory or supposition.

As a theory, evolution began as an explanation of how various forms of plant and animal life have developed out of simple early forms of life. Darwin's major contribution was that of showing how natural selection could account for the development of various species, including human beings, from simpler forms of life. The focus in his major work was on physiological characteristics and how they developed and changed over time. In the latter part of the twentieth century, sociobiology and evolutionary psychology were developed and explored. Scientists who initiated this research reasoned that evolution could not only explain the physiological development of creatures, but could also explain their social behavior. If the genetic constitution of creatures shapes the physical characteristics of bees, rats, apes, and human beings, so also could genetic material tend to control the individual and social behavior of these various creatures. The results of this research have been impressive.[9]

Evolutionary psychology and sociobiology have established a number of widely accepted conclusions. I will develop them in no particular order of importance and then examine the question of the relationships between these conclusions and morality. A major advance in evolutionary theory was clearly expressed by Richard Dawkins in his *The Selfish Gene*.[10] The major idea in that work is that organisms, such as human beings, are not the central actors in evolutionary process. Instead, genes—molecules of DNA—are the basic units of natural selection. Organisms have their place in the process since each can be seen as "gene machines" that help to propagate, not the organism itself, but various genes carried by that organism. My own body, for instance, does not and cannot replicate itself; but it can, with the help of another body of the opposite sex, function to replicate some of my genes. My child will carry copies of half of my own genes. A "successful" organism, from this point of view, is one that maximizes the number of copies of its genes that are passed on. These genes survive in other organisms, but the parent organism dies. These genes are "selfish" in the sense that they seek their own welfare at the cost of the organism that functions as the gene machine, and often at the cost of other genes as well. Cancer, for instance, can be thought of as rebellious cells shaped by rebellious genes that seek to replicate themselves but at great cost to the organism they inhabit. Paradoxically, if these cancer cells are too "successful" they finally bring about their own demise by ending the life of the host body. Truly successful genes are those that inhabit organisms that have the capacity to pass the genes on through reproduction.

From the "selfish gene" perspective, evolutionary theory is entirely compatible with the common sense notion that the individual is dispensable in evolutionary terms. Species and genes tend to be preserved, but the individual creature ultimately faces certain death. (With the exception of some simple creatures such as amoebas that can, in theory, keep on dividing and avoid individual death.) On the other hand, the individual is important as a link to the next generation and as a means of passing on a genetic pattern. Genes, if they are to replicate, require gene machines that have the capacity to do the replicating. Hence, the individual must survive long enough to bring in the new generation. The fear of death or the fear of being attacked would be a genetic trait that could help an individual to survive long enough to propagate its kind. An individual or a species without such a fear would have little chance of surviving in the contest for life. Spiders, perhaps, do not *experience* a fear of death, and they may not even experience a *fear* of being attacked. Nevertheless, they have inherited through their genes various strategies that lead them to avoid and escape from danger. Human beings, on the other hand, not only have a fear of being attacked, but they also have a fear of dying--a fear that may be peculiar to the human species. One scholar argues that this fear of death shapes much of human activity.[11]

Another feature of human beings that contributes to the survival of the individual in the early months of life is selfishness—a behavior encoded in our genes. Richard Dawkins notes that "we are born selfish."[12] One might object that it seems unfair to label a baby as "selfish," but Dawkins uses the word in a behavioral sense and not as a psychological term describing a motive. Thus, for Dawkins, babies *act* in selfish ways—especially during the early months of life—in that they seem not at all concerned about the needs of others but insist on expressing their own needs. This is what we have come to expect of babies, and their behavior no doubt helps them to survive. Parents often agree that it is fortunate that babies are "cute" since it would be difficult to tolerate their demands if they were not. If adults were to act like babies they would be intolerable.

This selfish behavior is not confined to human infants but is displayed in many animal species. In a litter of pigs, for instance, there is considerable competition for milk from the mother. If the litter is large and there happens to be a smaller and weaker runt that piglet may very well die. Such a death would leaves more food for the remaining siblings leaving them stronger and better able to replicate their genes. In bird species, competition for food from the parents is also intense. The baby bird with the loudest cry and raised mouth is most apt to get fed. There is some evolutionary wisdom in that scene since feeding the strong is an advantage to the genetic line. (Poverty stricken mothers in South America sometimes use their meager resources to feed the stronger children and thereby allow a weaker one to die. A tragic but not irrational choice.) The most striking example of "selfishness" in bird species is various kinds of fratricide where baby birds will eject other eggs from the nest before they hatch. The female in some bird species will lay her egg in a "foster" bird's nest where the resulting chick will destroy other eggs or baby birds. This picture is not pleasant, but it is another means for a species to survive and replicate its genes.[13]

Selfishness is not the whole story, however, since in the long run pure selfishness will not succeed. In the human species, parents are often gratified to notice that children do develop a sense of sympathy. In many species it is common for individuals to exhibit "altruistic" actions in the sense that these actions benefit other individuals without any immediate benefit to the altruist. For instance, in some monkey species and bird species an individual may give a warning cry as a sign of danger so that others might take cover. The warning cry itself may even increase the danger of the one giving the cry since a predator would more easily identify the presence of that individual. This altruism was difficult to understand in traditional evolutionary theory since it appears to work against the survival of the altruistic individual. This altruism is more easily explained by evolutionary psychology with its focus on the "selfish gene" since such altruism may enhance the reproductive success of the genes shared by the monkey or the birds though it may reduce the survival chance of the altruist. These actions are understood in terms of kin selection and/or reciprocal altruism, both of which have the advantage of maximizing the reproduction of genes even at the cost to an individual.

The concepts of *kin selection* and *reciprocal altruism* require a brief description at this point. Kin selection altruism occurs when altruistic actions—such as sharing food with a related individual—takes place only with a relative, not with a non-related individual. Related lions in the same pride will share food with each other as long as there is enough food to go around. (When food is scarce, the adult lions always eat the kill before the cubs have a chance. This makes survival sense since if the adults die the cubs cannot survive. And if the cubs die but the adults survive, more cubs can be produced.) But a lion with genes for purely altruistic acts may not survive. Consider: If a lion with purely altruistic genes gave handouts to lions from other prides when food was scarce, that altruism would work to the disadvantage of the altruist. In the competition for food that altruistic lion would not survive. Hence, we would expect that altruistic gene to be eliminated from the population. But since lions in the same pride share genes, their kin-altruism results in advantage for the pride and, hence, for successful replication of its shared genes. This point is clearly illustrated in many species, including human beings. We are much more apt to share our resources with those closely related to us than with those completely unrelated. In general, we are more inclined to share out resources with our children, who share half of our genes, than with a cousin who shares a smaller fraction. Such kin-selection altruism helps maximize the replication of our genes.

Reciprocal altruism takes place when individuals share resources with others, at some cost to themselves, even when the others are not related. Such altruistic actions make evolutionary sense only if these actions help ensure that the recipient will someday repay the altruist in kind and thus enable the altruist to maximize her genetic replication. If an altruist gave away her resources to just anyone without any hope that it would some day be returned, the altruist would find it hard to survive and her undiscriminating altruistic genes would be eliminated. She would be "too good for her own good." Such an altruist would be a "sucker" in evolutionary terms. I may, for instance, be willing to help my unrelated neighbor; but if I continue to do so and he never reciprocates, I am very apt to stop helping that neighbor. If I continued to help, I would be classified as a sucker. But if my altruistic actions are reciprocated and I am helped in return, then I may better prosper and the chances of maximizing my genetic replication would be enhanced. "If you scratch my back, I'll scratch yours." Employers and employees regularly illustrate such reciprocal altruism, even though the tradeoffs may not be entirely equal. Vampire bats are known to regurgitate blood in order to feed a neighbor, back in the cave, who failed to feed that night. This saves the neighbor from starving. However, the starving bat will get such help only from a bat who recognizes that he or she has been helped by the needy bat on an earlier occasion. Others refuse to supply the food. This bat behavior is clearly a case of mutual back scratching. Whether or not such reciprocal altruism is "true altruism" is a question that has generated considerable discussion.[14] Indeed, truly altruistic self-sacrificing actions can be seen as evolutionary mistakes.[15] If altruism is understood in terms of psychological motive or intention, then the word does not apply to insects and probably not to most animal species. While kin-selection and reciprocal altruism are demonstrated among human beings, both reflect what David Hume called "confined generosity."

If evolutionary psychology explains various forms of altruistic behavior in terms of kin-selection and reciprocal altruism and its related qualities (goodwill, humility, faith, hope, charity), then it should also be able to explain the darker side of human and animal nature (envy, deceit, hate, anger, ferocity, enmity). This, of course, can be done by the same appeal to the selfish gene theory. In a world where resources are often limited, the organisms that most successfully maximize their genes are those that can defend themselves against enemies of various kinds. For human beings, two kinds of enemies are confronted. First there are those enemies that use human flesh for their own nourishment—various large carnivores and omnivores, as well as bacteria and virus. We have largely overcome the danger from carnivores and omnivores, and are fighting a continuing battle against our smaller enemies. The second enemy we confront are other human beings, those within our own societies and those we consider to be enemy nations or groups. Human beings, and many other species, without some genetically provided capacity for deceit, hate, anger, and ferocity would certainly lose their competitive advantage in the race for genetic replication. It seems, then, that any group struggling for survival would have its chances enhanced by practicing kin-selection and reciprocal altruism within the group while expressing various forms of enmity toward competing groups. Evolution appears to have resulted in various forms of tribalism with human tribalisms of nation, religion, and race resulting in disastrous forms of the "struggle for existence" that Thomas Malthus once described. Most animal species will defend their territories or feeding grounds, but only human beings, with their special ingenuity, have learned how to reek general havoc on their enemies.

The question to be examined now is whether or not these tendencies developed through the evolutionary process can give us any moral direction. If the genes we have inherited control the color of our eyes and skin as well as our height and intelligence, do they also make us selfish? Do the phenomena of kin selection and reciprocal altruism direct our moral decisions? Charles Darwin believed that a biological explanation can be given for humanity's moral proclivities.

> Any animal whatever, endowed with well-marked social instincts, the parental and filial affections being here included, would inevitably acquire a moral sense or conscience, as soon as its intellectual powers had become as well, or nearly as well developed, as in man.[16]

Contemporary biologist E. O. Wilson believes that "scientists and humanists should consider together the possibility that the time has come for ethics to be removed temporarily from the hands of the philosophers and biologized."[17] Granting that our moral proclivities may be rooted in our evolutionary heritage, the important question in current discussion is whether this heritage can tell us what we *ought* to do. An examination of that question and related issues follows.

Most scientists and philosophers agree that while our genetic heritage may incline us toward certain actions and relationships, it does not *determine* our actions. They reject a completely biological deterministic view that would claim that our genetic heritage *alone* causes our behavior just as that heritage causes the color of our eyes. This rejection reflects the view that nurture has an important role in modifying nature. Good parenting and good schools can make some difference. The socializing influences in our lives help shape our behavior. Just as a dog that may be inclined to join you on the couch can be "taught" to remain on the floor, even so some patterns of a child's behavior—or an adult's—can be altered through social processes such as teaching. Belief systems can play a significant role in behavioral change through a change in beliefs, as the Civil Rights movement demonstrated.

The question of *determinism* does raise the old issue of *psychological egoism*, the philosophical theory that human beings are always motivated by what they believe to be in their self-interest. If this theory is true, then it follows that it is impossible for a human being to choose to act in a truly altruistic way. A classic articulation of psychological egoism is found in Thomas Hobbes (1588-1779) who has been identified as the "first sociobiologist two hundred years before Darwin."[18] Hobbes claimed that all deliberate human actions are motivated by desires and that all human desires are self-interested. What we ultimately want is our own well-being and all rational acts aim at that well-being. Even apparent acts of altruism were, for Hobbes, merely forms of disguised self-love. His theory, like all formulations of psychological egoism, is not a normative theory designed to show how persons *ought* to act. It is, rather, a psychological theory about human nature which seeks to explain just *why* persons act in the way they do. Later, the founders of utilitarianism, Jeremy

Bentham and John Stuart Mill, both espoused a form of psychological egoism. Ethical egoism, however, differs from psychological egoism. Ethical egoism as a normative theory tells us we *ought* to pursue our own self-interests; while psychological egoism—a descriptive theory that seeks only to describe what *is* the case, not what *ought* to be—maintains that we always *do*, in fact, pursue what we believe to be in our self-interest.

A major difficulty in proving that the theory of psychological egoism is either true or false is that the theory is about motives, not about actions. Are all motives self-interested or selfish? It is difficult to discover what motives actually lie behind an action. Psychological egoism is certainly not a scientific theory that can be tested by way of empirical evidence. What kind of empirical evidence would count one way or another? Some formulations of psychological egoism result in a theory that appears to be patently false. Philosopher Joel Feinberg, for instance, defines psychological egoism as the theory that "all human actions when properly understood can be seen to be motivated by selfish desires."[19] While James Rachels, another philosopher, has the psychological egoist claim that "Each person is so constituted that he will look out *only* for his own interests.... In the final analysis, we care nothing for other people."[20] If psychological egoism is formulated in such terms, then it is easily defeated for there are a multitude of counter examples which show that such a theory must be false. A parent staying up all night to care for a sick child can hardly be accurately assessed as looking out "only for his own interests" or "motivated by selfish desires."

If psychological egoism is to have any credence, it must have a different formulation. I have proposed the following:

> Psychological Egoism is the theory that all deliberate human actions involve a motive that is either self-regarding or, if other-regarding, involve a self-referential stimulus without which the action could not have taken place.[21]

More simply, psychological egoism is the theory that no deliberate action is purely altruistic; instead, all such actions are motivated by either a self-interested or a self-referential element. The parent, for instance, may act out of concern for the sick child (not a "selfish" motive), but the action is clearly *self-referential* in that the child's well being constitutes an important element in the parent's flourishing. While this formulation of psychological egoism cannot be conclusively proven to be true, it avoids the easy refutation of the formulation proposed by Feinberg and Rachels.[22] It is of some interest to note that my formulation of the theory is compatible with the categories of kin selection and reciprocal altruism espoused by theories of evolutionary psychology. Both behavior patterns are clearly self-referential in terms of genetic interests.

A major reason for claiming that evolution cannot give us any moral advice comes from the work of 18th century philosopher David Hume. In his *A Treatise of Human Nature*, Hume argued that no empirical fact can, by itself, lead to some value claim or to some normative rule.[23] In short, he argued that no "is" can, by itself, yield some "ought." This is Hume's duly famous "is-ought" distinction. For instance, the following are two statements of empirical fact: 1) A human fetus is a living entity. 2) A human fetus has the potential, under the right conditions, to develop into an adult human being. But these two statements of fact do not, by themselves, entail any type of normative claim such as, "Abortion is morally wrong." (Note that 1) does not state that a human fetus is a person. Even if 1) *did* state that, no normative or moral claim could be logically derived from it.) In order to conclude "Abortion is morally wrong" from either 1) or 2), an additional premise that includes a moral judgment must be posited, such as 3) It is wrong to kill a human fetus. Furthermore, premise 3) is not itself derived from any empirical fact but is, itself, a moral judgment usually derived from other non-empirical claims such as a theological assertion. Given Hume's point, it follows that no biological fact, by itself, can ever yield a moral assertion. It may be a biological fact that human beings have a genetic propensity to have sympathy for others, especially their kin. But that fact, in itself, does not yield the normative rule "Have sympathy for others." Neither does the biological fact that human beings have some genetic propensity to kill those they see as dangers to themselves or their "tribe" yield the normative rule "Kill your enemies."

The genetic fallacy or the fallacy of origins may be applied to the evolution and ethics issue. This fallacy is committed when one claims that proposition X is false because it originates from a dubious source. For instance, if Joe made claim X, and I claimed that X must be false because Joe is a liar, then I have committed the genetic fallacy. Joe may, indeed, be a liar, but liars sometimes utter truths. Whether or not X is true or false will depend on other data, not on the fact the Joe uttered X. Sigmund Freud recognized that fallacy when he claimed that religious beliefs may be true even though their origins are rooted in psychological needs. Freud did claim that religious beliefs are false, but not because of their origins. In much the same way, one can claim that moral patterns may be "true" even if they are rooted in human evolutionary history. On the other hand, these moral patterns may be "false." (I put the quotation marks around "true" and "false" to indicate that the question of just how one validates or falsifies moral claims is open.) At any rate, the truth or falsity of moral patterns do not depend, it seems, on their evolutionary origins.

Finally, the role of *nurture* must be recognized since it is clear that beliefs can lead one to override a genetic predisposition. The choice of celibacy would be an example. Men and women of normal sexual drives elect to be celibate in a variety of religious traditions—Buddhism, Jainism, and some forms of Christianity—because of certain beliefs drawn from their traditions. From an evolutionary point of view, elected celibacy would appear to be a mistake since it eliminates the possibility of replicating the celibate's genes. On the other hand, if one insists that the theory of evolution is a theory of (almost) everything, then one would propose some evolutionary strategy even for elected celibacy. One possible theory would hold that such behavior by a small group of persons within a society might influence others by example. Such celibacy is usually accompanied by other forms of asceticism as a pledge of poverty, isolation from relatives, and an expressed compassion for all human beings and other creatures.

These "saint" figures may, by example, influence others in that society to live a more generally altruistic life in relation to others in their community. Among ordinary citizens, it may well be that we look for ways of encouraging just a bit more altruism in our neighbors than we, ourselves, would wish to express. Great saint figures may help us to encourage just such altruism in others. Furthermore, this caring within a community would certainly strengthen that community and enable it to survive in the face of attacks from other communities. Religions often provide a powerful bond in the believing community that can aid in that community's struggle against enemies. In this way religions can have an evolutionary value for that community.

On the other hand, one could argue that such behavior need not be explained in evolutionary terms at all. Evolutionary psychology, after all, suggests that evolutionary "strategy" is designed to maximize the replication of a gene pool and that self-sacrificing actions not designed to assist your family or clan would be a rejection of such strategy. But there are religious beliefs that show no interest whatsoever in extending a gene pool or maximizing genetic offspring in some form. These beliefs may run counter to what is deemed as evolutionary "success," but this, in itself, would not falsify such beliefs. The religions of India—Hinduism, Buddhism, and Jainism—have as their fundamental goal "release" from the endless round of rebirth or reincarnation into the problematic existence of earthly life. Maximizing their genetic offspring would have the unfortunate result of casting more "souls" into the suffering of earthly life. Jainism expresses this view vividly in what appears to be a "rigorously world-denying" spiritual outlook.[24] The Jain saint is thoroughly ascetic and their great saints escaped from embodied life by starving themselves to death. Their aim is to achieve release from embodied existence and find supreme bliss as a conscious soul at the top of the universe. Not all Jains (or Buddhists or Hindus) pursue the heroic spiritual pathways and, instead, marry and bring in the next generations. This enables such belief systems to stay off the endangered species list. A different fate faced the Shakers, a sect imported to the United States from England, who expected the return of Christ and also valued celibacy above marriage. After gaining a rather large of adherents in the 1800s, the sect declined and in July, 2001, seven women remained as members.

Another example of how beliefs would run counter to evolutionary "success" would be that of pacifism and the teaching to "love your enemies." The biologist-philosopher Sir Arthur Keith put the matter forcefully: "Christ annihilates the law of evolution, he throws a bomb right into the very heart of the machinery by which and through which nature has sought to build up races or breeds of mankind."[24] Pacifism and universal benevolence has been explained in evolutionary terms as an adaptive behavior among conquered or vulnerable people. Jesus taught, after all, when the Jews were under the heel of the Roman Empire that took no pity on those who resisted their rule. In that setting, cooperative and acquiescent behavior may be an effective survival strategy.[26]

On the other hand, beliefs may trump evolutionary inclinations. If a theistic worldview is embraced, then pacifism, universal benevolence, and some forms of asceticism may be appropriate responses to such beliefs and an evolutionary explanation need not be employed to account for such behavior. (Whether or not such beliefs are true is quiet another question.) We need to remember, however, that such pacifism, universal benevolence, and asceticism are not viewed as self-sacrificing *in the long run* by those who pursue these practices on religious grounds. From within these belief systems the promise of fulfillment for those who persevere is always there. A German Roman Catholic nun working hard at cleaning guest facilities put the matter succinctly: "Heaven is not cheap." The Muslim suicide bombers from radical Islamic sects evidently also see such acts of devotion to be a means of immediate pathway to Heaven. These last two examples, of course, are illustrations of what Michael Ruse meant when he wrote, "Furthermore the way our biology enforces its ends is by making us think that there is an objective higher code, to which we are all subject."[27] Conflicting worldviews clearly stand behind many of these claims and arguments. Ruse would, evidently, not only explain the phenomena of religion in evolutionary terms but would also suggest that such explanations show religious beliefs, as such, to be false. In doing this he appears to be committing the genetic fallacy which Freud avoided. As one would expect, other philosophers disagree with Ruse.[28] No doubt lively exchanges regarding the relationship between evolutionary theory and ethics will continue.

CHAPTER TEN

ISSUES IN RELIGION-BASED MORALITY

Do the gods love holiness because it is holy, or is it holy because the gods love it?   Plato[1]

The Good is simply what God wills that we should do, . .
                                      Emil Brunner[2]

    The analyses and arguments provided throughout this book are philosophical in nature, not theological. This implies that any claims made or criticisms offered are supported by reason and evidence, not by some claim to revealed truth based on an authoritative book (Torah, Bible, Koran), organization or person. Consequently, this chapter will examine religion-based morality from a philosophical point of view to identify any weaknesses or strengths that such a morality might reflect. The religion-based morality under scrutiny will be that derived from the dominant monotheistic traditions of the West: Judaism, Christianity, and Islam. The arguments put forward may well apply to other religious traditions, but there will be no attempt to cover those traditions given the limited intent of this work.
    If a moral system is to be deemed rational in its nature, then it follows that the foundations or basic assumptions of such a system ought also to be rational. Since the religion-based moral systems to be analyzed are those which claim that God exists, then that belief itself should have some rational basis. This brings us to a major problem of religion-based morality: Can belief in God be established as rational? What kind of evidence or argument could

establish this belief? Since this book is not a work in philosophy of religion, close scrutiny of various arguments will not be attempted. Instead, some general observations about efforts to provide proofs will be made.

Arguments for God's existence go back as far as Plato and Aristotle, and were either adopted or refined by philosophers in the monotheisms under scrutiny. Moses Maimonides (1135-1204) and Thomas Aquinas (1225-1274) are standard examples from the Jewish and Christian traditions of philosophers who presented serious arguments for the existence of God. Both, however, supplemented philosophical reason with beliefs grounded in scriptures they considered authoritative. Both believed that there is no necessary conflict between faith and reason; but neither believed that reason alone gave adequate expression of a fully developed faith.

Later, the arguments for God's existence came under robust philosophical fire from such influential thinkers as David Hume (1711-1774) and Immanuel Kant (1724-1804). Hume was most clearly an atheist, while Kant—who believed that God's existence cannot be proven—posited the existence of God as necessary for morality. Attacks leveled by Hume and Kant on the various arguments have challenged later attempts to reconstruct them.[3] The argument from necessary being and the design argument are still supported by some philosophers; but the general mood of current philosophy suggests that the standard arguments, however restated, convince only those who are already inclined to believe. As Hume demonstrated, the "God" that results from these arguments is devoid of the traditional attributes of the God of Judaism, Christianity, and Islam and has little to attract religious devotion. Most human beings would not be inclined to bend the knee to some "necessary being" or some ill-defined "designer." The current situation would be compatible with the Protestant Reformers, Luther and Calvin, who generally held that human reason creates idols instead of the true God whose nature, they believed, can be known only through the revelation of scripture.

The absence of proof, however, is not the proof of absence—as many have noted. But the problem of suffering, so powerfully confronted in the Biblical book of *Job*, still stands as a challenge to the rationality of believing in a God who is at once all-powerful and all-good.[4] Most philosophers would grant that belief in God is not necessarily a mark of irrationality, but the failure of the arguments for God's existence leaves religious belief in the realm of *faith*, not of *knowledge*. Hence any morality that is based on such belief must also be seen as an act of faith. That conclusion, however, would not be offensive to Aquinas, Luther, Calvin or the 20th century theologian Karl Barth.

If God exists to give moral guidance, another question appears. Which God exists? Many views of God have competed for human allegiance. The classic arguments for God's existence provided, at most, a highly abstract view of God with little content that would engage religious devotion. But religions flesh out their deity with stories, rituals and concepts that attract allegiance and commitment. Most believers are inducted into their faith by the cultural system in which they were raised, or they convert to a tradition for a variety of reasons. But the choice of a particular faith is seldom if ever the result of conclusive arguments or evidence since faith judgments have no such solid rational grounding. For believers, then, the challenge of "which God?" is answered by personal commitments that grow out of family, culture, groups, friendships and specific needs or longings. All of this roughly explains the basis for a religion-based morality; but this explanation does not constitute a rational justification of such a morality.

Another challenge to a religion-based morality has its origins in Plato's dialogue *Euthyphro* where Socrates constructs a dilemma to defeat his opponent. In effect, Socrates attacks the claim that morality is founded on the commands of God. A reconstruction of the argument has Euthyphro assert that some act X is morally good because it was commanded by God. Socrates then poses the dilemma with its two "horns": 1) Is act X morally good *just because* God commanded X, or 2) does God command X *because* it is morally good? If the first horn is affirmed, then it would appear that anything that God happened to command would be morally good just because God so commanded. But that would appear to make morality quite arbitrary. If God commanded, for instance, the abuse of innocent children, then such abuse would be seen as good because of God's command. If the second horn is affirmed, then it would appear that the morally good is independent of God's command, and that God commanded X because X was morally good for some reason other than the fact that God commanded X. This would imply that the morally good was somehow independent of God's will or command. Traditional Jewish, Christian or Islamic thought would reject both resulting conclusions.

Can a religion-based morality escape Plato's dilemma?[5] A Theist might break the first horn of the dilemma by arguing that God's commands cannot be arbitrary since God is good—meaning that God desires the fulfillment of the human beings created—and God's goodness implies that God would command only that which would be fulfilling for human beings. That is, since God created human beings, God would know full well the kind of moral pathway that would be fulfilling for human beings; and God, being good, would want human beings to be fulfilled. Hence God's commands are not arbitrary. Furthermore, since God created the universe and the creatures within it, all of the divine commandments given would be an aspect of this creation. Persons are created such that their fulfillment is best achieved by following God's commandments. Therefore, the morally good is not independent of the creative will of God. While this argument may escape Plato's dilemma, it does assume that God is good and that creation is the result of God's active creative will. Both of those are generally considered to be assertions of faith, not some form of knowledge grounded in argument or evidence. Defeating Plato's dilemma in this way does not, therefore, constitute a rational justification of a religion-based morality.

Religion-based morality has also been criticized as being immature and childlike since it is authority-driven and infantile in its basic nature. These critics allude to various research showing that small children are dependent on others not only for their protection and sustenance, but also as guides for living. This early stage of development has been described as "authority-bound and dualistic."[6] In this stage, "what a person really trusts, knows, and believes is finally based on some Authority 'out there.'" Sources of that authority could include particular persons, such as parents, teachers or religious leaders, as well as films, television, newspapers, magazines, popular entertainers and community customs. This stage is "dualistic" in that clear distinctions are made between what is true and untrue and what is right and wrong. "There is little or no tolerance for ambiguity."[7]

All this, so these critics point out, describes religion-based morality where God, through the Church or the scriptures, is the authority regarding moral right and wrong. Furthermore, the rules are often considered to be clear and unambiguous. The role of the believer-child is to accept and submit. Various religious traditions reflect this mood, as in the prayer, "In God's will is our peace," and "Not my will but thine be done." In Islam, a "Muslim" is one who finds peace through submission to God's will. The result of this authority-driven approach to morality, according to this criticism, is that the believer rejects his or her own responsibility for making a moral choice by giving it over to the authority. This believer can claim, "I am not responsible because I am only doing what authority X told me to do. Blame X, not me." In the end, then, the authority-driven nature of a religion-based morality results in an immature, childlike approach that, at the same time, rids the believer of personal responsibility.[8]

Two defenses can be proposed against the criticism that religion-based morality is authority-driven and immature. First, the defense would point out that in most areas of our lives we readily accept the advice and direction of those who properly hold authority as in the case of doctors, lawyers, investment counselors or scientists. As William James once pointed out, most of our beliefs are held solely because others hold them. For instance, the reader probably believes that the sun is at the center of our solar system solely because of the claims made by various authorities. Few of us have done the empirical research that can establish the truth of that theory. That being the case, it would appear to follow that getting moral guidance from some authority may also be respected. A second defense, related to the first, is to assert that

ISSUES IN RELIGION-BASED MORALITY

...the aim of moral reflection is that of discovering the most fulfilling way to live the human life. So if one believes in God, then it would generally follow that the believer would look to God for guidance in gaining such a life. God, after all, should be in the best position to give just such advice. These defenses, then, grant that religion-based morality is authority-driven, but contend that deferring to authority is, at times, appropriate. The question remains, of course, as to whether or not there are good reasons for submitting to the authority selected.

Perhaps the most radical attack on religion-based morality is made by those who claim that such morality is an expression of weakness and inferiority. Friedrich Nietzsche (1844-1900) put this charge in vivid terms when declaring that Christian morality was a *slave* morality that undercuts the basic human drive for power and self-affirmation.[9] In calling for kindness, humility, forgiveness, patience and friendliness, Christian morality, he asserted, was the reflection of the mediocre values of the "herd" mentality of those who hold deep resentment against people of strength. Such a morality was, for him, a denial of life itself. Christian morality inverted the life-affirming values of the Greeks, making what was once noble into vice and the qualities of weakness into virtues. With his proclamation that "God is dead," Nietzsche hoped for a freer and more vigorous type of humanity once belief in God was given up.

A less strident attack on Christian morality came from British philosopher Fitzjames Stephen. He rejected J. S. Mill's claim that the natural feeling for oneself and for one's friends could be gradually transformed into a general love for the human race Stephen called, instead, for a utilitarianism that teaches love of neighbor and hatred of enemies—with qualifications:

> Love your neighbor in proportion to the degree in which he approaches yourself and appeals to your passions and sympathies. In hating your enemy, bear in mind the fact that under immediate excitement you are very likely to hate him more than you would wish to do upon a deliberate consideration of all his relations to yourself

ISSUES IN RELIGION-BASED MORALITY

and to your friends, and of your permanent and remote as compared with your immediate interest.[10]

A more contemporary rejection of Christian morality comes from Richard Taylor who urges a return to the ethics of Aristotle and calls for the virtues of superiority--strength of mind, body and spirit.

> We have been taught that meekness is a virtue, that ignorance and stupidity are not moral faults, that the gods look upon the vulgar with the same favor as upon the wise. As a result our morality has become a kind of petty clockwork way of behaving, the point of which appears to be nothing nobler than innocence.[11]

A defense of a religion-based morality against the charges of Nietzsche, Stephen, and Taylor would admit that each raises the fundamental question about the meaning of human life and each gives a plausible response in the light of their non-religious worldviews. Such an observation would be fully in keeping with the central theme of this work.

Worldview choices are fundamental in shaping values and moral perspectives. On the other hand, historians could also suggest that many devoutly religious figures have reflected considerable strength of spirit, body, and mind in the face of adversity and challenge. St. Paul, Augustine, Bernard of Clairvaux, Jan Hus, Martin Luther, and more recent figures as Dorothy Day and Dr. Martin Luther King, Jr., come to mind. Each possessed great personal strength as well as a nobility of spirit.

The final criticism offered here is that of the evils done throughout history in the name of religion. These evils include the bloody wars within religious traditions, as the Thirty Years War (1618-1648) in early modern Europe, as well as those between religious groups, such as the Christian Crusades against the Muslims as well as the Muslim attacks on Christian lands. Currently, the carnage wrought by radical sects in a variety of countries calls to mind the possibilities of religiously motivated horrors.[12] All this raises the question of whether human history has benefited at all from its religious dimensions. In Chapter Six, the divisive nature of religion was described in some detail and need not be repeated here. One could argue that persons with evil intentions can make use of religion for their purposes just as persons may use science to perpetrate evil deeds. But the problem lies at a deeper level, since there is some evidence that the propensity for evil and divisiveness lies near to the center of many great religious traditions. The cry "God wills it!" that rallied Christian crusaders illustrates how the perceived anger of God has too often been an instrument wielded against various enemies. The image of the warrior God of the Old Testament who, at times, orders ethnic cleansing cannot be easily dismissed.

One defense of a religion-based morality against this charge suggests that the charge itself assumes the adequacy of religious morality in order to condemn the violence. The critic must stand on some moral ground to make such judgments, and the moral ground used appears to be that of traditional Western religious values: love, justice, peace, kindness, gentleness. To be sure, religious persons and movements have failed by their own standards, but the standards themselves can still be affirmed.

This same line of defense could grant that while some religious persons appear to justify conspicuously immoral deeds in the name of their religion, they have failed to understand or follow the basic moral precepts of their faith. Those who hold that love of neighbor is the basic commandment argue that no one honoring that commandment could justify the various forms of violence against a neighbor. "Love does no wrong to the neighbor; therefore, love is the fulfilling of the Law."[13] On the current world scene, for instance, many traditional Muslim scholars argue that terrorist acts against civilians are forbidden by Islamic law. This line of analysis brings some Jews, Christians, and Muslims to the conclusion that those who do violence in the name of God misrepresent the true traditions.

There are, however, a thicket of interpretive problems involved, not the least of which is that of deciding just who speaks truly for the faith. Perpetrators of violence openly express the belief that they are following the will of God (Yahweh, Allah) as understood in their traditions. Furthermore, these traditions are haunted by two questions: 1) "Who is my neighbor?" and 2) "How can I love both my neighbor and those who attack my neighbor?" These questions reveal the tribalistic tendencies in all traditions and indicate the difficulty in pursuing love as the basic principle of morality.

Proponents of a religion-based morality would present a series of arguments designed to show the advantages of such a morality. Even atheist J. L. Mackie contends, in his *Ethics: Inventing Right and Wrong*, that a

> theistic position...could make a significant difference to moral philosophy... the good for man might be more determinate, more unitary than we have allowed... and our task might be less that of making or remaking morality than of finding out, with the help of some reliable revelations, what God's creative will has made appropriate for man and what his prescriptive will requires of us.[14]

Mackie, himself, does not go the theological route, however, since he believes the theistic position is neither coherent nor correct. Others who assume that belief in God can be rationally justified in some way, could follow Mackie's lead and suggest a number of ways in which theism could provide an advantageous approach to ethics.

One difference theism could make would be that of overcoming the tension between "practical reason" (self-interest) and "moral reason" (duty). Practical reason maintains that the pursuit of one's own long-term interests is rational, while moral reason claims that the pursuit of moral duty is rational. The tension arises when it appears that some decisions will offend against either practical reason or moral reason. There may well be times when moral reason will lead us to conclude that our own interests must be set aside. And, at other times, practical reason may reveal that we need to set aside moral reason in order to achieve certain long-term interests. But proponents of a religion-based morality may point out that practical reason and moral reason are never in conflict since the pathway of morality based on religion is the surest way to long-term fulfillment. English theologian William Paley (1743-1805) makes just such a claim when he defined virtue as "the doing good to mankind, in obedience to the will of God, and for the sake of everlasting happiness."[15] While Paley's position may seem a bit crude, contemporary non-religious philosopher William Frankena concedes the point.

> ... it seems clear to me... that a universal coincidence of being moral and achieving the best score can be shown to be false—unless it is posited that there is a hereafter in which God will readjust the balance.[16]

Paley's definition of "virtue" is consistent with the claim put forward in this book—that all serious moral systems assert that the moral pathway is the fulfilling one. For the theist, then, there is no need to choose between practical and moral rationality, since they are fundamentally linked in a religious worldview. The theist might well grant that the believer, while walking the moral pathway, may appear to be forfeiting significant aspects of human experience. But in the final summation of things, in the life to come, the believer rests assured that true fulfillment is to be found, as Paley put it, in "everlasting happiness." The reality of such delayed gratification is a crucial element in traditional theistic worldviews.

A similar argument would claim that if Theism is true, then goodness—as defined by that theistic worldview—will eventually win out and one can take the high moral road with the expectation that, in the end, one's vision of things will prevail. This vision enables the believer to hold to a high moral ideal, in spite of the difficulties faced in life, and guards against despair, guilt, and cynicism. Faith, hope, and love are companions on life's journey. From this perspective, moral reasons can always trump non-moral reasons. William James makes a similar suggestion when he wrote that religion teaches two things.

> First, she says that the best things are the more eternal things, the overlapping things, the things in the universe

that throw the last stone, so to speak, and say the final
word. . . . The second affirmation of religion is that we are
better off even now if we believe her first affirmation to be
true.[17]

Finally, theists could claim that a theistic worldview allows a foundation for the belief that all human beings are to be treated as persons of equal dignity and worth. Chapter Six analyzed the link between the idea of equal dignity and worth and the concept of justice. Thomas Jefferson, for instance, reflected a theistic tradition in the Declaration of Independence: ". . . all men are created equal and are endowed by their creator with certain unalienable rights." Given his Enlightenment mindset, Jefferson could not be considered an orthodox theist; nevertheless, his worldview contained strong elements of that tradition. The claim of equal dignity would have been rejected by Aristotle, Nietzsche, and the contemporary Richard Taylor—largely because they reject a theistic worldview. And Epicurus—along with modern followers—would have found the claim of equal dignity to be without rational foundation or ethical implications.

John Mackie may well be correct when he notes that "the theological frontier of ethics remains open."[18] In the meantime, serious religious believers continue to apply their moral convictions to the activities of their own lives and the needs of their communities. They generally believe that morality is discovered, not invented. Equally serious non-believers who conclude with John Mackie that religious belief is neither coherent nor correct continue to invent a moral point of view that will provide a rational approach to the demands of our human situation as they perceive it. No doubt the debate between non-religious and religious believers will continue to be an aspect of our culture. While I have made no claim for the superiority of either of these beliefs, I have argued that these beliefs can shape our moral convictions in various ways—again, for good or ill.

Having followed William James in developing the point of morality in Chapter Two, it seems fitting to close with a summary of this most irenic philosopher's position regarding religious belief.[19] A thoroughly committed empiricist, James held that we are warranted to hold beliefs that are verified by scientific method but should reject those beliefs that are falsified by scientific method or logical contradiction. On the other hand, he argued that some religious beliefs—such as the existence of God—can neither be falsified nor verified by science or purely logical deductions. Such beliefs therefore require some other basis for rejecting or accepting them. Reflecting his interest in psychology as well as philosophy, James defended the following thesis: "Our passional nature not only may, but must, decide an option between propositions, whenever it is a genuine option that cannot by its nature be decided on intellectual grounds."[20] James used moral questions as examples of those that must be decided on passional grounds, since no particular empirical facts or logical truths can, by themselves, lead to a moral judgment. In this, James reflects the view of David Hume who was largely responsible for drawing the distinction between fact and value. For Hume, as for James, moral convictions are rooted in feelings or emotions, not in facts.

Making a parallel argument regarding religious beliefs, James asserted that these must be decided on the basis of feelings or "passions." Religious beliefs, he maintained, constitute a "genuine option" for some persons. He defined a "genuine option" as a choice between two propositions that is forced (not avoidable), live (not dead), and momentous (not trivial). A proposal for marriage is an example of a forced choice. The response to a proposal must be either "Yes' or "No" since "I'm not sure" or "Let me think it over" both effectively constitute a "No." Religious beliefs are, in like manner, forced options for *all* persons. Since beliefs, for James, are "rules for actions," religious beliefs necessarily lead to certain kinds of actions—such as prayer or perhaps worship with some believing community. In like manner, non-religious beliefs also represent rules for actions or the lack of—such as non-prayer or non-worship. Each day of our lives we commit ourselves to one set of actions or another, and by that commitment we demonstrate our beliefs. We cannot *not* choose; hence, belief is forced one way or another—religious or non-religious. We can, of course, change our beliefs from time to time and express that change in our actions.

An option is "momentous" if the choice involved leads to significant changes in life patterns and experiences. A marriage proposal would be a momentous option for most persons. James would consider the choice between holding and not holding religious beliefs to be momentous. He no doubt had in mind serious religious beliefs that implied certain life patterns and commitments. Furthermore, he argued that such beliefs are momentous whether or not they are true since the holding of the beliefs leads to significant differences in one's life. Consider, for instance, the life experience that follows from the monastic vow of obedience, poverty, and chastity.

An option that is "live, not dead," is one that has at least some appeal to what James refers to as our passional nature—to our wants, needs, and desires. He granted that religious belief may strike no living chords whatsoever for some persons so religious belief would not be a live option for them. Nevertheless, James held, the absence of a some living response to a religious message is, itself, an emotional factor which nullifies the "will to believe" in such persons. Their rejection of belief is not based altogether on fact or logic. But if the religious message has some emotional appeal to a person, then religious belief is live, forced, and momentous—a "genuine option" for that person.

James concluded that if religious belief is a genuine option for a certain person, then he or she has the "right to believe" on the basis of the emotional attraction of the belief. Furthermore, James maintains that such a believer cannot be faulted on evidential or logical grounds. The desire to hold the belief justifies holding the belief. Some caution must be introduced at this point. James did not claim that my desire to hold a belief somehow makes the belief true. Nor do I have the right to believe just anything I feel like believing just because I am attracted to it. James insisted that beliefs must always stand the test of empirical evidence and logical construction when such evidence is available. Some belief I might like to hold must be rejected if factual evidence counts against it.

Finally, James grants the same "right to believe" to the atheist as well as the theist since neither conviction can be falsified by way of scientific evidence or logical relations. The believer and the atheist stand on the same ground in that both hold their beliefs on the basis of their emotional inclinations—their "passions"—not on the basis of empirical fact or logical deduction.

Perhaps this is also where we must rest our moral convictions—or lack of them. As James asserted, "If your heart does not want a world of moral reality, your head will assuredly never make you believe in one."[21] We find in William James a reflection of existentialist thinkers who hold that all of us believe and act beyond what scientific evidence or formal logic can show us to be the case. James also reflected the influence of David Hume who maintained some two hundred years before James that "reason is and ought only to be the slave of the passions."[22]

END NOTES

CHAPTER ONE: A THEORY ABOUT MORAL THEORIES

1. Clifford Geertz, "Ethos, World-view and the Analysis of Sacred Symbols," in *A Reader in Modern Cultural Anthropology*, eds. Eugene Hammel and William Simmons (Boston: Little Brown and Co., 1970), 326.
2. W. D. Hudson, *Modern Moral Philosophy* (Garden City, N.Y.: Anchor Books, 1970), 321.
3. Richard Taylor, *Ethics, Faith and Reason* (Englewood Cliffs, New Jersey: Prentice-Hall, Inc., 1985), xiii. For his attack on religious ethics, see pp. 22-23.
4. John L. Mackie, *Ethics: Inventing Right and Wrong* (New York: Penguin Books, 1977), 232.
5. For a summary of such research, see Alan Wolfe, The Transformation of American Religion (New York: Free Press, 2003), 150 ff.
6. Recent and contemporary philosophers who defend the view that moral claims are related in some way to human wants, needs, desires, fulfillment or flourishing include: G. J. Warnock, *Contemporary Moral Philosophy* (London: Macmillan, 1967); Philippa Foot, "Moral Beliefs," and G. E. M. Anscombe, "Modern Moral Philosophy," both to be found in W. D. Hudson, ed., The Is/Ought Question (London: Macmillan, 1967); W. D. Hudson (1970): Alasdair MacIntyre, *After Virtue*, 2nd ed. (Notre Dame, Indiana: University of Notre Dame Press, 1964); John L. Mackie, *op. cit.*; and for a view tied to social contract theory, David Gauthier, *Morals By Agreement* (Oxford: Clarendon Press, 1986).
7. For an explanation of why systems of morality vary so much, see Wayne G. Johnson, "Explaining Diversity in Moral Thought: A Theory," *The Southern Journal of Philosophy* Vol. XXVI, No. 1, (1988): 115-133.

CHAPTER TWO: THE POINT OF MORALITY

1. R. D. Alexander, *The Biology of Moral Systems* (New York: Aldine DeGruyter, 1987), 1.
2. W. D. Hudson, *Modern Moral Philosophy*, 326.

3. William James, "The Moral Philosopher and the Moral Life," in *The Will to Believe and Other Essays in Popular Philosophy* (New York: Dover Publications, Inc., 1956). This analysis was also used by Richard Taylor in his *Good and Evil: A New Direction* (New York: The Macmillan Company, 1970) 125 ff.

CHAPTER THREE: MORAL THEORIES AND WORLDVIEWS

1. Leo Tolstoy, "Religion and Morality," in *Leo Tolstoy: Selected Essays*, trans. Aylmer Maude (Random House, 1964), 31 ff.
2. Richard Taylor, *Ethics, Faith, and Reason*, xiii.
3. Plato, *Theaetetus*, 152a.
4. Plato, *Crito*, 50b.
5. Plato, *Laws*, Book X, 885 ff.
6. W. K. C. Guthrie, *The Greeks and Their Gods* (Boston: Beacon Press, 1955), 364.
7. Frank Thilly and Ledger Wood, *A History of Philosophy* (New York: Holt, Rinehart and Winston, 1963), 110.
8. *Ibid*, 109.
9. An extended description of this 'excellent man" is given in *Nicomachean Ethics*, Book IV.
11 Richard Taylor, *Ethics, Faith and Reason*.
12 F. R. Barry, *Christian Ethics and Secular Society* (London: Hodder and Stoughton, 1966), 93.
13 R. E. O. White, *Christian Ethics* (Atlanta: John Knox Press, 1981), 100.
14 *The Gospel According to Matthew* 27:37-39.
15 *Romans* 13:10.
16 Brian Davies, *The Thought of Thomas Aquinas* (Oxford: Clarendon Press, 1992), 18.
17 David Hume, *An Enquiry Concerning Human Understanding*, in *The English Philosophers from Bacon to Mill*, ed. E. A. Burtt (New York: The Modern Library, 1939), 689.
18 David Hume, *A Treatise on Human Nature*, II, 3, 3., London, 1739.
19 S. E. Stumpf, *Socrates to Sartre: A History of Philosophy*, 3rd edition (New York: McGraw-Hill Book Company, 1982), 278.
20 David Hume, *The Philosophical Works of David Hume*. Edited by T. H. Green, and T. H. Grose. 4 vols. (London: Longman, Green, 1875), IV, 246.

21 Annette C. Baier, "David Hume," in *Encyclopedia of Ethics*, ed. L.C. Becker (New York: Garland Publishing, Inc, 1992), Vol. I, 569-570.
22 Alasdair MacIntyre, *A Short History of Ethics*, 2nd edition (Notre Dame: University of Notre Dame Press, 1998), 171.
23 Immanuel Kant, *Grounding for the Metaphysics of Morals*, trans. J. W. Ellington (Indianapolis: Hackett Publishing Company, 1981), 3.
24 George F. Thomas, *Religious Philosophies of the West* (New York: Charles Scribner's Sons, 1965), 249.
25 *Ibid.*, 250.
26 Jeremy Bentham, *An Introduction to the Principles of Morals and Legislation*, in E. A. Burtt, *op, cit.*, 791.
27 *Ibid.*, 793.

CHAPTER FOUR: RELIGION-BASED MORALITY: AN OVERVIEW

1 Clifford Geertz, *op. cit.*, 326.
2 See Becker, L. C., and Becker, C. B., eds. *Encyclopedia of Ethics* (New York: Garland Publishing, Inc. 1992) for helpful survey essays on ethics, philosophical and religious.
3 This imagery is adapted from J. S. Whale, *The Protestant Tradition* (Cambridge: Cambridge University Press, 1955), 140 ff. Whale acknowledges that he drew from a Buddhist source.
4 For a survey of the ethical theories of the Christian tradition, see R. E. O. White, *Christian Ethics: The Historical Development* (Atlanta, Georgia: John Knox Press, 1981). For a veiw of the ethics of non-Christian religions in the context of their own belief systems, see Noss and Noss, *A History of the World's Religions* (Upper Saddle River, New Jersey: Prentice-Hall, 1994).
5 Romans 13:10.
6 Augustine, *The Confessions of St. Augustine*, F. J. Sheed, translator (New York: Sheed and Ward, 1942), Book Two, Chapters iv-x.
7 Paul Tillich, *Systematic Theology* (Chicago: The University of Chicago Press, 1963), Volume III, 249 ff., and Paul Tillich, *The Protestant Era* (Chicago: The University of Chicago Press, 1957), 44 ff., and 55 ff.

CHAPTER FIVE: HOW "GOD" MAKES A DIFFERENCE

1 J. L. Mackie, *Ethics: Inventing Right and Wrong* (New York: Penguin Books, 1977), 232.

2. Richard Taylor, *Ethics, Faith, and Reason* (Englewood Cliffs, New Jersey: Prentice-Hall, Inc., 1985), 1-2.
3. Ibid., xviii.
4. William H. Halverson., *A Concise Introduction to Philosophy* (New York: Random House, Fourth Edition, 1981), Part XIV. I am indebted to Halverson for much of this analysis.
5. Richard Taylor, "The Meaning of Life," IN *The Meaning of Life*, ed. E. D. Klemke (New York: Oxford University Press, 1981, Chapter 10.
6. See Ernest Hemingway, *The Complete Short Stories of Ernest Hemingway* (New York: Charles Scribners Sons/Macmillan Publishing Company, 1987), 291.
7. John Henry Newman, in *Minister's Service Book*, compiled and edited by J. D. Morrison (New York: Harper and Brothers, Publishers, 1937), 215.
8. Bertrand Russell, "A Free Man's Worship," in E. D. Klemke, *op. cit.*, 61-62.
9. For a clear introduction to Kierkegaard's thought, see John Douglas Mullen, *Kierkegaard's Philosophy: Self Deception and Cowardice in the Present Age* (New York: New American Library, 1981).
10. Albert Camus, *The Fall*, Justin O'Brian,Translator (New York: Alfred A. Knopf, 1957).
11. See Paul Tillich, *The Courage To Be* (New Haven: Yale University Press, 1952) for his analysis of existential anxieties.
12. The data is from Raymond F. Paloutzian, *Invitation to the Psychology of Religion*, Second Edition (Boston: Allyn & Bacon, 1996).
13. Ernest Becker, *Escape From Evil* (New York: The Free Press, 1975) 4.
14. Blaise Pascal, *Pensees and Other Writings*, trans. Honor Levi (New York: Oxford University Press, 1995), 26 and 73.
15. See Paul Tillich, *The Courage to Be* (New Haven: Yale University Press, 1952) for a distinction between existential and neurotic anxiety.
16. See Peter Berger, *The Sacred Canopy: Elements of a Sociological Theory of Religion* (Garden City, New York: Doubleday Publishers, 1967), for this analysis of religious belief systems.
17. Ernest Becker, *The Denial of Death* (New York: The Free Press, 1973), ix.
18. Plato, *Phaedo* 64Z, in *Plato: Five Dialogues*, Translated by B. Jowett (Roslyn, N.Y., Walter J. Black, Inc., 1942), 92-93.

19. See David Noss, and John Noss, *A History of the World's Religions* (Upper Saddle River, New Jersey: Prentice Hall, Inc., 1994) 178 ff.
20. I Corinthians 15: 26.
21. Sigmund Freud, *The Future of an Illusion* (New York: Anchor Books Edition, 1964), Chapters 3 and 4.
22. See C. Bailey, *The Greek Atomists and Epicurus* (New York: Oxford University Press, 1928).
23. See Robert J. Lifton, *The Life of the Self: Toward a New Psychology* (New York: Simon and Shuster, 1976).
24. See Paul Tillich, *The Courage To Be*, for his analysis of end of age anxieties.
25. David Noss, and John Noss, *op. cit.*, 103.
26. *Ibid.*, 189 ff.
27. Ernest Becker, *The Denial of Death*, 5.

CHAPTER SIX: SELF, OTHERS, AND RIGHTS

1 Henry Sidgwick, *The Methods of Ethics* (New York: Dover Publications, Inc.), 246.
2 See Peter Singer, *Practical Ethics* (Cambridge: Cambridge University Press, 1993), and John Mackie, *Ethics: Inventing Right and Wrong* (New York: Penguin Books, 1977).
3 Jeremy Bentham, *An Introduction to the Principles of Morals and Legislation*, in *The English Philosophers From Bacon to Mill*, ed. E. A. Burtt (New York: The Modern Library, 1939), 791.
4 Robert Bellah, *Habits of the Heart* (Berkeley: University of California Press, 1985), 282.
5 MacIntyre, Alasdair, *After Virtue* (Notre Dame: University or Notre Dame Press, 1981), 201. For an observation that links our various stories with religion and nationalism, see Richard Alexander, *The Biology of Moral Systems* (New York: Aldine De Gruyter, 1987), 201 ff.
6 Ninian Smart, *Beyond Ideology* (San Francisco: Harper and Row, 1981) 227.
7 *Ibid.*, 234.
8 *Ibid.*, 222. For a link between evolutionary psychology and national loyalty by way of kinship metaphors, see Steven Pinker, The Blank Slate (New York: Viking Press, 2002), 247. ". . . people are more convinced by a political speech if the speaker appeals to their hearts and minds with kinship metaphors."

9   Robert Bellah, *op. cit*, 56.
10 See, for example, Mark Juergensmeyer, *Terror in the Mind of God* (Berkeley: University of California Press, 2000).
11 Galatians 3:28.
12 R. E. O. White, *Christian Ethics* (Atlanta: John Knox Press, 1981), 249 ff.
13 *Ibid.*, 256.
14 Mark Juergensmeyer, *op. cit.*
15 Jon Krakauer, *Under the Banner of Heaven: A Story of a Violent Faith* (New York: Doubleday, 2003).
16 Mark Juergensmeyer, *op. cit.*, 243.
17 Thomas Hobbes, *Leviathan*, in E. A. Burtt, *op. cit.*, 163.
18 Michael Ignatieff, *Human Rights As Politics and Idolatry* (Princeton: Princeton University Press, 2001), xxv.
19 Paul Lauren, *The Evolution of International Human Rights* (Philadelphia: University of Pennsylvania Press, 1998), 20.
20 *Ibid.*, 19.
21 See Michael J. Perry, *The Idea of Human Rights: Four Inquiries* (New York: Oxford University Press, 1998).
22 Brian Orend, *Human Rights: Concept and Content* (Peterborough, Canada: Broadview Press, 2002), 87.
23 J. S. Mill, *Utilitarianism* (1861), ed. George Sher (Indianapolis: Hackett, 1979), 52.
24 Brian Orend, *op. cit.*, 70. See, also, Richard Rorty, *Philosophy and Social Hope* (New York: Penguin Books, 1999), 83-88.
25 Joel Feinberg, *Social Philosophy* (Englewood Cliffs, New Jersey: Prentice-Hall, Inc., 1973), 94.

CHAPTER SEVEN: THE CHALLENGE OF ETHICAL RELATIVISM

1   William James, *The Will to Believe* (New York: Dover Publications, Inc., 1956), 23.
2   See Sharon Parks, *The Critical Years* (San Francisco: Harper Collins, 1991) for this argument.

CHAPTER EIGHT: WHY BE MORAL?

1   C. J. Ducasse, *A Critical Examination of the Belief in Life After Death.* (Springfield, Illinois: Charles C. Thomas, 1961), 24
2   Alasdair MacIntyre, *After Virtue* (Notre Dame, Indiana: University of Notre Dame Press, 1981), 67.

3 For extended analyses of the question "Why be moral?" see, for instance, William Frankena, *op. cit*, 114 ff; Ronald Green, *Religious Reason* (New York: Oxford University Press, 1978), chapters two and three; Peter Singer, *Practical Reason*, second edition (Cambridge: Cambridge University Press, 1933), chapter three.
4 Ronald Green, *op. cit.*, 20.
5 W. D. Hudson, *Modern Moral Philosophy* (Garden City, New York: Anchor Books, 1970), 326.
6 William Frankena, *op. cit.*, 115.
7 Richard Taylor, *Ethics, Faith, and Reason*, 108.
8 William Frankena, *op. cit.*, 19. Peter Singer makes much the same point in his *Practical Ethics*, 2nd edition (Cambridge: Cambridge University Press, 1993), 10 ff.
9 John Mackie, *op. cit.*, 190.
10 David Gauthier, "Morality and Advantage," in *20th Century Ethical Theory*, eds. S. Cahn and J. Haber (Englewood Cliffs: Prentice Hall, 1995), 438.
11 Kurt Baier, quoted in Gauthier, *ibid.*, 438.
12 William Frankena, *op. cit.*, 113 ff.
13 William Frankena, *Thinking About Morality* (Ann Arbor, Michigan: University of Michigan Press, 1980), 87.
14 *Ibid.*, p. 91.
15 William Frankena, *Ethics*, 113 ff. For Baier's complete argument see Kurt Baier, *The Moral Point of View* (New York: Random House, 1965), Chapter 5.
16 R. M. Hare, "Universalizability," in *Encyclopedia of Ethics*. For an extended discussion of the topic, see J. L. Mackie, *op. cit.*, and R. M. Hare, *Freedom and Reason* (Oxford: Oxford University Press, 1963), and *Moral Thinking* (Oxford: Oxford University Press, 1981).
17 Alasdair MacIntyre, *Whose Justice? Which Rationality?* (Notre Dame, Indiana: University of Notre Dame Press, 1988), 3.
18 *Ibid.*, 146 ff., for the development of the argument to follow. The quotations are from that work.
19 As quoted in S. E. Stumpf, *Socrates to Sartre* (New York: MacGraw-Hill, 1982), 111.
20 Alasdair MacIntyre, *Whose Justice? Which Rationality?*, 147.
21 Ibid., 148.
22 Ronald Green, *op. cit.*
23 G. E. M. Anscombe, "Modern Moral Philosophy," *Philosophy*, 33, No. 124 (January, 1958).
24 Richard Taylor, *op. cit.*, 89-90.

END NOTES

25 Stephen Prothero, *American Jesus: How the Son of God Became a National Icon* (New York: Farrar, Straus and Giroux, 2003), 30.

CHAPTER NINE: EVOLUTION AND ETHICS

1   Charles Darwin, *The Descent of Man and Selection in Relation to Sex*, 2 vols. (New York: Appleton, 1871) 500.
2   Richard Alexander, *The Biology of Moral Systems* (New York: Aldine DeGruyter, 1978), xvi.
3   Daniel Dennett, *Darwin's Dangerous Idea* (New York: Simon and Schuster, 1995), 21.
4   Ibid, p. 21.
5   Major contributors would include (in alphabetical order): R. D. Alexander, R. Axelrod, Richard Dawkins, Daniel Dennett, Anthony Flew, Stephen Jay Gould, Holmes Rolston, III, Michael Ruse, Peter Singer, R. L. Trivers, George C. Williams, Edward O. Wilson.
6   Edward O. Wilson, *On Human Nature* (Cambridge, Massachusetts: Harvard University Press, 1978), 167.
7   Michael Ruse and Edward O. Wilson, "The Evolution of Ethics." *New Scientist*, vol. 17, October, 1985, 51. Quoted in Daniel Dennett, *op. cit.*, 470.
8   Richard D. Alexander, *op. cit.*, 141.
9   See endnote 5, above, for a list of major contributors.
10 Richard Dawkins, *The Selfish Gene* (Oxford: Oxford University Press, 1976).
11 For an impressive development of the fear of death and its consequences for human beings, see Ernest Becker, *The Denial of Death* (New York: The Free Press, 1973).
12 Richard Dawkins, *op. cit.*, 3.
13 *Ibid.*, 130 ff.
14 See, for instance, E. Sober and D. S. Wilson, *Unto Others: The Evolution and Psychology of Unselfish Behavior* (Cambridge MA: Harvard University Press, 1988).
15 Richard Alexander, *op. cit.*, 191.
16 Charles Darwin, *The Descent of Man and Selection in Relation to Sex*, Chapter 4.
17 E. O. Wilson, *Sociobiology: The New Synthesis* (Cambridge Massachusetts: Harvard University Press, 1975), 27.
18 Daniel Dennett, *op. cit.*, 453.
19 Joel Feinberg, "Psychological Egoism," in *Moral Philosophy*, ed. George Sher (New York: Harcourt Brace Jovanovich, 1987), 5.

20 James Rachels, *The Elements of Moral Philosophy* (New York: Random House, 1986), 53-54. (My emphasis.)
21 Wayne Johnson, "Psychological Egoism: *Noch Einmal*," *Journal of Philosophical Research*, Vol. XVII, 1992, 243.
22 For an extended analysis of the entire issue, see the article listed in the above endnote. See also E. Sober, *From A Biological Point of View* (Cambridge: Cambridge University Press, 1994).
23 See David Hume, *A Treatise of Human Nature* (Oxford: Clarendon Press, 1978), 469.
24 David Noss and John Noss, *A History of the World's Religions* Ninth Edition (New Jersey: Prentice-Hall, Inc., 1994) 162 ff.
25 Sir Arthur Keith, *Evolution and Ethics* (New York: G. P. Putnam's Sons, 1947), 65.
26 Richard Alexander, *op. cit.*, 176.
27 Michael Ruse, *op. cit.*, 51.
28 For example, see Holmes Rolston, III, *Genes, Genesis and God* (Cambridge: Cambridge University Press, 1999).

CHAPTER TEN: ISSUES IN RELIGION-BASED MORALITY

1 Plato, *Euthyphro*, Transl. William Jowett (New York: Charles Scribner's Sons, 1889).
2 Emil Brunner, *The Divine Imperative*, Transl. Olive Wyon, (Philadelphia, The Westminster Press, 1947), 117.
3 For a review of the classical arguments see John Hick, *Arguments for the Existence of God* (New York: Herder and Herder, 1971), and John Mackie, *The Miracle of Theism* (Oxford: Clarendon Press, 1982). For a current restatement of some of the arguments, see Richard Swinburne, *Is There A God* (New York: Oxford University Press, 1996). David Hume's attack is in *Dialogues Concerning Natural Religion,* ed. N. K. Smith (New York: Social Science Publishers, 1948).
4 See, for instance, John Hick, *Evil and the God of Love* (New York: Harper and Row Publishers, 1966).
5 For a view that claims Plato's dilemma undermines the view that the good is what God commands, see Peter Singer, *Practical Ethics*, second edition (Cambridge: Cambridge University Press, 1993), 3. Atheist John Mackie gives a lively defense of religion-based morality against Plato's dilemma in his *Ethics: Inventing Right and Wrong,* (London: Penguin Books, 1990) 229 ff.

6   See Sharon Parks, *The Critical Years: Young Adults and the Search for Meaning, Faith, and Commitment* (San Francisco, Harper Collins Publishers, 1991).
7   *Ibid.*, 45.
8   For a case study of this form of morality, see the description of some Mormon fundamentalists in Jon Krakauer, *Under the Banner of Heaven: A Story of a Violent Faith* (New York: Doubleday, 2003).
9   See Chapter Three for a more developed discussion of Nietzsche's morality in the context of his wider philosophical position.
10 Quoted by John Mackie, *Ethics: Inventing Right and Wrong*, 171.
11 Taylor, Richard, *op. cit.*, xiii.
12 For examples from many religious traditions in the modern world, see Mark Jeurgensmeyer, *Terror in the Mind of God* (Berkeley: University of California Press, 2000).
13 Romans 13:10.
14 John Mackie, *Ethics: Inventing Right and Wrong*, 232.
15 *Ibid.*, 227.
16 William Frankena, *Thinking About Morality* (Ann Arbor, Michigan: Michigan University Press, 1980), 91.
17 William James, *The Will to Believe and Other Essays in Popular Philosophy* (New York, Dover Publications, Inc., 1956), 25-26.
18 John Mackie, *Ethics: Inventing Right and Wrong*, 232.
19 William James develops his position in "The Will To Believe," *op. cit.*
20 *Ibid.*, 11.
21 David Hume, *The Philosophical Works of David Hume*, eds. T. H. Green and T. H. Grose. 4 vols. (London: Longman, Green, 1875) IV, 246.

BIBLIOGRAPHY

Alexander, Richard. *The Biology of Moral Systems.* New York: Aldine De Gruyter, 1987.

Anscombe, G. E. M. "Modern Moral Philosophy." In *The Is/Ought Question,* edited by W. D. Hudson. London: Macmillan, 1967.

Aristotle. "Nicomachean Ethics." In *Classics of Western Philosophy,* Fourth Edition, edited by Steven Cahn. Indianapolis: Hacket Publishing Company, Inc., 1995.

Augustine. *The Confessions of St. Augustine.* Translated by F. J. Sheed. New York: Sheed and Ward, 1942.

Baier, Annette. "David Hume." In *Encyclopedia of Ethics,* edited by L. C. Becker, New York: Garland Publishing, Inc., 1992.

Baier, Kurt. *The Moral Point of View.* Ithaca, New York: Cornell University Press, 1958.

Bailey, C. *The Greek Atomists and Epicurus.* New York: Oxford University Press, 1928.

Barry, F. R. *Christian Ethics and Secular Society.* London: Hodder and Stoughton, 1966.

Becker, Ernest. *The Denial of Death.* New York: Free Press, 1973.

------------------. *Escape From Evil.* New York: The Free Press, 1975.

Becker, L. C., and Becker, C. B. eds. *Encyclopedia of Ethics.* New York: Garland Publishing, Inc., 1992.

Bellah, Robert. *Habits of the Heart.* Berkeley: University of California Press, 1985.

Bentham, Jeremy. "An Introduction to the Principles of Morals and Legislation." In *The English Philosophers from Bacon to Mill,* edited by E. A. Burtt. New York: Modern Library, 1939.

Berger, Peter. *The Sacred Canopy: Elements of a Sociological Theory of Religion.* Garden City, New York: Doubleday Publishers, 1967.

Bible, The Oxford Annotated, Revised Standard Version. New York: Oxford University Press, 1962.

Broad, C. D. "Egoism as a Theory of Human Motives." In *Egoism and Altruism.* Edited by R. D. Milo. Belmont, California: Wadsworth Publishing Co., 1973.

Brunner, Emil. *The Divine Imperative.* Translated by Olive Wyon. Philadelphia: The Westminster Press, 1947.

Burtt, Edwin A. ed. *The English Philosophers from Bacon to Mill.* New York: Modern Library, 1939.

Butler, Joseph. *Five Sermons*. New York: Bobbs-Merrill, 1950.
Cahn, Steven M. ed. *Classics of Western Philosophy*. Fourth Edition. Indianapolis: Hackett Publishing Company, 1995.
Camus, Albert. *The Fall*. Translated by Justin Obrian. New York: Alfred A. Knopf, 1957.
Carmody, D. L., and Carmody, J. T. *How to Live Well: Ethics in the World Religions*. Belmont, California: Wadsworth Publishing Company, 1988.
Darwin, Charles. *The Descent of Man and Selection in Relation to Sex*. New York: Appleton, 1871.
——————. *On the Origin of Species*. First Edition. Cambridge: Harvard University Press, 1964.
Davies, Brian. *The Thought of Thomas Aquinas*. Oxford: Clarendon Press, 1992.
Dawkins, Richard. *The Selfish Gene*. Oxford: Oxford University Press, 1976.
Dennett, Daniel. *Darwin's Dangerous Idea*. New York: Simon and Schuster, 1995.
Ducasse, C. J. *A Critical Examination of the Belief in Life After Death*. Springfield, Illinois: Charles C. Thomas, 1961.
Feinberg, Joel. "Psychological Egoism." In *Moral Philosophy*. Edited by George Sher. New York: Harcourt Brace Jovanovich, 1987.
——————. *Social Philosophy*. Englewood Cliffs, New Jersey: Prentice-Hall, Inc., 1973.
Foot, Philippa. "Moral Beliefs." In *Proceedings of the Aristotelian Society*, LIX, 1958-59.
——————. "Morality as a System of Hypothetical Imperatives." In Philippa Foot, *Virtues and Vices*. New York: Oxford University Press, 1978.
Frankena, William. *Ethics*. Englewood Cliffs, New Jersey: Prentice-Hall, Inc., 1963.
——————. Thinking About Morality. Ann Arbor, Michigan: University of Michigan Press, 1980.
Freud, Sigmund. *The Future of an Illusion*. New York: Anchor Books Edition, 1964.
Gauthier, David. "Morality and Advantage." In *20th Century Ethical Theory*, edited by S. Cahn and J. Haber. Englewood Cliffs: Prentice Hall, 1995.
——————. ed. *Morality and Rational Self-Interest*. Englewood Cliffs, New Jersey: Prentice Hall, Inc., 1970.

———. *Morals By Agreement*. New York: Oxford University Press, 1986.
Gaylin, Willard. *Hatred: The Psychological Descent into Violence*. New York: Public Affairs, 2003.
Geertz, Clifford. "Ethos, World-view and the Analysis of Sacred Symbols." In *A Reader in Modern Cultural Anthropology*, edited by E. Hammel and W. Simmons. Boston: Little Brown and Co., 1970.
———. "From Sine Qua Non to Cultural Systems." In *Ways of Understanding Religion*, edited by Walter Capps. New York: MacMillan Co., 1972.
———. "Religion as a Cultural System." In *Reader in Comparative Religion: An Anthropological Approach*, edited by Lessa and Vogt. New York: Harper and Row, 1958.
Green, Ronald. *Religion and Moral Reason*. New York: Oxford University Press, 1988.
———. *Religious Reason*. New York: Oxford University Press, 1978.
Guthrie, W. K. C. *The Greeks and Their Gods*. Boston: Beacon Press, 1955.
Halverson, William. A *Concise Introduction to Philosophy*. Fourth Edition. New York: Random House, 1981.
Hare, R. M. *Freedom and Reason*. Oxford: Oxford University Press, 1963.
———. *The Language of Morals*. New York: Oxford University Press, 1952.
———. *Moral Thinking*. Oxford: Oxford University Press, 1981.
Heil, John. *Rationality, Morality, and Self-Interest*. Lanham, Maryland: Rowman & Littlefield Publishers, Inc., 1993.
Hemingway, Ernest. *The Complete Short Stories of Ernest Hemingway*. New York: Charles Scribners Sons/Macmillan Publishing Company, 1987.
Hick, John. *Arguments for the Existence of God*. New York: Herder and Herder, 1971.
———. *Evil and the God of Love*. New York: Harper and Row Publishers, 1966.
Hobbes, Thomas. *Leviathan*. In *The English Philosophers from Bacon to Mill*, edited by E. A. Burtt. New York: The Modern Library, 1939.
Hudson, W. D. *The Is/Ought Question*. London: Macmillan, 1967.

——————. *Modern Moral Philosophy*. Garden City, New York: Anchor Books, 1970.

Hume, David. *Dialogues Concerning Natural Religion*. Edited by N. K. Smith. New York: Social Science Publishers, 1948.

——————. "An Enquiry Concerning Human Understanding." In *The English Philosophers from Bacon to Mill*. Edited by E. A. Burtt. New York: The Modern Library, 1939.

——————, *The Philosophical Works of David Hume*. Edited by T. H. Green and T. H. Grose, 4 volumes. London: Longman, Green, 1875.

——————. *A Treatise of Human Nature*. Oxford: Clarendon Press, 1978.

Ignatieff, Michael. *Human Rights As Politics and Idolatry*. Princeton, New Jersey: Princeton University Press, 2001.

James, William. "The Moral Philosopher and the Moral Life." In William James, *The Will to Believe and Other Essays in Popular Philosophy*. New York: Dover Publications, 1956.

——————. *Pragmatism and the Meaning of Truth*. Cambridge: Harvard University Press, 1978.

Johnson, Wayne G. "Explaining Diversity in Moral Thought: A Theory." In *The Southern Journal of Philosophy*, Vol. XXVI. No. 1, 1988.

——————. "The Freight of God." In *The Existence of God: Essays from the Basic Issues Forum*, edited by Jacobson and Mitchell. Lewisten, Maine: Edwin Mellen Press, 1988.

——————. "Psychological Egoism: *Noch Einmal.*" In *Journal of Philosophical Research*, Vol. XVII, 1992.

Juergensmeyer, Mark. *Terror in the Mind of God: The Global Rise of Religious Violence*. Berkeley: University of California Press, 2001.

Kant, Immanuel. *Grounding for the Metaphysics of Morals*. Translated by J. W. Ellington. Indianapolis: Hackett Publishing Co., 1981.

Keith, Sir Arthur. *Evolution and Ethics*. New York: B. P. Putnam's Sons, 1947.

King, Winston L. *In the Hope of Nibbana: The Ethics of Theravada Buddhism*. LaSalle, Illinois: Open Court, 1964.

Krakauer, Jon. *Under the Banner of Heaven: A Story of a Violent Faith*. New York: Doubleday, 2003.

Lauren, Paul. *The Evolution of International Human Rights*. Philadelphia: University of Pennsylvania Press, 1998.

Lifton, Robert J. *The Life of the Self: Toward a New Psychology.* New York: Simon and Schuster, 1976.

MacIntyre, Alasdair. *After Virtue: A Study in Moral Theory.* Notre Dame, Indiana: University of Notre Dame Press, 1981.

------------. *A Short History of Ethics.* New York: Macmillan Co., 1966.

------------. *Three Rival Versions of Moral Inquiry.* Notre Dame, Indiana: University of Notre Dame Press, 1990.

------------. Whose *Justice? Which Rationality?* Notre Dame, Indiana: University of Notre Dame Press, 1988.

Mackie, John. *Ethics: Inventing Right and Wrong.* New York: Penguin Books, 1977.

------------. *The Miracle of Theism.* Oxford: Clarendon Press, 1982.

Mill, J. S. *Utilitarianism.* Edited by George Sher. Indianapolis: Hackett Publishers, 1979.

Mitchell, Basil. *Morality: Religious and Secular.* Oxford: Oxford University Press, 1980.

Mullen, John Douglas. *Kierkegaard's Philosophy: Self Deception and Cowardice in the Present Age.* New York: New American Library, 1981.

Nielsen, Kai. *Ethics Without God.* Buffalo, New York: Prometheus Books, 1973.

Nietzsche, Friedrich. The *Joyful Wisdom.* Translated by Thomas Common. London: George Allan and Unwin Ltd., 1910.

Noss, D. S., Noss, J. B. *A History of the World's Religions.* Upper Saddle River, New Jersey: Prentice Hall, 1994.

Nowell-Smith, P. H. *Ethics.* Baltimore, Maryland: Penguin Books, 1969.

Orend, Brian. *Human Rights: Concept and Content.* Peterborough, Canada: Broadview Press, 2002.

Paloutzian, Raymond. *Invitation to the Psychology of Religion*, Second Edition. Boston: Allyn and Bacon, 1996.

Pascal, Blaise. *Pensees and Other Writings.* Translated by Honor Levi. New York: Oxford University Press, 1995.

Parks, Sharon. *The Critical Years: Young Adults and the Search for Meaning, Faith, and Commitment.* San Francisco: Harper Collins Publishers, 1991.

Perry, Michael. *The Idea of Human Rights: Four Inquiries.* New York: Oxford University Press, 1998.

Plato. *Complete Works of Plato*. Edited with introduction and notes by John M. Cooper, associate editor P. S. Hutchinson. Indianapolis: Hackett Publishing Company, Inc., 1997.

Prothero, Stephen. *American Jesus: How the Son of God Became a National Icon.* New York: Farrar, Straus and Giroux, 2003.

Rachels, James. *The Elements of Moral Philosophy*. New York: Random House, 1986.

Rawls, John. *A Theory of Justice*. Cambridge, Massachusetts: Harvard University Press, 1971.

Rolston, Holmes, III. *Genes, Genesis and God*. Cambridge: Cambridge University Press, 1999.

Rorty, Richard. *Philosophy and Social Hope*. London, England: Penguin Books, 1999.

Russell, Bertrand. "A Free Man's Worship." In *The Meaning of Life*. Edited by E. D. Klemke. New York: Oxford University Press, 1981.

——————. *Why I Am Not A Christian*. New York: Simon and Schuster, 1967.

Scheibe, Karl. *Beliefs and Values*. New York: Holt, Rinehart and Winston, 1970.

Schneewind, J. B. ed. *Reason, Ethics, and Society*. Chicago, Illinois: Open Court, 1996.

Sidgwick, Henry. *The Methods of Ethics*. New York: Dover Publications, Inc., 1966.

——————. *Outlines of the History of Ethics*. Boston: Beacon Press, 1960.

Singer, Peter. *Practical Ethics*. Cambridge: Cambridge University Press, 1993.

Smart, Ninian. *Beyond Ideology*. San Francisco: Harper and Row, 1981.

——————. *Worldviews: Crosscultural Explorations of Human Beliefs*. New York: Charles Scribner's Sons, 1983.

Sober, E. *From A Biological Point of View*. Cambridge: Cambridge University Press, 1994.

——————, and Wilson, D. S. *Unto Others: The Evolution and Psychology of Unselfish Behavior*. Cambridge MA: Harvard University Press, 1988.

Stark, Rodney. *For the Glory of God*. Princeton: Princeton University Press, 2003.

Stout, Jeffrey. *Ethics After Babel: The Languages of Morals and Their Discontents*. Boston: Beacon Press, 1988.

———————. *The Flight From Authority: Religion, Morality, and the Quest for Autonomy*. Notre Dame, Indiana: University of Notre Dame Press, 1981.

Strauss, Leo. *Natural Right and History*. Chicago: University of Chicago Press, 1953.

Stumpf, S. E. *Socrates to Sartre*. New York: MacGraw-Hill, 1982.

Swinbourne, Richard. *Is There a God?* New York: Oxford University Press, 1996.

Taylor, Richard. *Ethics, Faith, and Reason*. Englewood Cliffs, New Jersey: Prentice-Hall Inc., 1985.

———————. *Good and Evil*. New York: The Macmillan Company, 1970.

———————. "The Meaning of Life." In *The Meaning of Life*, edited by E. D. Klemke. New York: Oxford University Press, 1981.

Thilly, Frank, and Wood, Ledger. *A History of Philosophy*. New York: Holt, Rinehart and Winston, 1963.

Thomas, George F. *Religious Philosophies of the West*. New York: Charles Scribner's Sons, 1965.

Tillich, Paul. *The Courage to Be*. New Haven: Yale University Press, 1952.

———————. *Love, Power, and Justice*. New York: Oxford University Press, 1954.

———————. *The Protestant Era*. Chicago: The University of Chicago Press, 1957.

———————. *Systematic Theology*. Three Volumes. Chicago: The University of Chicago Press, 1963.

Tolstoy, Leo. "Religion and Morality." In *Leo Tolstoy: Selected Readings*, translated by Aylmer Maude. New York: Random House, 1964.

Waley, Arthur. *Three Ways of Thought in Ancient China*. Garden City, New York: Doubleday and Company, 1939.

Warnock, G. J. *Contemporary Moral Philosophy*. London: Macmillan, 1967.

———————. *The Object of Morality*. London: Methuen, 1971.

Whale, J. S. *The Protestant Tradition*. Cambridge: Cambridge University Press, 1955.

White, R. E. O. *Christian Ethics*. Atlanta, Georgia: John Knox Press, 1981.

Williams, Bernard. *Ethics and the Limits of Philosophy*. Cambridge, Massachusetts: Harvard University Press, 1985.

Wilson, Edward O. *On Human Nature*. Cambridge, Massachusetts: Harvard University Press, 1978.

———. *Sociobiology: The New Synthesis*. Cambridge, Massachusetts: Harvard University Press, 1975.

Wilson, James Q. *The Moral Sense*. New York: Simon and Schuster, 1993.

Wolfe, Alan. *The Transformation of American Religion*. New York: Free Press, 2003.

BIOGRAPHICAL SKETCH

Wayne G. Johnson received a degree in civil engineering at Iowa State University in Ames, Iowa, and was then employed as a bridge design engineer at the Iowa Highway Commission. His life interests changed when he faced important questions he could not solve with mathematical equations and his slide-rule. After receiving a Bachelor of Divinity degree from Andover Newton Theological School and a Ph. D. from the University of Iowa, he taught at Carthage College and then at the University of Wisconsin-Parkside. He received outstanding teaching awards at both institutions, has published two other books and a number of scholarly articles, and is now Emeritus Professor of Philosophy at UW-Parkside. Since retirement, he has chaired two peace and justice organizations in Racine. The father of four children, he and his wife, Jeanne, reside in Racine, Wisconsin.

INDEX

Note: Some entries that appear throughout the book, such as God, Allah, Yahwey, are not consistently listed in the Index.

absolutist
  principle, 98
  rule, 98
agnostic, 4
altruism, 166
altruism, reciprocal, 188
altruistic behavior, 167
Alexander, R. D., 17, 181, 184, 213, 217, 220-223
Ambrose, 56
Aquinas, Thomas, 4, 26, 56-58, 62, 64, 141, 166-167, 179, 200-201
analytic proposition, 65, 66
Anscombe, G. E. M., 178, 213, 219, 223
Apollo, 84
Aristotle, 5, 9, 12, 26, 50-56, 58, 59, 92, 123, 166, 167, 179, 205, 223
atheism, 92
Atomists, 35, 120
Augustine, 4, 45, 56-58, 60, 102, 162, 166-167, 179, 205, 215, 223
autonomy, 102-103
Axelrod, R., 220
Ayer, A. J. 87-89
Baha'i, 132
Baier, Annette, 215, 223
Baier, Kurt, 169-170, 172, 219
Bailey, C. 217, 223
Barry, F. R., 214, 223
Barth, Karl, 201, 223

Becker, Ernest, 117-118, 124, 216-217, 220, 223
Bellah, Robert, 129, 217-218, 223
Bentham, Jeremy, 75-77, 128, 167, 171, 179, 192, 215, 217, 223
Berger, Peter, 116, 216
Bhagavad-Gita, 136
Bible, 98, 223
Bill of Rights, 138
Boswell, James, 69
Brahmin, 121
Broad, C. D., 223
Broad Theory, My 7-8
Brunner, Emil, 199, 221, 223
Buddha, 93, 118, 122
Buddhism, 11-12, 91, 102, 122, 131, 135, 179, 195
Burtt, E. A., 214-215, 217, 223
Butler, Joseph, 224
Calvin, John, 5, 58, 62, 96, 101, 179, 200-201
Camus, Albert, 113, 216, 224
Carvaka, 37
categorical imperative, 13, 72
category of the mind, 70
cat hold model, 95
cause-effect, 70
Christianity, 3, 91, 100, 109, 179
Cicero, 176
city state, 38-39
class struggle, 81
cognitive meaning, 88

Communist, 137
Corinthians, Letter to, 217
cosmic meaning, 108, 115
contract, 64
cultural relativism, 147
Crusades, 205
Darwin, Charles, 82, 181-182, 190, 220, 224
Davies, Brian, 214, 224
Dawkins, Richard, 185-186, 220, 224
death anxiety, 118
Declaration of Independence, 97, 139, 143, 209
Demiurgos, 40
Dennett, Daniel, 182, 220, 224
deontological, 10-11
despair, 113-114
determinism, 80, 191
divine command theory, 10-11, 45
Divine Craftsman, 40-41
divine law, 59
divine law: functions of:
    saving, 100
    civil, 100
    normative, 100-101
    theological, 100-101
Dionysus, 84
Don Juan, 113
Dostoevsky, F., 85, 92
dualism of practical reason, 127
DuCasse, C. J., 161, 218, 224
duty, 71
egoistic hedonism, 35
emotive theory, 87
entelechy, 53
Epicurus, 5, 9, 12, 24-25, 34-37, 92, 119-120, 148, 159, 162, 166-167

eros, 45
ethical absolutism, 146-147
ethical egoism, 26, 159, 192
ethical relativism, 145-160
eudaemonia, 54
Euripides, 38
evolution, 182-197
evolutionary psychology, 185
experiential transcendence, 120
Euthyphro, 201
fact, 6
faith, 115
Fall, The, 100
Far East, 9
Feinberg, Joel, 143-144, 192, 218, 220, 225
Flew, Anthony, 220
Foot, Philippa, 213, 224
forms, Platonic, 40, 44, 50
forms of intuition, 70
Fox, George, 134
Frankena, Wm., 165, 168, 170-173, 208, 219, 222, 224
Freud, S. 16, 119, 179, 197, 217, 224
fulfillment, 8-9, 26, 60, 69
Galatians, Letter to, 218
Gandhi, M., 135-136, 140
Garden of Eden, 22
Gauthier, David, 168, 170, 213, 219, 224
Gaylin, Willard, 225
Geertz, Clifford, 1, 91, 213, 215, 225
Genesis, Book of, 15
genetic fallacy, 16, 194
genuine option, 210
God, death of, 83
God, proofs of, 200-201
golden mean, 54
Goldstein, Baruch, 136

INDEX

Gould, Stephen J., 220
Green, Ronald, 163, 167, 219, 225
Guthrie, W. K. C., 214, 225
Halverson, W. H., 216, 225
happiness, 8, 54, 58, 73-75, 77
Hare, R. M., 215, 225
Heaven, 96, 179
Hebrew Bible, 30
Hebrew Prophets, 30-31
Hegel, 79
Heil, John, 22
Hell, 96, 179
Hemingway, E., 109, 216, 225
heroism, 124
Hesiod, 32
heteronomy, 102-103
Hick, John, 221, 225
Hill, Rev. Paul, 136
Hinduism, 11, 15, 91, 122, 135, 179, 195
historical materialism, 79
Hobbes, Thomas, 62-65, 80, 139, 191, 218, 225
Homer, 31-32
Hudson, W. D., 1, 17, 164, 213, 219, 225
Hume, David, 65-70, 89, 126, 189, 193, 200, 210, 214, 221-222, 226
ideologies, 129
Ignatieff, M., 218, 226
ignorance, 102
Iliad, 32
immortality, 50, 74
  symbolic, 120
Islam, 3, 91, 109, 179
Jainism, 11, 135, 195
James, William, 2, 18, 181, 203, 208-212, 214, 218, 222, 226
Japan, 131, 134

Jews, 97
Job, 201
John, Gospel of, 134
Johnson, Wayne, 213, 221, 226
Judaism, 3, 91, 109, 179
Juergensmeyer, Mark, 218, 222, 226
justice, 42, 74
Kant, I., 10, 12-13, 24, 70-74, 92, 167, 171, 177, 200, 215, 226
Karma, 11, 15, 19, 43, 95, 100, 121, 135
Keith, Sir Alfred, 196, 221, 226
Key, Francis Scott, 125
Kierkegaard, Soren, 84-86, 111-115, 117, 121, 216
King, M. L., Jr., 135, 205
King, Winston, 226
kin selection, 188
Krakauer, Jon, 218, 222, 226
Language, Truth, and Logic, 87
Lauren, Paul, 218, 226
law, 59
Laws (Plato), 38-39, 41
Leviticus, 31
Lifton, Robert, 120, 217, 227
light of Christ, 134
Locke, John, 92, 141-142, 179
love, 57, 61
Luther, Martin, 5, 44, 58, 62, 96, 200-201, 205
lying, 72
MacIntyre, Alasdair, 129, 161, 170, 174-177, 213, 215, 217-219, 227
Mackie, John, 5, 105-107, 168, 170, 207, 209, 213, 215, 217, 219, 221-222, 227
Maimonides, 179, 200
Malthus, Thomas, 181-182

Marx, Karl, 79-80, 86
master morality, 83
Matthew, Gospel of, 125, 214
meaninglessness, 121
meaning of life, 108-117
   cosmic meaning, 108-110
   nihilism, 108-109, 115
   temporal meaning, 108, 110, 115
Middle East, 131
Mill, J. S., 26, 75-79, 128, 142, 167, 171, 179, 192, 204, 227
Mitchell, Basil, 227
Moksha, 96
monkey hold model, 95
moral point of view, 162, 171
moral rationality, 163
moral theories:
   deontological, 10-11
   discovered, 11
   emotive theory, 14, 87
   invented, 11, 13
   normative, 8, 9
   projection theory, 14-16
   teleological, 10
morality, point of, 24
Mormons, 136
mortality, 117, 123
Moses, 11, 30
Muhammad, 134
Mullen, Douglas, 216, 227
Muslims, 97, 134, 196
Nada, 109
national identity, 130-131
natural law, 59, 97, 141
natural right, 63
naturalism, 2-4, 29, 38
Nazi, 86, 99, 137, 148
Neoplatonism, 56
Newman, J. H., 216
Newton, Isaac, 6-7, 120

Nicomachean Ethics, 53, 214
Nielsen, Kai, 227
Nietzsche, F., 5, 82-85, 123, 204, 227
nihilism, 108-109, 115
nihilist, moral, 155
Nirvana, 94, 96
Noss, David and John, 215, 217, 221, 227
ontological materialism, 79
opium of the people, 80
Orend, Brian, 218, 227
original sin, 106
Orphics, 38
Osama bin Laden, 136
our moral setting, 21, 23
Owen, Robert, 135
Paine, Thomas, 140
Palestinians, 131
Paley, William, 208
Paloutzian, R. F., 216, 227
Parks, Sharon, 218, 222, 227
Pascal, B., 117, 216, 227
Penn, William, 135
Perry, M. J., 218, 227
philosopher king, 47
Pinker, Steven, 220, 227
Plato, 1, 13, 26, 29, 37-50, 118, 121, 166, 179, 199, 200-201, 214, 216, 221, 227
pleasure, 35-36
predestination, 57, 60
Pre-Socratics, 30
Prothero, Stephen, 220, 227
polytheism, 38
postulate of practical reason, 73
Prime Mover, 51
principle of utility, 76
promising, 72
Protagoras, 13, 32-34, 145, 150
Protestantism, 96-97, 100-101

prudence, 161
psychological egoism, 26, 62, 68, 128, 191-192
psychological hedonism, 75
purpose in life test, 116
Pythagoreans, 38
Quakers, 134-135
Qur'an, 98
Rachels, James, 192, 221, 227
Romans, Letter to, 214-215, 222
rational egoism, 162-163, 165
Rawls, John, 228
reincarnation, 119
religion of humanity, 78
Republic, 39, 42, 47
resurrection, 119
Ricardo, 79
rights, 137-144
rights:
    civil, 138
    human, 138-139
    legal, 138
    natural, 138
Robin Hood, 23
Rokeach, Milton, 116
Rolston, Holmes III, 220-221, 228
Roman Catholic, 95, 97, 100, 131
Rorty, Richard, 143, 228
Ruse, Michael, 183, 196-197, 220-221
Russell, Bertrand, 111, 123, 216, 228
Saint Paul, 97, 010, 119, 133, 177, 205
Saint-Simon, 79
salvation, models of, 94-96
sanctions, 9, 60, 76, 162, 179-180

Sartre, Jean Paul, 13, 85-87, 92
Scheibe, Karl, 228
Schneewind, J. B., 228
sea turtle model, 94
selfish, 126, 165
selfishness, 187
self-interested, 165
self-referential, 126, 165
Selfish Gene, The, 185
Shakers, 195
Shinto, 131, 134
Sidgwick, Henry, 126-127, 217, 228
Sisyphus, 108-110
situation ethics, 98, 148
Slavery, 49
Smart, Ninian, 130, 217, 228
Sober, E., 220-221, 228
Society of Friends, 134
Socrates, 46-47
Sophists, 38
sociobiology, 185
soul, 43-45, 52-53
Spinoza, B., 26
Stark, Rodney, 228
state, 38-39, 61
stages on life's way
    aesthetic, 111-113
    ethical, 111, 114
    religious, 111, 114
Stephen, Fitzjames, 204
Stoics, 48, 141, 175-176
Stout, Jeffrey, 228
Straus, Leo, 229
Stumph, S. E., 214, 219, 229
superman, 85
Swinburne, R., 221, 229
sympathy, 67
synthetic proposition, 66
Taoism, 91
Tartarus, 46

Taylor, Richard, 5, 29, 105-108, 110, 167, 178, 205, 213-214, 216, 219, 222, 229
temporal meaning, 108, 115
Ten Commandments, 11, 98
theism, 2-4, 9, 29
theonomy, 102
theories, 6-7
Thilly, Frank, 214, 229
Thomas, George F., 215, 229
Tillich, Paul, 102, 118, 215-217, 229
tolerance, 151
Tolstoy, Leo, 29, 120, 214, 229
Torah, 98, 177,
transmigration, 119
tribalism, 128-129, 132, 175-176
Trivers, R. L., 220
Universal Declaration of Human Rights, 139
universality, 72
universalizing, 173
utilitarianism, 10, 75-76, 148, 167, 204

value survey, 116
verifiability principle, 88-89
Waley, Arthur, 229
Warnock, G. J., 213, 229
Whale, J. S., 215, 229
White, R. E. O., 214-215, 218, 229
Williams, Bernard, 229
Williams, George, 220
will to power, 83
Wilson, D. S., 220
Wilson, E. O., 183, 190, 220, 230
Wilson, James, Q., 230
WNDs, 18, 20-26, 107
Wolfe, Alan, 213, 230
Women, 50, 54-55, 62
Wood, Ledger, 214, 229
Woolman, John, 135
World Soul, 40-41
Worldview, 2, 93
Zeus, 32
Zionist, 131